CW01653565

The TOLLESBURY BRANCH

Six months after nationalisation, and Class J69/1 No. 8636 still bears the legend LNER on her tank sides. The 'Buck Jumper' is waiting on the main single line, by the run-round loop, south of Tollesbury Station, before pulling into the platform on 26th June 1948. This was prior to setting off for Kelvedon with her train, which was composed of two light railway vehicles and a main line six wheel brake vehicle.

H. C. Casserley

The TOLLESBURY BRANCH

Peter Paye

Oxford Publishing Co.

Copyright © 1985 Peter Paye & Oxford Publishing Co.

ISBN 0-86093-327-X

All rights reserved. No part of this book may be reproduced or transmitted in any form or by any means, electronic or mechanical, including photocopying, recording or any information storage and retrieval system, without permission in writing from the Publisher.

Acknowledgements

The publication of this history would not have been possible without the help of many people who have been kind enough to assist. In particular I should like to thank:

The late Mr A. R. Cox
The late Mr W. Fenton
The late Mr G. Woodcock
Mr B. D. J. Walsh
Mr J. Watling
Dr I. C. Allen
Mr D. Taylor
Mr D. Hoser
Mr G. Pember
Mr R. C. Riley
Mr H. C. Casserley
Mr M. Brooks
Mr P. Webber
Mr F. Hennessey
Mr J. Bosley
The late Mr S. Orrin
Mr K. Townroe
Mr A. Lawrence
Mr M. Petchey
Mr G. Manning
Mr N. Woriker
Mr P Tillett

also staff of the former Colchester Motive Power Depot and the many other active and retired railway staff, some of whom worked on the Tollesbury Light Railway.

Thanks are also due to:

The Public Record Office
British Rail Eastern Region
The House of Lords Record Office
The British Museum Newspaper Library
Essex County Record Office, Chelmsford
Great Eastern Railway Society

Special thanks go to my mother who typed the manuscript, and to my wife, Madge, who assisted in checking the text.

Typesetting by:
Aquarius Typesetting Services, New Milton, Hants.

Printed in Great Britain by:
Biddles Ltd., Guildford, Surrey.

Published by:
Oxford Publishing Co.
Link House
West Street
POOLE, Dorset

KEY TO DRAWINGS

Sb..........Station Buildings
Smh..........Stationmaster's House
Sc..........Signal Box
cp..........cattle pens
gs..........goods shed
olc..........open level crossing
glc..........gated level crossing
sp..........signal post
wt..........water tank
wc..........water crane
lg..........loading gauge
pwh..........permanent way hut
cb..........carriage body
fb..........footbridge
fp..........footpath
ld..........loading dock
bb..........bus body

Contents

	Page
Acknowledgements	4
Introduction	7
Chapter One — Advent of the Light Railway	9
Chapter Two — Great Eastern Administration	25
Chapter Three — Amalgamation and Nationalisation	33
Chapter Four — The Route Described	49
Chapter Five — Timetables and Traffic	87
Chapter Six — Locomotives and Rolling Stock	103
Appendix — Kelvedon to Tollesbury Pier : Bridges and Culverts	126

Bibliography

General Works

Allen, C. J. — *The Great Eastern Railway* Ian Allan
Gordon, D. I. — *Regional History Railways of Great Britain Volume 5 - Eastern Counties* David & Charles
Gordon, W. J. — *Our Home Railways Volume 1*
Joby, R. S. — *Forgotten Railways of East Anglia* David & Charles
Tatford, B. — *Story of British Railways*
R.C.T.S. — *Locomotives of LNER (Various Volumes)*
Aldrich C. L. — *GER Locomotives*

Periodicals

Bradshaws Railway Guide
Bradshaws Railway Manual
British Railways (Eastern Region) Magazine
Buses
East Anglian Magazine
Essex Countryside
Essex Review
Great Eastern Railway Magazine
Locomotive Carriage and Wagon Review
Locomotive Magazine
LNER Magazine
Railway Magazine
Railway World
Railway Year Book
Trains Illustrated

Newspapers

Essex County Standard
Maldon and Burnham Standard

Also

Minute books of:

Great Eastern Railway
London & North Eastern Railway

Working and Public Timetables: GER, LNER and BR (ER)
Appendices to Working Timetables: GER, LNER and BR (ER)

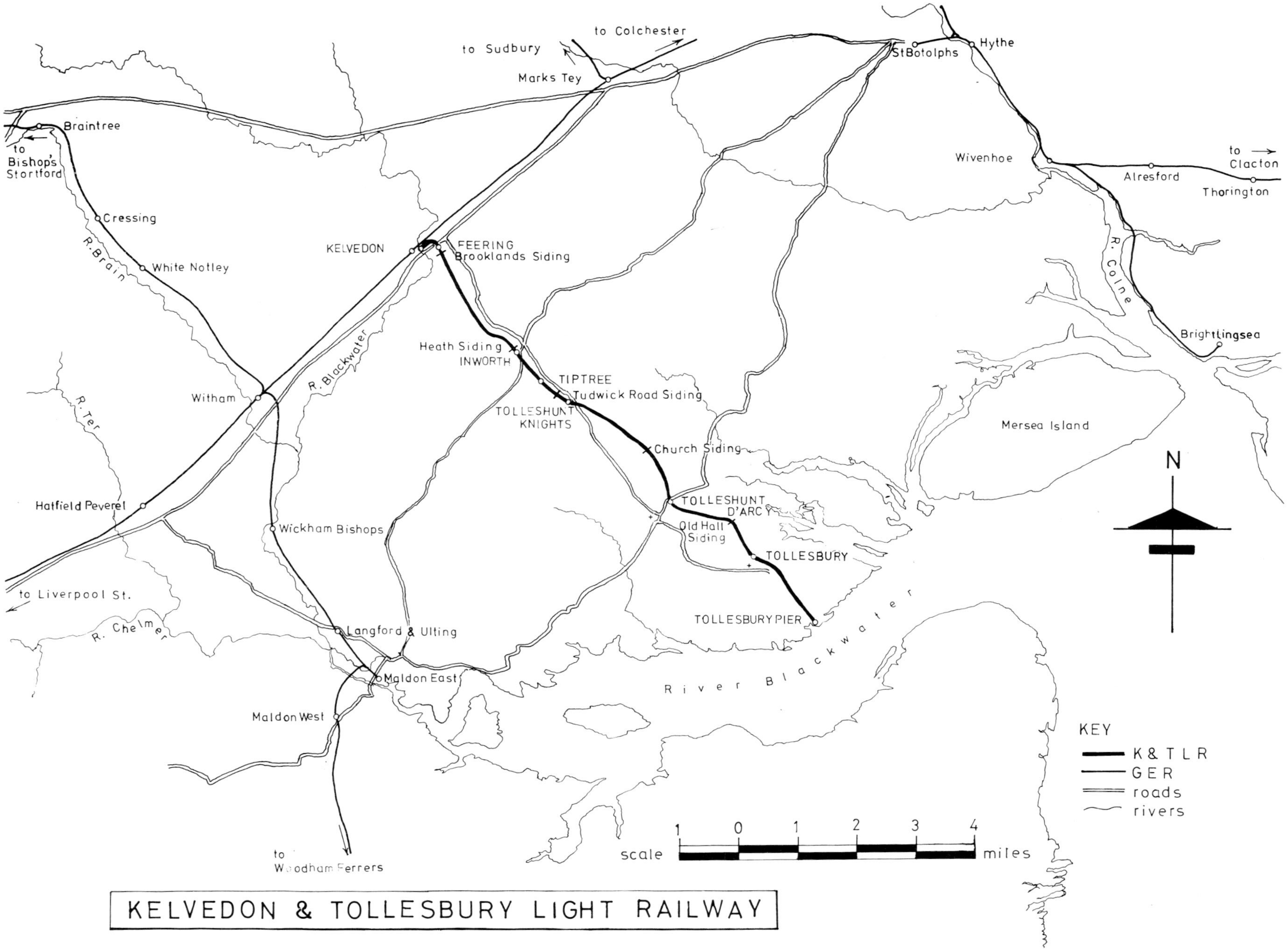

KELVEDON & TOLLESBURY LIGHT RAILWAY

Introduction

Like many of the branch lines of East Anglia, the Kelvedon & Tollesbury Light Railway was conceived by local farmers, landowners and businessmen to improve transportation of their produce to London and the provincial markets. After many abortive attempts, the scheme to build the railway south from the Great Eastern Railway station at Kelvedon, on the Liverpool Street to Norwich main line, to serve the fruit-growing area around the small Essex town of Tiptree and also tap the fishing and oyster industry around Tollesbury, on the banks of the River Blackwater, only came to fruition after the passing of the Light Railways Act in 1896, as the locality was limited in its potential, and expensive construction costs were considered prohibitive. Local landowners then gave freely of their land whilst the Treasury and, to a greater extent the Great Eastern Railway Company, finally provided the necessary financial backing.

The opening of the Kelvedon & Tollesbury Light Railway in 1904 brought the expected freight receipts and, indeed, goods traffic increased steadily until the mid-1930s, but after the introduction of motor lorries on an increasing scale, decline set in. With a catchment area of around 5,000 inhabitants, passenger receipts on the branch never showed the healthy returns of freight. The gamble to develop the area round Tollesbury Pier into a yachting centre, on a par with Brightlingsea or Burnham-on-Crouch, met with early failure and doomed this section of the line to early closure.

During the depressed days of 1930, when the LNER was seeking economies, the passenger services on the 'Crab and Winkle' line (so-called because of its early maritime aspirations) were lucky to escape withdrawal.

After World War II, road improvements and the end of petrol rationing brought further decline, as traffic turned to the internal combustion engine for door-to-door service. Passenger services, operating with antiquated locomotives, and rolling stock, was little changed from when the line originally opened to traffic. It was often noted in the national press for its quaintness and was withdrawn in May 1951, well before the Beeching era. Freight traffic beyond Tudwick Road Siding suffered a similar fate, in October of the same year, reducing the north end of the branch to the status of a siding serving the jam factory at Tiptree. This truncated section remained until 1962 when dwindling traffic receipts rendered it unremunerative to continue, and the branch was closed.

An attempt has been made at tracing the history of the line. Details have been checked with documents that are available but apologies are offered for errors which might, inevitably, have occurred.

P. PAYE

Class J67/1 No. 7169 (ex-GER Class R24 No. 169) stands by the run-round loop to the south of Tollesbury Station, after forming its mixed train for the return run to Kelvedon, on 6th March 1939.

G. Pember Collection

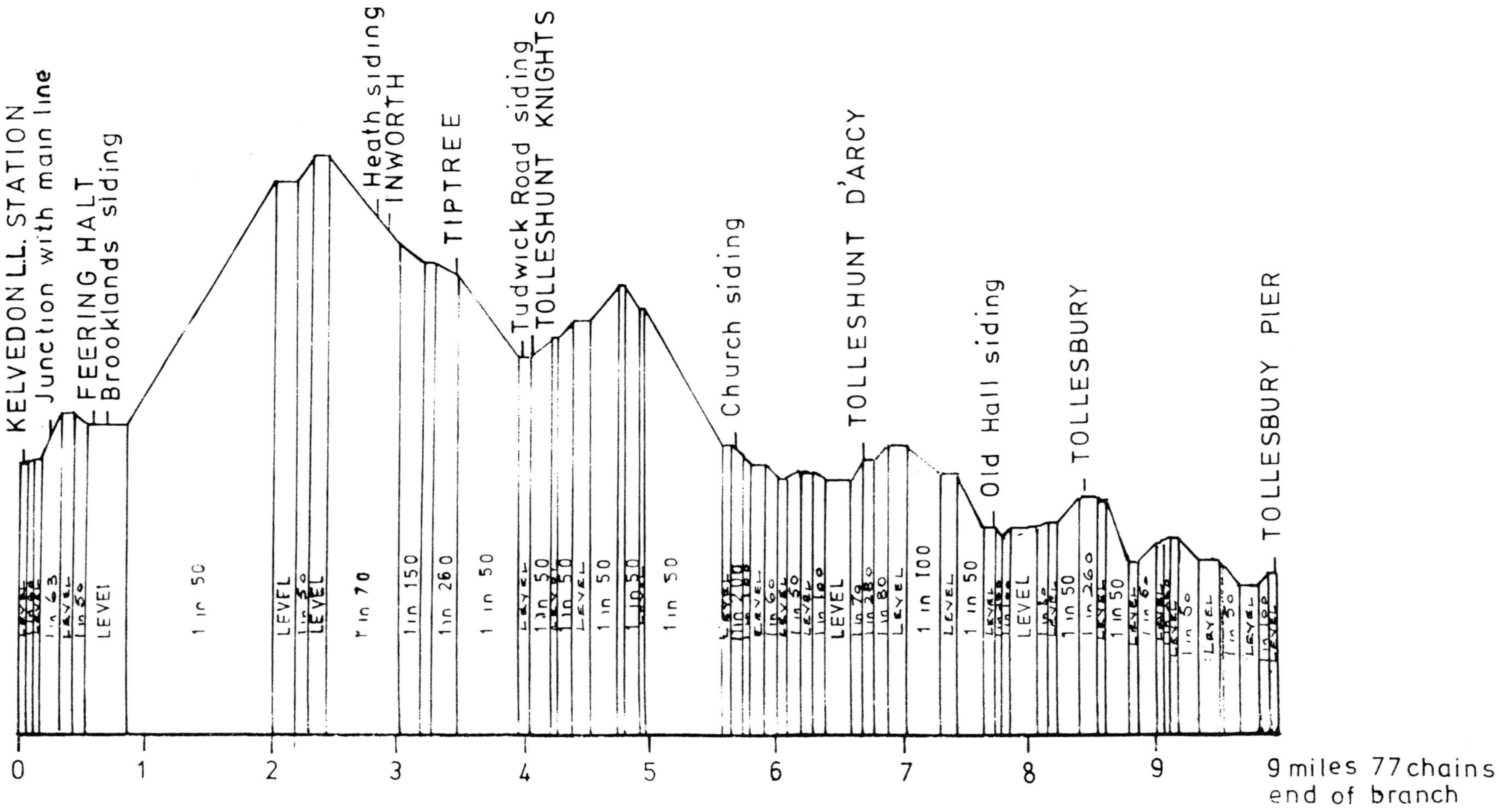

KELVEDON - TOLLESBURY — GRADIENTS

Chapter One

Advent of the Light Railway

The River Blackwater, known in its upper reaches as the 'Pant', rises in the near 500ft. high flattened chalk hills a few miles south-east of Saffron Walden in the north-west corner of Essex. In its subsequent journey to the sea the river passes through vastly contrasting scenery, before forming a broad tidal estuary in the south-east of the county, and is last bridged in the seaward direction at the ancient town of Maldon. Beyond the marshy north bank of the muddy estuary, the river has long winding channels striking inland with inlets that, for centuries, were the haunt of smugglers and fishermen, and were later famed for oysters and shrimping.

North of the undulating coastline and away from the marshes the land is fertile, dotted with small villages and hamlets including Tollesbury, Tolleshunt D'Arcy and Tiptree. Unfortunately the locality was particularly hard hit during the agricultural depression in the early nineteenth century, when land values fell by as much as forty per cent.

The advent of the railway initially brought little relief to the area with the Eastern Counties Railway, incorporated on 4th July 1836, to provide a line from Shoreditch to Norwich and Yarmouth, via Colchester, taking an inland route which followed closely the main turnpike road through Chelmsford and Witham, opening for goods to Colchester on 7th March 1843 and to passengers on 29th March. The company at least provided a station at Kelvedon to serve as a railhead. Two years later the Maldon, Witham & Braintree Railway was promoted, essentially to develop the harbour at Maldon. Parliamentary authority was granted in 1846 but the ECR, taking great interest in the proposal, deceitfully promised dividends of eight to ten per cent at the same time spreading rumours that the venture would not pay. The ECR later successfully absorbed the local company. The line was opened for goods on 15th August 1848 and for passenger traffic on 2nd October, with the ECR making no effort to improve the harbour facilities or to deepen the Blackwater.

By the mid-1850s the fertile land south of Kelvedon was again attracting growers and in 1859 Arthur C. Wilkin settled at Trewlands Farm, Tiptree, where he commenced fruit farming five years later. Others followed suit, and it was not long before smallholdings and small farms were increasing output. Adjacent to Trewlands Farm was Tiptree Hall Farm where John Joseph Mechi began an energetic programme for better farming, trying out new theories, implements and new ideas. So successful was he in the agricultural sphere that he founded the Royal Agricultural Benevolent Institution, became Alderman of the City of London, Sheriff of Middlesex and provided Tiptree with a church and a school.

Wilkin in the meantime had not been idle as his orchards and soft fruit farms continued to expand, with greengages, cherries, plums, quinces, damsons, strawberries, blackcurrants, gooseberries, loganberries, apples and crab apples being grown. Also, in 1885 jam making commenced in an old corn barn, but fruit cultivation was not the only development in the area for vegetables were grown in abundance, with potatoes and green peas forming the basic commodities. Despite two summer droughts followed by a wet summer, all of which contributed to poor harvests, local landowners and growers were showing healthy returns but, like their fishing colleagues from the Blackwater Estuary at Tollesbury, they were finding the absence of a local railway with rapid transport of their goods to London and local markets of considerable hinderance. In addition, local farmers and growers in the Tollesbury and Tiptree areas were compelled to herd their cattle and convey their produce in horse-drawn waggons along the narrow byways to Kelvedon, Maldon and Colchester. In wet or adverse weather these byways were deep in mud with crops often deteriorating before reaching the railhead, this cumbersome method of transportation not being conducive to the advancement and growth of the industry.

In 1862 the Eastern Counties Railway had ceased to exist. Having leased or taken over the working of many major lines in East Anglia a scheme was prepared for the amalgamation of the ECR, East Anglian, Newmarket, Norfolk and Eastern Union Railways to form the Great Eastern Railway. The sanctioned Act - the GER Act 1862 (25 & 26 Vic Cap CCXX111) obtained the Royal Assent on 7th August 1862, but took effect retrospectively from 1st July 1862. The new company gradually improved services between London and Colchester and also on the Maldon branch but, despite several complaints to the railway authorities, facilities at Kelvedon left much to be desired and few attempts were made to encourage the collection and delivery of produce and commodities from the surrounding area. The local gentry and farmers, therefore, decided on the only alternative course of action; that of endeavouring to engender support for the building of a railway from Kelvedon to Tiptree and Tollesbury.

Several promoters of the proposed railway requested a meeting with the GER Board and finally a deputation was received at 12 noon, on 4th December 1889, to speak in favour of a railway serving the Tollesbury area. Those attending included C. W. Gray, MP, A. C. Wilkin, Dr Salter, G. R. J. Bloare-Barker, C. W. Chatterton and Messrs Potter and Rann. The promoters brought to the attention of the Directors a memorandum, signed by 400 to 500 of the principal gentry, landowners and farmers of the district, requesting the construction of a branch railway from Kelvedon Station to Tollesbury. After listening to the proposals the Board advised the deputation that the GER Company, because of works already proposed and in hand plus other financial commitments, could not take steps to provide the required railway. However, if independent construction was undertaken and finished to a good standard, the main line company would be prepared to work the line at reasonable costs.

Evidently encouraged by the response, the promoters held further discussions to strengthen their argument for the line. Thus in the new year another audience was sought and on 4th March 1890 a further deputation was received when Messrs Wilkin, Hudson, H. & W. Frost, A. Chatterton and Ward made representation to the Way and Works

In 1948, J69/1 No. 8636 approaches Tollesbury with a 'down' mixed train, formed of two tram coaches and freight brake van.
Dr I. C. Allen

Committee of the GER. As a result of their submission the Chairman of the committee advised that he and others would visit the locality, the committee later requesting that the GER Engineer survey the area between Kelvedon and Tollesbury, through which the proposed line would pass. Although these visits took place no action was taken, and again local interested parties became restless because of the inactivity, and on 21st February 1893 the Tollesbury Improvement Association wrote to Bishopsgate asking if the GE Directors would be prepared to build the railway to Tollesbury if it were independently promoted.

The GER authorities continued to show disinterest, and delayed replying under the pretext that they required more definite proposals. Two years elapsed before local gentry resurrected plans for a railway and early in May 1895, in the homely parlour of the rectory at Tiptree, a group of four interested people, including A. C. Wilkin and Dr Salter, who had mooted the proposal six years earlier, met to discuss the possibility of providing a railway from Kelvedon to serve Tiptree and Tollesbury. The idea received the formal approval of those present and within weeks the following landowners formed themselves into a committee to further the scheme; Sir William Abdy, Alex P. McMullen, Mayor and brewer of Hertford, James N. Paxman, JP, John Henry Salter, JP, and Arthur C. Wilkin, owner of the Britannia Fruit Preserving Company of Tiptree.

On 5th May 1895, a deputation again visited the GER headquarters, and advised the Board of their independent plan for a light railway linking Kelvedon with Tiptree and Tollesbury. They also sought official backing for the line from the main line company, but the Board were adamant that no undertaking could be given until further investigations were made. Despite the cool reception received from the GER the local committee continued to strive and engender support for the proposed railway, and a public meeting was held at the White Hart Assembly Rooms, at Witham, in March 1896. Several prominent advocates of the line gave details to the assembly, of the aim of the promoters, and received the general approval of those present. In the same year, Parliament gave agreement to a statute that was to help their problem.

The Light Railways Act of 1896 was promoted to alleviate the distress of agricultural depression by allowing inexpensive railways to be constructed in rural areas, with the proviso that those so constructed would be freed from the obligations to build to the high standards laid down by the Board of Trade for main lines. Section 5 of the Act stated that where the Board of Agriculture certified that the making of a light railway would benefit agriculture, the Treasury might agree to aid the building of the line out of public money. Another significant feature was that application to the Light Railway Commissioners for an order,

Tollesbury Station, with Class J69/1 0-6-0T No. 8636 simmering at the platform, whilst waiting to depart with a mixed train for Kelvedon. Although the photograph was taken on 26th June 1948, the locomotive still bears the legend LNER on the side tanks.

H. C. Casserley

could be made by the County, Borough or the district through which the railway would pass, or by any company or individual. The latter was particularly relevant to those advocating the railway because, with persuasion and a strong enough argument, it was now possible to construct a line at a fraction of the cost and with subsidised support.

No time was lost in resurrecting plans and, in the absence of any formal reply to their earlier meeting, a further deputation visited the GER headquarters at 1.45p.m. on 4th November 1896. As well as pressing for the light railway linking Kelvedon with Tollesbury, a possible extension to Mersea Island was also discussed. The GER Board voiced their general approval of the Tollesbury scheme, but doubted the viability of the extension. The promoters, encouraged by the change of heart at Bishopsgate, made their first application for a light railway order in May 1897. They requested authority to build a railway 9 miles, 6 furlongs and 7 chains in length from Kelvedon to the terminus near Mill Creek, on the shore of the River Blackwater beyond Tollesbury. This total cost was estimated at £45,500 or £4,667 per mile. The main road at Feering, and two minor roads near Tolleshunt Knights, were to be provided with overbridges, whilst another at Tolleshunt Knights was to be crossed by an underbridge, with fifteen gated level crossings being needed at other road level crossings.

Negotiations were also opened with the Board of Agriculture and the Treasury, where stress was placed on the depressed state of the industry in the area. After deliberating with the Board of Agriculture, and following investigation into the light railway application, the Treasury finally agreed, in December 1897, to contribute the sum of £16,000 towards the proposed railway linking Kelvedon with the River Blackwater. The Light Railway Commissioners and the promoters were advised that payment was made on condition that the calculated 53 acres, 3 rod and 18 perches of land required for the line was provided free of charge by local landowners, and that the Great Eastern Railway Company would supervise construction and work the railway.

Protracted negotiations followed throughout the early months of 1898, until the GER finally agreed to build and work the railway. In May the GER Engineer and land agents were requested to prepare plans and submit costings, while landowners were approached regarding the takeover of property. With support in the district for the railway gathering momentum, success now depended on the Light

Railway Commission enquiry.

The Commissioner under the Light Railways Act held his enquiry into the scheme for the provision of the Kelvedon, Tiptree & Tollesbury Light Railway on Tuesday, 25th October 1898 in the public hall at Kelvedon, the same day as the enquiry into the proposed line linking Kelvedon, Coggeshall and Halstead. The Commissioners chairing the meeting were Gerald A. R. Fitzgerald and Colonel Boughey, CSI with Henry Allan Steward, acting as Secretary. The hall was crowded and amongst the general assembly with interest in the Tollesbury line were the Hon. C. H. Strutt, MP, James Round, MP, J. Moss, Dr J. H. Salter, Sir W. H. Abdy, (Bart), the Revd B. Abstey, A. P. McMullen, Joseph Wakelin and A. C. Wilkin. The Hon. C. H. Strutt, MP, gave evidence for the Kelvedon to Tollesbury line, and advised the Chairman that although there was a little opposition to the scheme such opposition would not attack the vital points of his case. He reiterated that the promoters had tried for years to get the GER to build a railway to serve the area and had met with no success. The passing of the Light Railway Order in 1896 had changed the situation when Clause 5 was found by Strutt and his colleagues to exactly suit their purpose. A further proposal for a light railway had been forwarded and the Treasury had tentatively agreed to provide £16,000 to assist finance the construction, and this had strengthened their case. The proposed light railway, 9¾ miles long and built to the standard gauge of 4ft 8½ in., would pass from Tollesbury through Tolleshunt D'Arcy, Tolleshunt Knights, Messing, Inworth and Feering to Kelvedon and a junction with the Great Eastern Railway. A possible extension from Tollesbury to Mill Creek on the River Blackwater was also contemplated, it being here that the river, at 1½ miles, was at one of its widest points. Strutt stated that witnesses for the proposal would advise on the need for a railway to assist local agricultural and fishing, whilst one or two industries would also benefit from the railway. Since the GER had promised to build the line slight alterations were planned; it was envisaged that no gates would be erected at level crossings and that simple halts would replace the substantial stations originally mooted. The small halts would have accommodation where people could get out of the rain, and as low platforms were to be provided, passengers alighting or joining the trains would use steps to gain access to the coaches. Strutt concluded his evidence by advising that more stations were to be built than originally proposed, and it was envisaged that the railway company would build even more if people desired them.

After listening to the lengthy discourse, the Chairman asked for the points of opposition against the scheme. J. C. Freeman, Clerk to Maldon Council, advised that his authority did not oppose the railway on the grounds of necessity but only asked the commission to consider the safety of the public when authorising open level crossings, and hoped all such crossings would be manned. F. C. Braintree, appearing on behalf of Mr R. E. Renn, stated his client was the owner of an estate to be crossed by the proposed railway near Messing, and that Mr Renn was not wholly in approval of the line and the way it was to be built. Strutt counteracted this allegation and said that the promoter had every confidence in the Engineer and that they were not being 'used as the cat's-paw by the GER'; it had taken long and difficult negotiations to get the main line company to act. John Moss, JP, Vice Chairman of Lexden & Winstree District Council, then stated that his authority approved of the scheme for the line subject to the protection of the rights of way across the railway.

Evidence in support of the railway was then proffered by John Wakelin, representing Essex County Council, who spoke of the necessity for the line in the area and stated that the County Council heartily approved of the scheme, although it was desirable that the line was fenced throughout its length. Dr J. H. Salter, a resident in the neighbourhood for thirty years, advised there was great backing from the local populace, and Mr Chatterton, a fish dealer from Tollesbury, and A. C. Wilkin of Britannia Fruit Farms, Tiptree, stated that they knew the railway would bring an increase in trade, the latter saying that the light railway was like a tramway, ideal for improving such a thinly-populated and rural district. Finally the GER representatives reminded the Chairman that although the main line company was not promoting the light railway, they were keen to assist. In such a guise J. Wilson, the Engineer, informed the gathering that it was contemplated his company would use 56lb. per yard rail on the line and work the service with the same type of coaching stock used on the Wisbech & Upwell Tramway. To reiterate the point made by the Hon. C. H. Strutt he said it was not intended to build normal height platforms but only those of sufficient height to enable people to get on or off using steps. It was also thought that at least three level crossings would have to be gated, with provision for cottages for the respective gatekeepers. Wilson then concluded his evidence by advising that the estimated cost of the line was £45,000.

The Chairman, before concluding, asked if anyone wished to question the GER Engineer. F. C. Braintree enquired if Renn's land would be 'cut to smithereens' by the new line, and received the terse reply that his client had known of the impending railway when he bought the estate and that it would be cut in almost two equal halves. When told that Renn would receive a reasonable price for his portion of land by the railway, the opposition was withdrawn.

After the lengthy hearing the Commissioners, much to the delight of the promoters, advised they would recommend the provision of a Light Railway Order to the Board of Trade. This decision later turned sour on the promoters of the Kelvedon, Coggeshall & Halstead Light Railway, for their order was refused. The Board of Trade enquiry into the application was duly held on 16th March 1899, under the Chairmanship of Sir Courtenay Boyle, KCB. The promoters were represented by Mr Frere and A. C. Wilkin, Secretary, whilst Sir William Birt, General Manager, gave evidence on behalf of the GER. Only one objection was raised regarding the safety of the public at open crossings, and the suggestion was made that all trains should be subjected to a maximum speed of 10m.p.h. within 300 yards of the ungated level crossings.

After the Board of Trade approval for the new line, further delays occurred. The Light Railway Commissioners duly granted the Kelvedon, Tiptree & Tollesbury Light Railway Order (1901) on 29th January 1901 and confirmed it on 27th February, authorising construction of a light railway linking Kelvedon with the River Blackwater in the County of Essex. The order granted powers to build a railway 9 miles, 6 furlongs and 7 chains, or thereabouts, in length, commencing in the Parish of Feering (County of Essex) by a junction with the Colchester main line of the Great Eastern Railway at Kelvedon Station, and terminating

Class J67/1 No. 68608 stands at Feering Halt, with the 12.50p.m. Tollesbury to Kelvedon train, on 30th September 1950. The fireman is descending from the footplate, to open the crossing gates to allow the train to cross the A12 London to Colchester main road.
LCGB/Ken Nunn Collection

Tiptree Station (3 miles and 31 chains from Kelvedon), viewed from the approach path in 1904. A Tollesbury to Kelvedon train, formed of the original four wheel coaching stock converted from main line vehicles and hauled by Adams Class K9 0-4-2T No. 25, waits at the platform. Behind the train is the goods siding, which is occupied by coal wagons, and to the left Wilkin's jam factory, served by a siding off the goods loop. The rose bushes and shrubs decorating the station gardens were provided by Wilkins.

at a point in property numbered 508 on the 1/2,500 scale Ordnance Survey map in the Parish of Tollesbury. Three years were allowed for the compulsory purchase of land, and five years for completion of works. Under Clause 11 of the Order the GER was not to purchase or acquire ten or more houses which, on 15th February 1901, were occupied by labouring classes as tenants or lodgers, and if they defaulted were liable to a penalty of £500 for each house purchased or acquired. Clause 15 required the Company to carry the public road in the Parish of Tolleshunt Knights over the railway by a bridge 20ft. wide, whilst Clause 16 bound the GER to erect gates over the railway at the following level crossings:

No. 6 in the Parish of Feering
No. 85 in the Parish of Inworth
No. 47 in the Parish of Tolleshunt Knights
No. 17 in the Parish of Tolleshunt D'Arcy
No. 54 in the Parish of Tollesbury

Because of its standing as a light railway, Clause 18 of the Order enforced the construction of cattle guards on each side of the road at ungated level crossings, to prevent cattle straying on to the line. Trains were to be limited to 10m.p.h. over ungated level crossings, and warning boards for drivers were to be erected 5ft. above the ground at 300 yards distance on the approach to each side of the crossing. Notices for road users to beware of trains were required 50 yards on each approach to the crossing. Level crossing inclinations were permitted to be altered at one level crossing each in the parishes of Feering, Inworth, Tolleshunt Knights and Tolleshunt D'Arcy, whilst the railway could divert two roads in the Parish of Inworth and one in the Parish of Tollesbury.

As 60lb. per yard rail was to be used on the light railway, the order limited the axle weight of locomotives and rolling stock used on the line to 14 tons, whilst the speed limit of trains was restricted to 25m.p.h. and 10m.p.h. within 200 yards of each approach to ungated level crossings. Finally a penalty clause stated that if the GER Company failed to open the line within the period stipulated by the Order, they were liable to a £20 fine per day. A forfeit of £20 was also payable if the railway opened without notice being given to the Board of Trade.

Of the various landowners who owned estates on the route of the proposed line Sir William Abdy, Lord of the Manor at Barn Hall, gave 5 acres, 3 rod and 5 perches, C. H. C. DuCann gave 4 acres, 3 rod and 6 perches, A. P. McMullen, Lord of the Manor of Tollesbury and a member of the brewing family of Hertford, 6 acres, 2 rod and 7 perches and the Britannia Fruit Company of Tiptree about 8 acres. Around £750 towards purchase of the remaining land was collected in the district, while Sir William Abdy offered £200, A. P. McMullen £100, the Hon. C. H. Strutt, MP, £65, Barclay & Co., H. T. Bailey and the Britannia Fruit Company £50 each, Mr DuCann £25 with a smaller sum from Thomas Moy Ltd., the coal merchants, who hoped to locate coal sidings on the proposed line. The money was duly handed over to the GER in January 1900. The proprietors of the GER were informed at their meeting, on 29th January 1901, that the Treasury had agreed to a free grant of £16,000 towards the cost of construction of the Kelvedon, Tiptree & Tollesbury Light Railway.

At the GER Board Meeting, on 15th October 1901, the General Manager submitted to the Directors three schemes for the proposed accommodation for the new light railway at Kelvedon. The initial plan 1, prepared in June 1898, was estimated to cost £12,216 whilst plans 2 and 3 submitted by the Engineer in June and August 1901, were estimated to cost £4,150 and £2,510 respectively, exclusive of a siding for goods traffic which would possibly be necessary. After considerable discussion it was estimated that little additional land was required for the siding, and £200 would cover the cost of purchase. Gooday reminded his fellow Directors that, under the original estimates for the railway, the GER had to find £16,534 for construction inclusive of land but, from the latest estimates, it appeared the company would have to find £21,284 exclusive of accomodation at Kelvedon. Gooday advised that from all reports Kelvedon was not a progressive place, and the GER would not contemplate spending any money were it not for the light railway. It was thought that any additional traffic accrued from the new line would be insufficient to pay interest on even the £2,510.

After a considerable and often heated discussion, it was resolved that good cross-platform facilities would be provided from the new line at Kelvedon, and that although a cut-back on costs was desirable, the merits of proper interchange facilities, with provision for attracting further passenger and freight traffic, would far outweigh savings on assets. Scheme 1, costing £12,216, was finally approved, and the promoters duly advised. At the Board Meeting on 8th January 1902 the Directors, as well as formally approving the construction of the light railway, sanctioned the building of a separate small station at Kelvedon to serve the line, estimated at a cost of £7,000.

Protracted negotiations for the transfer of the required land delayed the progress of the railway for nearly ten months. Once the necessary acreage had been made available, or acquired, for the railway, J. Wilson, the GER Engineer, lost no time in obtaining schedules of prices for the construction of earthworks and the formation of the railway. He reported to the Way and Works and Traffic Committees, on 3rd November 1902, of his negotiations with Messrs Scott & Middleton and C. J. Wills. With the approval of the General Manager he subsequently agreed to Scott & Middleton's tender being accepted, this being the firm that had built the GER extension to Southend and the branch connecting Woodham Ferrers with Maldon West and East, also the Southminster branch.

On 4th November 1902, the Traffic Committee discussed the provision of facilities at the junction, and fully concurred with the plan to provide the light railway with a separate station at Kelvedon. This would obviate unnecessary and expensive works in providing a bay platform alongside the 'up' main line platform, which would have involved bridge reconstruction and additional earthworks. The Engineer then revised his estimate for the small timber-built ground level station with low platform to £810. The Locomotive Superintendent also requested provision of a water supply for the branch locomotive, with the sinking of a well and provision of a water-tank being estimated at £750. The Goods Manager stipulated the provision of a small goods office and a permanent way weighbridge to handle goods traffic on and off the new light railway, at a total cost of £464. Approval was readily given to the expenditure of £2,024 on the new works.

Delighted with the progress being made, the promoters

The 10.35a.m. mixed train from Kelvedon to Tollesbury curves away from the main line at Kelvedon, up the 1 in 63 gradient towards Feering, hauled by Class R24 0-6-0 No. 267 on 9th April 1910. The 'Buck Jumper' is running as a 2-4-0T, with its front coupling rods removed.

LCGB/Ken Nunn Collection

Class J69/1 No. 8636 waits to depart from Tollesbury with a mixed train, formed of six wheel brake third No. E62262, bogie tram No. E60461, a van and open wagons on 8th January 1949.

John H. Meredith

LIGHT RAILWAYS ACT, 1896.

KELVEDON, TIPTREE AND TOLLESBURY LIGHT RAILWAY ORDER, 1901.

ORDER

MADE BY THE

LIGHT RAILWAY COMMISSIONERS,

AND MODIFIED AND CONFIRMED BY THE

BOARD OF TRADE,

AUTHORISING THE CONSTRUCTION OF A

LIGHT RAILWAY IN THE COUNTY OF ESSEX, BETWEEN KELVEDON AND RIVER BLACKWATER.

Presented to both Houses of Parliament by Command of His Majesty.

LONDON:
PRINTED FOR HIS MAJESTY'S STATIONERY OFFICE,
BY DARLING & SON, LTD., 34-40, BACON STREET, E.

And to be purchased, either directly or through any Bookseller, from
EYRE & SPOTTISWOODE, EAST HARDING STREET, FLEET STREET, E.C.,
and 32, ABINGDON STREET, WESTMINSTER, S.W.:
or OLIVER & BOYD, EDINBURGH:
or E. PONSONBY, 116, GRAFTON STREET, DUBLIN.

1902.

[Cd. 542.] *Price 2½d.*

The Kelvedon, Tiptree & Tollesbury Light Railway Order, 1901.

THE LIGHT RAILWAYS ACT 1896.

KELVEDON, TIPTREE AND TOLLESBURY LIGHT RAILWAY.

ORDER

Authorising the construction of a Light Railway in the County of Essex between Kelvedon and River Blackwater.

WHEREAS an application has been made to the Light Railway Commissioners by the promoters therein named for the construction of the light railway hereinafter described AND WHEREAS it has been arranged with the approval of the Light Railway Commissioners that the Order should be granted to the Great Eastern Railway Company in the place of the said promoters and the proprietors of the Great Eastern Railway Company at a meeting specially called for the purpose and held on the 29th day of January 1901 have approved that arrangement AND WHEREAS the Treasury have agreed subject to the fulfilment of certain conditions to make a free grant of a sum of sixteen thousand pounds for the purpose of the light railway NOW we the Light Railway Commissioners being satisfied after local inquiry of the expediency of granting the said application do in pursuance of the Light Railways Act 1896 and by virtue and in exercise of the powers thereby vested in and of every other power enabling us in this behalf ORDER as follows:— Preamble.

Preliminary.

1. This Order may be cited as "The Kelvedon Tiptree and Tollesbury Light Railway Order 1901" and shall come into force on the date on which it is confirmed by the Board of Trade and that date is hereinafter referred to as "the commencement of this Order." Short title.

2. Words and expressions to which by the principal Act or any Acts in whole or in part incorporated with this Order meanings are assigned have in this Order (unless the context otherwise requires) the same respective meanings and in this Order— Interpretation.

The expression "the Company" means the Great Eastern Railway Company;

The expression "the principal Act" means the Light Railways Act 1896;

The expression "the railway" means the railway and works by this Order authorised and the expression "the undertaking" means the undertaking by this Order authorised;

The expressions "the Plan" "the Section" and "the Book of Reference" mean respectively the Plan Section and Book of Reference deposited in respect of the application for this Order with the Board of Trade and signed by a secretary or an assistant-secretary of the Board of Trade;

The Kelvedon, Tiptree & Tollesbury Light Railway Order preamble.

held a ceremonial cutting of the first sod of the new railway attended by six people including Dr Salter, on 11th November 1902, in a field near Kelvedon Station owned by the Britannia Fruit Farms of Tiptree. Following acceptance of their tender, Walter Scott & Middleton Ltd. forwarded their final bill of estimates to the GER for the construction of the railway, on 25th February 1903, from their office at 25 Victoria Street in Westminster;

	£	s.d.
Fencing		
35,000 linear yards fencing	2,625	0 0
100 each 12ft. field gates	800	0 0
30 each footpath gates	90	0 0
Earthworks		
125,000 cu. yards excavation of soil	8,333	6 8
1,000 cu. yards excavation suitable for roads and approaches to level crossings, bridges etc.	100	0 0
4,000 cu. yards excavation of earthworks to raise roads approaching cattle docks	200	0 0
200 cu. yards excavation foundations of bridges and culverts	25	0 0
100 cu. yards dry rubble filling	15	0 0
Concrete		
200 cu. yards concrete for foundations	140	0 0
Brickwork		
800 cu. yards brickwork in greamer blue lias ground brick	1,120	0 0
200 cu. yards Portland cement	310	0 0
500 cu. yards Staffordshire blue brick coping for walls	18	15 0
Masonry		
300 cu. yards ashlar stonework	45	0 0
Asphalt		
500 sq. yards ¾ in. asphalt coating arches	56	5 0
Drainpipes		
200 linear yards 6in. pipes	30	0 0
200 linear yards 9in. pipes	37	10 0
200 linear yards 12in. pipes	50	0 0
100 linear yards 18in. pipes	60	0 0
200 linear yards 3in. agricultural drains	10	0 0
100 linear yards 6in. agricultural drains	20	0 0
500 cu. yards burnt ballast for filling in	100	0 0

Also included were prices for laying the permanent way;

Laying single line of permanent way	£ 0 1s 4d per yard
Laying points	£ 2 10s 0d per set
Laying points 3 way	£ 5 0s 0d per set
Laying double slip	£10 0s 0d per set
Laying single slip	£ 8 0s 0d per set

A busy time at Tollesbury Station, as a group of children, with parents and guardians, await the branch train in the late 1900s.

Kelvedon (Low Level) Station, with the platform 15in. above rail level. Passenger facilities included a timber waiting shed, whilst illumination during the hours of darkness was provided by three post type oil lamps.

M. Brooks Collection

Laying diamond crossing £ 6 0s 0d each
Laying gravel ballast 4s 0d per cu. yard but if the railway company supplied the ballast, the price would be reduced to 1s 3d per cu. yard.
Fixing point boxes complete with balance weights 7s 6d each.

The contractor later accepted the sum of 1s 6d per cu. yard for the excavation of the 'up' refuge siding at Kelvedon. The earth was subsequently loaded into wagons and offloaded on to the site of the new light railway station, to consolidate the site above the marshy land near the river. The contractor's engineer was responsible for the supervision of the work at Kelvedon, whilst the GER supplied locomotive power and wagons for which the contractor paid a nominal sum. The Engineer in charge of the construction of the new light railway was Edward A. Wilson, son of John Wilson, the Chief Engineer of the GER. Walter Scott & Middleton Ltd. of London and Newcastle, the contractors, were represented by D. F. Saunders, their Clerk of Works, and Engineer P. Riach.

Construction of the railway began from the Kelvedon end in the spring of 1903, the contractor employing over 200 men on the earthworks including Irishmen, Scotsmen and local men who left local farms to earn higher wages as navvies building the railway. Good progress was made, and by September earthworks had reached the site of Tudwick Road. During July and August 1903 the Essex Geologists Association obtained permission to walk along the length of excavation from Kelvedon to Tiptree, and made many interesting discoveries regarding the soil formation and topography of the area.

Soon after construction commenced Mr Moss, owner of land adjacent to the railway near Feering, requested the provision of a siding to serve his farm. On 6th October 1903 the Engineer reported on his negotiations with Moss and estimated the cost at £420, whereby Moss agreed to provide the land free of charge and pay an annual rent of £42. The GER agreed to construct the siding out of the capital account charged to the light railway, subject to the siding being made available for public use, and the siding was later known as Brooklands Siding.

The construction was considerably delayed by continuous wet weather in the autumn and winter of 1903/4 when nearly three month progress was lost, effectively cancelling all hopes of opening the railway in the summer of 1904. At the GER Board Meeting of 4th March 1904 a letter was received from Mr J. Hudson, of Tolleshunt D'Arcy, stating

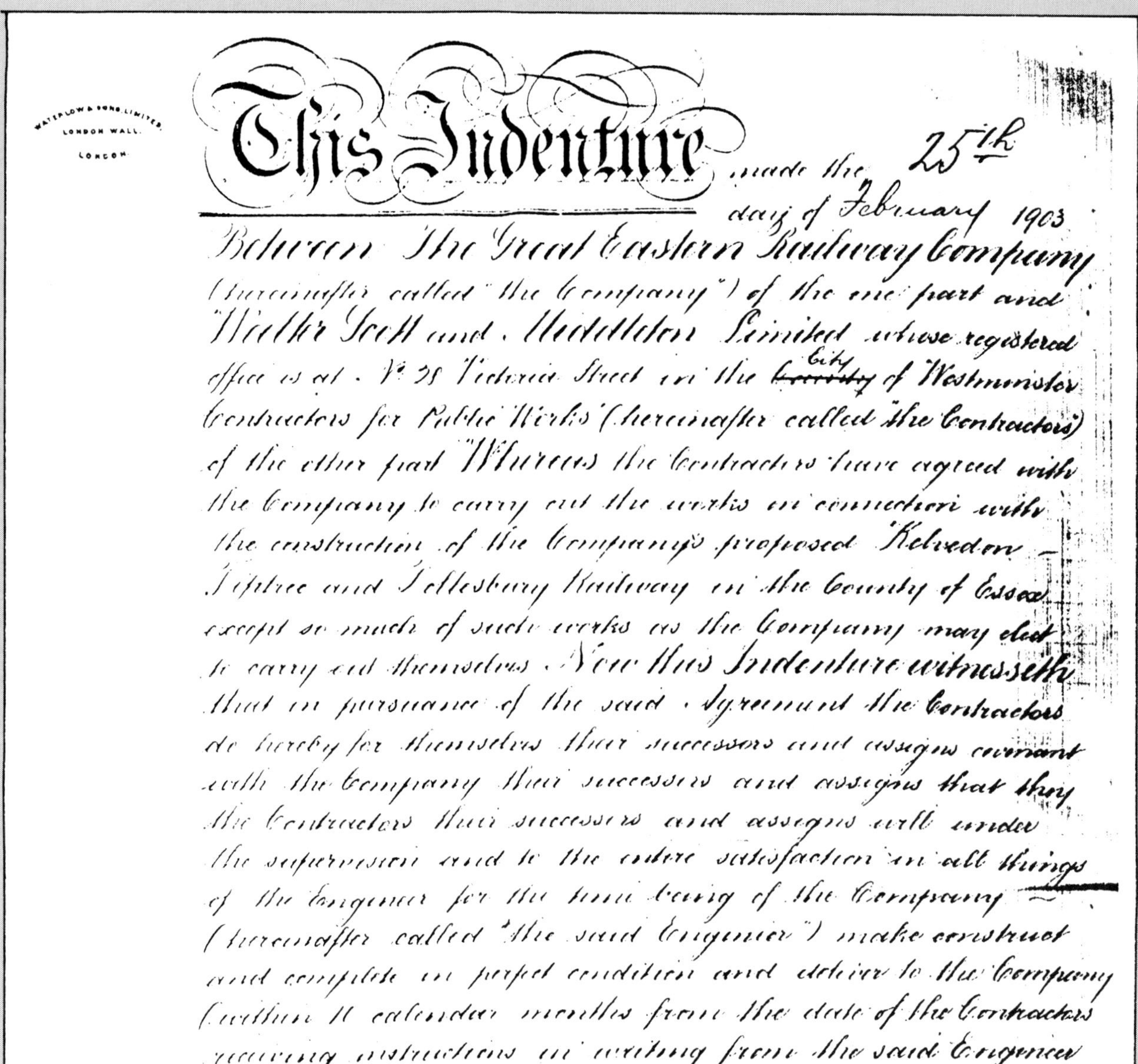

WATERLOW & SONS LIMITED, LONDON WALL, LONDON

This Indenture made the 25th day of February 1903 Between The Great Eastern Railway Company (hereinafter called "the Company") of the one part and Walter Scott and Middleton Limited whose registered office is at No. 28 Victoria Street in the ~~County~~ City of Westminster Contractors for Public Works (hereinafter called "the Contractors") of the other part Whereas the Contractors have agreed with the Company to carry out the works in connection with the construction of the Company's proposed Kelvedon – Tiptree and Tollesbury Railway in the County of Essex except so much of such works as the Company may elect to carry out themselves Now this Indenture witnesseth that in pursuance of the said Agreement the Contractors do hereby for themselves their successors and assigns covenant with the Company their successors and assigns that they the Contractors their successors and assigns will under the supervision and to the entire satisfaction in all things of the Engineer for the time being of the Company (hereinafter called "the said Engineer") make construct and complete in perfect condition and deliver to the Company within 11 calendar months from the date of the Contractors receiving instructions in writing from the said Engineer to proceed with the same the said proposed new Railway (including the Permanent Way) the whole of the said works to be in accordance with the Plans and Sections furnished or to be furnished by the said Engineer to the Contractors and shall to the satisfaction of the said Engineer maintain the said works except the Permanent way for the period of 1 year after the certified completion thereof by the said Engineer. The whole of the said works shall be in all respects subject to the description of materials and Schedule of Prices referred to in the Schedule hereunto annexed and shall be carried out in all respects in strict accordance with the General Conditions and Specification entered into by Charles Wills with the Company for the construction of

Indenture between the GER and Walter Scott and Middleton Ltd. for the construction of the Kelvedon, Tiptree & Tollesbury Light Railway.

that he was continually receiving enquiries regarding progress of the proposed railway. It was agreed that Mr Hudson should be invited to meet the General Manager, so that the latest information could be advised.

The heaviest construction work encountered by the contractor's navvies was the removal of 50,000 cu. yards of earth from the cutting near Tolleshunt Knights, and the construction of the two arch Blind Lane overbridge. The soil removed from the cutting was utilised to build up embankments on other parts of the formation. Unfortunately, after the wet weather, the earthworks were ankle deep in mud, and waggons and horses were bogged down in the quagmire. Once drier weather prevailed the narrow brown swath extended across the Essex fields towards Tollesbury, while laying of permanent way and ballasting continued unabated well into the late summer evenings, as the contractor's men attempted to make up for time lost in the winter months.

A further application for a siding alongside the new light railway near Inworth, between Feering and Tiptree, was made by Mr Thorne. The engineer estimated the construction cost of Heath Siding at £470 and, after negotiation with Thorne, approval was given on 19th April 1904 for the siding to be laid, provided Thorne supplied the land free of charge, and paid £47 towards construction subject to the usual 5 per cent allowance for traffic. With both Moss's application for Brooklands and Thorne's applications for Heath, provision was initially made, and subsequently agreed, that the GER would make the sidings available for general public traffic, and in that event the rental would be reduced to 5s 0d per week.

During the final stages of construction, the contractors used one of their Manning Wardle 0-6-0 tank locomotives to assist with the movement of ballast wagons along the new light railway, although all interchange work at Kelvedon, between the main line and the light railway, was carried out by a GER locomotive. By August all the permanent way, except for some sidings, had been laid and ballasted, whilst the stations were almost complete. After consultation with the contractor regarding progress of outstanding items, the GER duly notified the Board of Trade that the light railway was ready for inspection. Once ballasting was complete it appears local people were offered sample rides along the new railway on Whit Monday, in open wagons hauled by the contractor's locomotive, with A. C. Wilkin riding on the first train.

The Board of Trade inspection was carried out by Lt. Col. P.G. Von Donop, on 22nd September 1904. Initially the new work at Kelvedon was reviewed where Von Donop noted the new trailing connection into the 'up' line from the light railway, and the crossover provided between the 'up' and 'down' main lines. The points and signals on the main line and the connection to the low level were worked from the new station signal box, with its 42 lever frame which included four spare levers, while a fifteen lever ground, frame was also provided, this including four spare levers for yard work. This frame was bolt locked with the main line signal box, and the Inspector expressed his satisfaction that all interlocking was correct. Von Donop then turned his attention to the new light railway which was reported as being 8 miles 45.90 chains in length, with an average width of formation of 16ft. After inspecting the permanent way

Tolleshunt Knights Station (4 miles and 6 chains from Kelvedon) was located adjacent to a gated level crossing, and was opened by the GER on 12th December 1910 to serve as a railhead for this scattered parish. The station was unstaffed, and originally trains only called by request. View facing Kelvedon.

D. Trevor Rowe

GREAT EASTERN RAILWAY

OPENING

OF

A NEW LIGHT RAILWAY

BETWEEN

KELVEDON AND TOLLESBURY

A New Light Railway between Kelvedon and Tollesbury will be opened for Traffic on Saturday, 1st October, 1904, and Trains will run as under:—

DOWN TRAINS.		WEEK-DAYS.							
		a.m.		a.m.		p.m.		p.m.	p.m. Saturdays only
London (Liverpool Street)	dep.	8 55	...	10 55	...	...	...	4 18	
Chelmsford	„	9 57	...	11 56	...	...	...	5 10	
Witham	„	10 13	...	12 15	...	...	...	5 27	
Kelvedon	arr.	10 21	...	12 23	...	...	...	5 35	
Ipswich	dep.	8 55	...	...	...	1 29	...	3 30	
Colchester	„	9 41	...	...	...	2 25	...	4 9	4 57
Kelvedon	arr.	10 4	...	...	...	2 42	...	4 32	5 16
		Mixd.							
Kelvedon	dep.	10 45	...	12 30	...	2 45	...	5 40	
Tiptree	„	11 3	...	12 44	...	2 59	...	5 54	
Tolleshunt D'Arcy	„	11 19	...	12 56	...	3 11	...	6 6	
Tollesbury	arr.	11 25	...	1 2	...	3 17	...	6 12	

UP TRAINS.		WEEK-DAYS.							
		a.m.		a.m.		p.m.		Mixd. p.m.	
Tollesbury	dep.	8 25	...	11 40	...	2 [illegible]	...	6 20	...
Tolleshunt D'Arcy	„	8 32	...	11 47	...	2 [illegible]	...	6 31	...
Tiptree	„	8 44	...	11 59	...	2 19	...	6 47	...
Kelvedon	arr.	8 57	...	12 12	...	2 32	...	7 0	...
Kelvedon	dep.	10 21	...	12 23	...	3 40	...	7 43	...
Colchester	arr.	10 36	...	12 44	...	4 0	...	8 1	...
Ipswich	„	11 12	...	1 48	...	4 40	...	9 12	...
Kelvedon	dep.	9 8	...	1 7	...	2 42	...	7 33	...
Witham	arr.	9 18	...	1 19	...	2 53	...	7 45	...
Chelmsford	„	9 40	...	1 38	...	3 18	...	8 8	...
London (Liverpool Street)	„	10 26	...	2 25	...	4 20	...	9 6	...

NO TRAINS ON SUNDAYS.

FARES FOR THE SINGLE JOURNEY:—

KELVEDON AND	d.	TIPTREE AND	d.	TOLLESHUNT D'ARCY AND	d.
Tiptree	**4**	**Tolleshunt D'Arcy**	**3**	**Tollesbury**	**2**
Tolleshunt D'Arcy	**7**	**Tollesbury**	**5**		
Tollesbury ...	**9**				

Tickets will be issued on the Train.

Personal luggage not exceeding 60 lbs. in weight will be allowed to be taken by each Adult Passenger free of charge.

Parcels conveyed between **Kelvedon** and **Tollesbury** will be charged as under:—

Not exceeding 7 lbs. ... ... *3d.*
Over 7 lbs., but not exceeding 14 lbs. ... ... *5d.*
Over 14 lbs., but not exceeding 28 lbs. ... ... *7d.*
Over 28 lbs., but not exceeding 56 lbs. ... ... *9d.*
Excess weight above 56 lbs., 1d. for every 8 lbs. or part thereof.

London, September, 1904. J. F. S. GOODAY, General Manager.

The GER Timetable and Fare Chart, announcing the opening of the Kelvedon to Tollesbury Light Railway.

the fencing was checked, Von Donop noting that it was formed of wooden posts 6ft. apart connected by stretched steel wire throughout the whole length of the line. On journeying along the light railway, the Inspector noted that the drainage of the formation was by side ditches and under rail earthenware pipes. The gradients were steep and undulating, the maximum being 1 in 50 whilst the deepest cutting was 19ft. deep for 12 chains and the highest embankment 17½ft. high for 11 chains. The Lt. Col. then inspected the one overbridge at Blind Lane and tested deflections of the two stream underbridges, which were found to be satisfactory. Comment was passed on the four public road level crossings with gates, and the ten ungated level crossings, where close inspection of the fencing and cattle guards was carried out. The sidings at Kelvedon (Low Level) and three of the four stations were also inspected, together with the goods sidings at Brooklands, Heath, Church and Old Hall. The Inspector commented 'The sidings are properly trapped and at each end points are worked by two small ground frames of two levers locked by the key attached to the train staff'.

Von Donop requested the following, lamps to be provided at Kelvedon (Low Level), Tiptree, Tolleshunt D'Arcy, and Tollesbury Station, whilst at Kelvedon (Low Level) the spare siding required the provision of trap points. All points along the route of the railway required to be connected properly, and despite being erected and sited, the Inspector found the mile posts devoid of distances, and required these to be painted thereon. Most of the stations were devoid of notice-boards, and these required provision and erection. The rail connection used by the contractor near Heath level crossing was to be removed as a matter of urgency, while the reverse curves at 6 miles 27 chains from Kelvedon required alteration and easing to give a short straight section between the curves. At Tollesbury the Inspector required the completion of fencing on the 'down' side of the railway, and the fitting of trap points to the section of line leading to the proposed extension.

Under Clause 15 of the Light Railway Order the GER was required to provide gates at four level crossings across public roads in the parishes of Feering, Inworth, Tolleshunt Knights and Tolleshunt D'Arcy. The Lt. Col. found the contractor had also provided the gates, as specified in Clause 15, at level crossing No. 54 in the Parish of Tollesbury, on a section of line not scheduled for inspection. The level crossing gates on the Kelvedon to Tollesbury section closed across both road and railway, but in order to safeguard the public, Von Donop ordered the GER to provide gatekeepers to open and shut the gates at level crossing No. 6, in the Parish of Feering, and No. 85 in the Parish of Inworth. At the other two crossings, No. 17 in the Parish of Tolleshunt D'Arcy and No. 47 in the Parish of Tolleshunt Knights, the employment of gatekeepers could be dispensed with and the gates opened and closed by trainmen. Subject to the completion of the detailed remedial work, the Inspector authorised the light railway to open for traffic, but the GER contested the stipulation regarding the provision of gatekeepers at Feering and Inworth, and wrote to the Board of Trade requesting release from the obligation.

On receipt of the necessary certificate, notices announcing the opening of the new railway, and giving details of the train services from 1st October 1904, were posted at stations in the East Essex area. In the last week of September the specially modified coaching stock for the new light railway arrived at Kelvedon, whilst staff appointed to the stations at Tiptree, Tolleshunt D'Arcy and Tollesbury were advised of their new posts. The line was duly cleared of ballast wagons by the contractor's locomotive, whilst Adams 0-4-2T No. 25 was dispatched to Kelvedon Shed to take over the branch. Evidently the contractor attempted to outdo the GER by giving local people, especially children, an inaugural ride. Their locomotive hauled several flag-bedecked wagons and made a couple of runs, between Kelvedon and Tiptree, in the last week of September.

One of the GER's 'trespassers will be prosecuted', notices posted alongside the branch.

D. Trevor Rowe

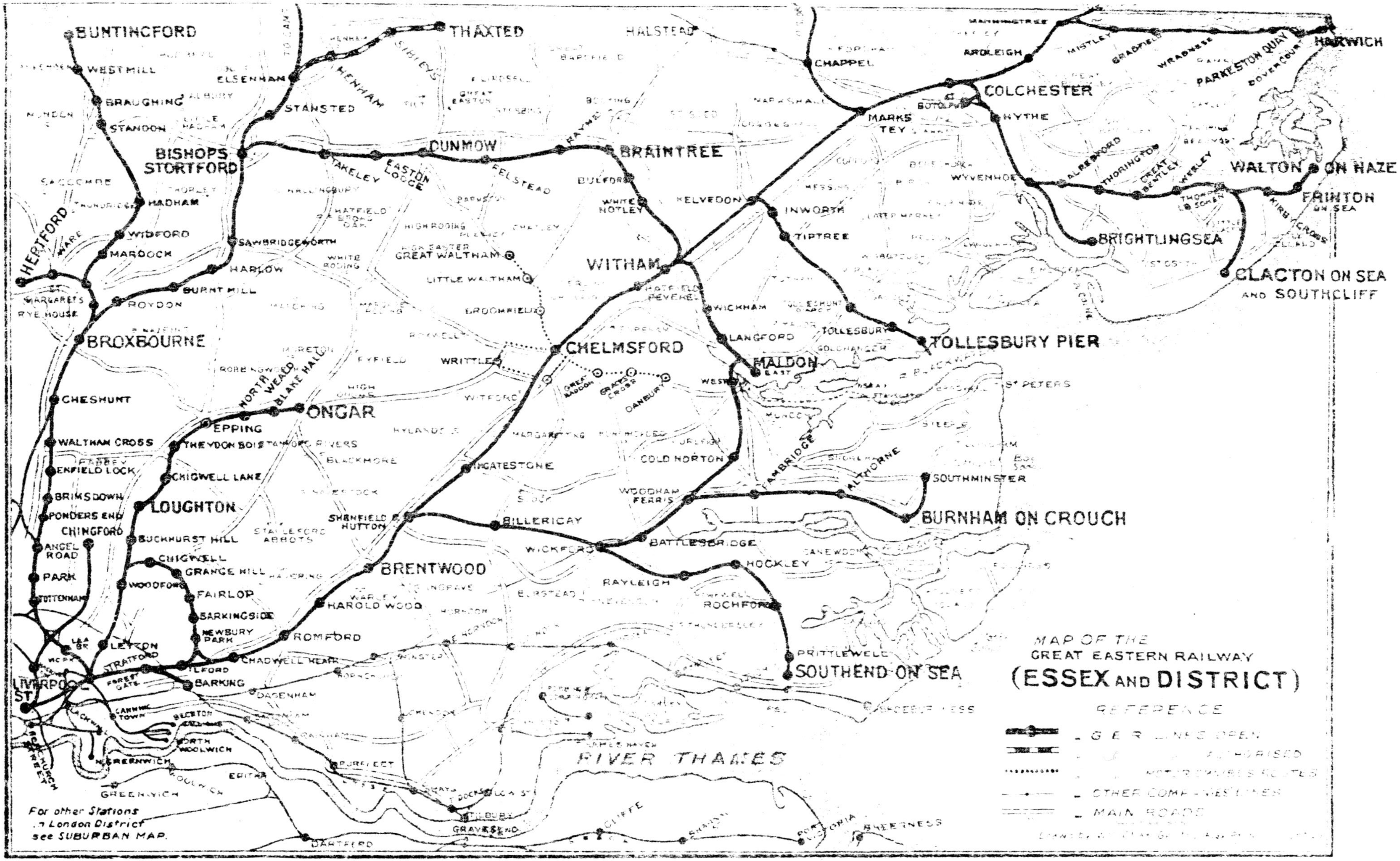

A 1910 GER map of Essex and district, showing the Tollesbury branch and the surrounding lines.

Chapter Two

Great Eastern Administration

On the morning of 1st October 1904 rain fell steadily as 120 passengers, including Edward Wilson, the GER Engineer, and Inspectors Chapman and Norman, joined the first train at Kelvedon. The train departed sharp to time at 10.45 a.m., without any formal ceremony, under the watchful eye of Stationmaster C. E. Jarvis.

Some enthusiasm was, however, shown by the employees of Wilkin's jam factory at Tiptree, who stopped work to cheer the train on its journey. Local people gathered at the lineside and farm workers stopped their labours in the fields to wave a greeting to the passing train. Special cheers were given at the gated level crossings, where the train halted to allow the fireman to open and the guard to close the gates. A large number of people gathered at Tollesbury to watch and cheer the arrival of the train, amongst whom was Captain Seymour, the racing master of the yacht *Shamrock III*, who had sailed his craft from Brightlingsea to Tollesbury especially for the event. The town of Tollesbury was not overawed by the occasion, and took the opening of the railway calmly. After leaving the train the special guests were taken by road to view the *Shamrock III* moored near the site of the proposed Tollesbury Pier Station, before returning to the flag-bedecked King's Head Hotel for lunch. The host, H. G. Wombwell, provided the small group with an excellent meal before speeches advocating success to the new line were rounded off with toasts. The party then returned to Tollesbury Station to journey on the afternoon train back to Kelvedon. The only disappointment to the successful day was the absence of three people who had done much to advocate and promote the railway; the Hon. C. H. Strutt, MP, who was away in Borneo, Dr Salter, whose wife had died recently and A. C. Wilkin, indisposed with a heavy cold. During the afternoon and early evening the branch train was packed with Tollesbury people making the return journey to Tiptree and Kelvedon, and with Tiptree folk journeying to the end of the line and back.

At a Board Meeting on 4th October 1904, the GER Traffic Committee discussed the Board of Trade report on Kelvedon Station and the Tollesbury line, and two weeks later received correspondence regarding the gatekeepers at certain level crossings on the line. Permission was granted for train crews to open and close the gates at Feering and Inworth, saving the Company the cost of residential crossing keepers.

After the novelty of riding on the first trains had ceased, the branch settled down to provide the district with a regular, if spasmodic, service, and carried most passengers on Saturdays for Colchester Market. The contractor retained some navvies on the line until December, as problems with bank slips required additional wagons of ballast and hardcore to consolidate embankments and cuttings at various locations. Most of the contractor's other staff retained on the payroll were put to work on the earthworks at the Tollesbury Pier extension, the number employed being far less than the original.

On 6th December 1904, the General Manager advised the Traffic Committee that for the month of October receipts on the Tollesbury Light Railway were £183, equal to 1s 6d per train mile. Working expenses of £259 had, however, meant a loss of £76, although contributive earnings on the main line, for traffic starting from or destined for stations on the branch, had amounted to £215, exclusive of passenger traffic. Receipts for the month of November showed a slight fall to £175, although the 1s 6d per train mile remained. Working expenses of £249 resulted in a direct loss of £74, the working expenses being affected by additional engineer's trains. Contributive earning on the main line increased to £338, inclusive of passenger traffic. Special trains, run for the benefit of the Engineer, again increased the working expenses total to £259 for December 1904, while receipts of £178, equal to 1s 6d per train mile, meant another loss of £81. Contributive earnings on the main line continued to improve and resulted in £310 including passenger revenue, and an additional £24 was received for goods traffic passing between the contractor and destinations on the light railway. Figures for January 1905 showed receipts of £172 equal to 1s 6d per train mile, offset by working expenses of £253, but despite the loss of £81 the GER Board was satisfied with the traffic generated to and from the new railway. Contributive earnings on the main line reached a new figure of £407, with an additional £35 for contractor's goods traffic being sent for the extension work beyond Tollesbury. The GER Accountant estimated that allowing for 60 per cent of these figures for working expenses, the goods receipts showed a profit of £96. In February 1905, the light railway showed a deficit on actual earnings, but when this was compared with contributive earnings towards the traffic carried by the railway company, the line showed a profit of £92.

Receipts £183
Per train mile 1s 6d
Working expenses £237
Loss £54

The following month showed an improved train mile earning figure, although actual working expenses still exceeded receipts.

Receipts £213
Per train mile 1s 10d
Working expenses £239
Loss £26

In March 1905 the Goods Manager reported that due to an increase of heavy traffic, including large quantities of coal, grain and root crops, the roadways in Tiptree and Tollesbury yards were unsafe to work over. When the railway was constructed, the roadways to goods yards were never made up, so the wet weather and increased loading left deep ruts in the surface, resulting in two waggons shedding their loads and one waggon breaking its axle. The Engineer was requested to investigate as a matter of urgency, and reported to the Way and Works Committee on 18th April 1905 that costs to make good the damage were estimated at £915.

The Committee and, indeed, the GER Board were rather unhappy, as the cost of the light railway was continually increasing over estimate. The original estimate for the light railway was £33,284 but actual work, including the cost of Kelvedon Station, together with the additional expenditure now proposed was £60,000, of which only £16,000 was given by the Treasury and £750 contributed by local landowners. Despite the remaining £43,000 being borne by the GER the railway authorities decided to maintain good faith with their customers by inducing further trade, and authorised the repair work to the sidings to proceed. No work, however, was carried out.

After the basic service had been operating for a few months it became clear that additional traffic would be obtained at Inworth, after several local people had voiced a desire for a halt to be located near the village. The GER, in the spring of 1905, arranged for the contractor to provide a suitable halt similar in style to the other station on the line and subsequently, on 1st May 1905, Inworth Station was opened for traffic on the 'down' side of the line, adjacent to Heath Siding, but over two miles from Inworth Village.

Early in 1905 the Britannia Fruit Company, ever in need of manure for enriching the soil of their fruit farms, approached the GER to seek their assistance in conveying manure traffic from London by rail. The railway authorities, who were eager to assist, investigated the matter and estimated the provision of the necessary sidings would incur expenditure of £815. The traffic conveyed since the opening of the line had exceeded expectations, and on several occasions it had been necessary to delay traffic by holding wagons in other sidings on the branch. It was thought that such delays would seriously affect the fruit and green pea traffic loaded at various sidings. At a meeting of the Way and Works Committee, on 2nd May 1905, advice was given that the Britannia Fruit Company were prepared to convey to the railway company the necessary land, reserving for themselves a strip of land 60ft. long by 15ft. wide to locate the manure bins, access being obtained by a gate in the existing fence. The fruit company also guaranteed the GER a movement of 2,000 tons per annum for three years, on the understanding that the siding could be used by the general public when use of the factory siding at Tiptree was discontinued for manure traffic. The necessary authority was duly given to construct the siding at Tudwick Road.

During the period April to September 1905, receipts actually showed a slight profit, with takings of £1,335 at 2s 1d per train mile against working expenses of £1,325. The results for six months ending 31st December 1905, were again satisfactory to the GER authorities because although receipts of £1,316 were exceeded by working expenses of £1,406, a deficit of £90, the earning per train mile of 1s 11d was 5d in excess of the 1s 6d average for GER branches and secondary routes. After taking into account the contributive earnings (eliminating the estimated value of traffic diverted from Kelvedon to the light railway amounting to £1,548, and deducting 60 per cent for working expenses with the loss of £90) the total working showed a net profit of £529 to the Company, equal to 2 per cent per annum on GER proportion of capital outlaid on the new railway.

The GER Board continued, however, to express concern regarding the excessive costs of building the line from Kelvedon to Tollesbury, and in April 1906 again requested details of expenditure on both the light railway and the rebuilt Kelvedon Station. On 1st May 1906 the General Manager produced the following figures;

	Estimated	*Actual*
Kelvedon to Tollesbury Railway	£39,851	£53,308
less Treasury grant	16,000	16,000
	23,851	37,308
Kelvedon (new station)	9,024	4,834
	£32,875	£42,142

The Directors were gratified to learn that the overspending of £13,457 on the Tiptree Railway had been partially offset by the saving of £4,190 on Kelvedon Station, but requested

A mixed train from Tollesbury to Kelvedon, formed of the original 4-wheel passenger coaches modified for the line, approaches Tiptree hauled by K9 class 0-4-2T, No. 25. The photograph portrays the station shortly after the line opened for traffic in 1904.

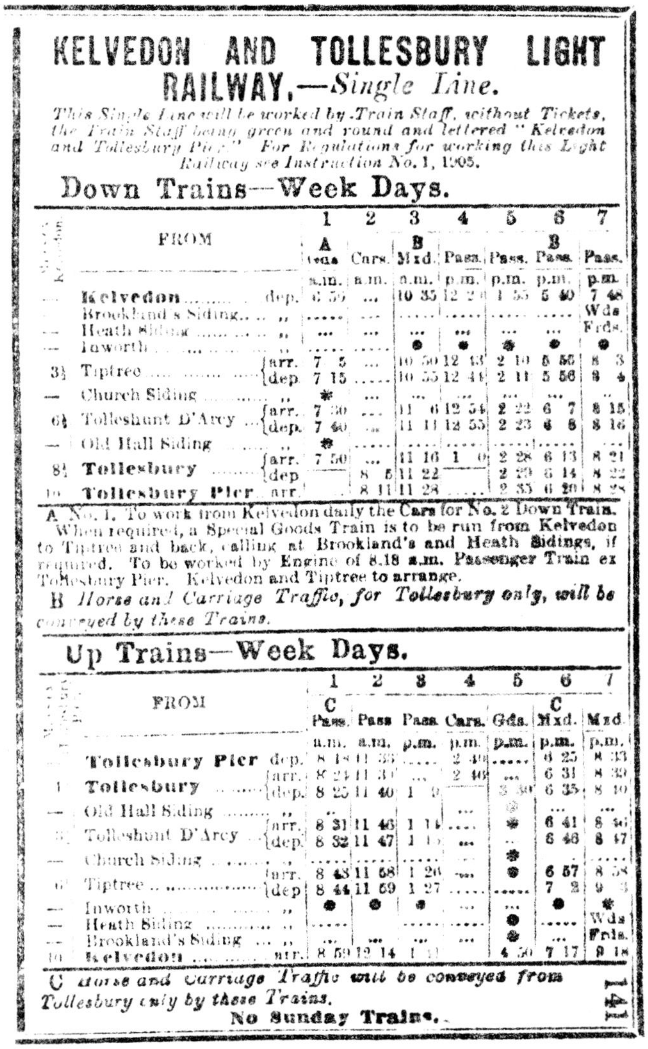

KELVEDON AND TOLLESBURY LIGHT RAILWAY.—*Single Line.*

This Single Line will be worked by Train Staff, without Tickets, the Train Staff being green and round and lettered "Kelvedon and Tollesbury Pier." For Regulations for working this Light Railway see Instruction No. 1, 1905.

Down Trains—Week Days.

Miles	FROM		1 A Pass	2 Cars.	3 B Mxd.	4 Pass.	5 Pass.	6 B Pass.	7 Pass.
			a.m.	a.m.	a.m.	p.m.	p.m.	p.m.	p.m.
—	**Kelvedon**	dep.	6 5[illegible]	...	10 35	12 2[illegible]	1 55	5 40	7 48
—	Brookland's Siding	„	.....	.....	.....	.....	.....	.....	Wds
—	Heath Siding	„	...	...	...	...	...	...	Frds.
—	Inworth	„	.....	.....	*	*	*	*	*
3½	Tiptree	arr.	7 5	...	10 50	12 43	2 10	5 55	8 3
		dep.	7 15	.....	10 55	12 44	2 11	5 56	8 4
—	Church Siding	„	*	...	...	...	...	...	..
6¾	Tolleshunt D'Arcy	arr.	7 30	...	11 6	12 54	2 22	6 7	8 15
		dep.	7 40	...	11 11	12 55	2 23	6 8	8 16
—	Old Hall Siding	„	*	.....	.....	.....	.....	.....	...
8½	**Tollesbury**	arr.	7 50	...	11 16	1 0	2 28	6 13	8 21
		dep.		8 5	11 22		2 29	6 14	8 22
10	**Tollesbury Pier**	arr.	...	8 11	11 28	.....	2 35	6 20	8 28

A No. 1. To work from Kelvedon daily the **Cars for No. 2 Down Train.**

When required, a Special Goods Train is to be run from Kelvedon to Tiptree and back, calling at **Brookland's and Heath Sidings,** if required. To be worked by **Engine of 8.18 a.m. Passenger Train ex** Tollesbury Pier. Kelvedon and Tiptree **to arrange.**

B *Horse and Carriage Traffic, for* ***Tollesbury only, will be*** *conveyed by these Trains.*

Up Trains—Week Days.

Miles	FROM		1 C Pass.	2 Pass	3 Pass.	4 Cars.	5 Gds.	6 C Mxd.	7 Mxd.
			a.m.	a.m.	p.m.	p.m.	p.m.	p.m.	p.m.
—	**Tollesbury Pier**	dep.	8 18	11 35	.....	2 40	.....	6 25	8 33
1	**Tollesbury**	arr.	8 24	11 3[illegible]	...	2 46	...	6 31	8 39
		dep.	8 25	11 40	1 [illegible]		3 30	6 35	8 40
—	Old Hall Siding	„	..			...	*	...	...
3[illegible]	Tolleshunt D'Arcy	arr.	8 31	11 46	1 1[illegible]	.....	*	6 41	8 46
		dep.	8 32	11 47	1 1[illegible]	...	..	6 46	8 47
—	Church Siding	„	.....	.....	.....	.....	*		.....
6[illegible]	Tiptree	arr.	8 43	11 58	1 26	...	*	6 57	8 58
		dep.	8 44	11 59	1 27	.....	.....	7 2	9 3
—	Inworth	„	*	*	*	...	...	*	*
—	Heath Siding	„	.....		.....	.....	*	.....	Wds
—	Brookland's Siding	„	...	...	...	...	*	...	Frds.
10	**Kelvedon**	arr.	8 59	12 14	1 [illegible]		4 [illegible]	7 17	9 18

C *Horse and Carriage Traffic* ***will be conveyed from*** *Tollesbury only by these Trains.*

No Sunday Trains.

The GER Working Timetable, 1907.

Kelvedon 'up' fixed branch distant signal, of typical GER design, located on the 'down' side of the line near Feering level crossing on 30th September 1950. The original finial has been replaced by a post cap.

LCGB/Ken Nunn Collection

An October 1904 view of Tollesbury Station with the branch line train approaching behind K9 class 0-4-2T, No. 25. The three open wagons, covered van and brake van in the yard siding indicate that the morning freight has made its run.

Lens of Sutton

a closer watch be kept on the working expenses of the line with a view to savings being made.

Tenders for the construction of the pier and ancillary works at Tollesbury were considered by the Way and Works Committee on 2nd October 1906. Eight tenders were received ranging from £4,048 19s 10d to £5,781 6s 2d and, after considerable discussion, the offer of Bott & Stennett Ltd. of Victoria Street in Westminster, at £4,048 19s 10d, was accepted.

Many farmers and smallholders, delivering produce to the sidings for transit to market or collecting railborne items, continued to complain of the poor state of the gravel roadways and approaches in station yards and goods sidings on the line. After the two winters of 1904 and 1905 and the failure of the railway company to carry out any remedial work, the wet weather in the spring of 1906 aggravated the situation and the roadways were again deep with ruts. Matters came to a head when two waggons overturned, spilling their produce on the ground. Remonstrations to the railway authorities produced rapid plans for metalling the roads in station yards and work was completed in October 1906 at a cost of £422, a saving of £268 on the revised estimate of £690, the original estimate being £915.

An electrical storm passed across East Anglia on 27th July 1906 and the resultant heavy rain caused flooding on the extension works to Tollesbury Pier, forcing the contractor's men to delay progress for almost a week until water was pumped away. The rain also caused minor flooding on the light railway, and trains were forced to proceed with caution over several sections of line. Work on the extension line to Tollesbury Pier progressed slowly, partly because of the marshy terrain near the terminus which required consolidating, and also because of the fewer navvies allotted to the task. By the end of March 1907 construction of both railway station and pier were almost completed, and the GER notified the Board of Trade the railway was ready for inspection. The new pier at Tollesbury and ancillary work cost a total of £4,652, against the Engineer's estimate of £5,300.

On 13th May 1907, Lt. Col. P. G. Von Donop returned to the light railway to carry out the Board of Trade inspection of the extension from Tollesbury to Tollesbury Pier. He found the 1 mile 36 chain long new line substantially constructed, with permanent way similar to that provided on the existing light railway. The steepest gradient was again 1 in 50, with the sharpest curve being one of 20 chains radius, and three public level crossings were provided, two protected by cattle guards and one with gates. The Lt. Col. exempted the GER from employing a gatekeeper at the latter, and authorised the gates to be opened and closed by trainmen. The station at Tollesbury Pier was complete except for the provision of a platform lamp, and the Inspector concluded that he had no objection to the line opening for traffic provided the run-round loop at the terminus was never used for the storage of wagons. The GER authorities assured the Board of Trade on this point and therefore no trap points were provided, the points being securely padlocked with the key kept in the possession of the porter in charge.

On Wednesday 15th May 1907, with the departure of the 8.18a.m. train to Kelvedon, the railway from Tollesbury to the new terminus at Tollesbury Pier was officially opened to traffic. Flags were flying from various buildings in Tollesbury, and a small group of officials visited the rather bleak site to promenade down the pier. The structure, extending 1,770ft. in length into the River Blackwater, was constructed mainly of timber with earthworks at the shore end. During spring tides the depth of water at the pierhead was 25ft. at high tide and 10ft. at low tide, affording shallow draught vessels to load and unload at all states of the tide. Alongside the pier, steps descended to water level 1,500 ft. from the station, where the depth of water at high tide was 8ft. Other steps were available 66ft. from the station, where 5ft. of water at high tide allowed small boats to offload. The width of the pier was 8ft 10in. along its entire length, whilst the pierhead promenade and stage was 50ft. wide by 18ft. deep. The whole structure, except for the pierhead end, was protected by a wooden fencing 6ft. 6in. in height.

The object of the pier extension was essentially to afford accommodation and mooring for yachts as well as tapping the resources of the local shrimp, oyster beds and other fish traffic, with ready access to the London market using the railway via Kelvedon. The railway company and promoters advertised that the area in the locality of the pier was suitable for the erection of yachting accommodation and bungalows.

Having taken the gamble of opening the line to the pier, the GER hoped Tollesbury Pier would add to the yachting and fishing facilities of the River Blackwater, offering boatmen ready access to Brightlingsea, Burnham-on-Crouch and the coastal resorts of Clacton and Harwich which were all served by the railway company. To attract yachtsmen and other custom to Tollesbury Pier, the GER issued cheap weekend tickets from Liverpool Street, with holders being permitted to return from other yachting stations on the East Coast on payment of a small surcharge. Even the possible use of the pier as a point for steamer services to the Continent was advocated.

Work on Tudwick Road Siding, located between Tiptree and Tolleshunt D'Arcy, was completed by early autumn of 1907 at a cost of £687, a saving of £137 on the £815 estimated by the Engineer. Lt. Col. P. G. Von Donop again visited the light railway, on 28th October, to inspect the new connection provided from the main single line to the siding. He duly authorised the opening of the siding after being satisfied that the points facing 'up' trains, worked by a two lever ground frame, would be released by Annett's key attached to the train staff.

For the six months ending 31st December 1907, receipts of £1,428 were wholly overtaken by £1,891 working expenses, the additional expenditure being incurred by the Engineer making good a bank slip between Tiptree and Tolleshunt D'Arcy. By June 1908, receipts again exceeded working expenses. Takings of £1,712, compared with outgoings of £1,614, meant a profit of £98, but at the end of the year receipts had slumped to £1,511, whilst working expenses had fallen to £1,583 leaving a loss of £72.

As passenger traffic steadily increased it became evident to the railway authorities that the hamlet of Tolleshunt Knights might provide some additional revenue, as several complaints had been made that intending passengers from the village had to walk or travel by horse and cart to Tiptree Station to catch the train. The GER authorities realised that as all trains had to stop for the crew to open and close the level crossing gates across the road, it was feasible to construct a halt to serve the locality. Sited adjacent to the Tiptree to Tolleshunt D'Arcy Road, on the 'down' side of the line north of the crossing, the station was built with the usual low platform and was provided with a coach body for waiting accommodation. Tolleshunt Knights opened for traffic on 12th December 1910, with trains initially only calling if required to pick up or set down passengers.

The increasing output of Wilkin's jam factory brought additional traffic to the line. Unfortunately the meagre siding accommodation meant that empty wagons had to be taken to other yards on the branch, or be held at Kelvedon until they could be accepted at Tiptree for loading. By March 1910 delays were causing production problems, and Wilkin complained to the GER early in April about the traffic congestion with a request being made for an additional siding serving the factory, and such was the urgency of the matter that Wilkin's offered to lay the siding on their portion of land. The Engineer estimated the cost as £330, and reported to the Traffic Committee on 21st April 1910. The cost on the GER property was £30 and the committee subsequently authorised the expenditure of £130, £100 to assist Wilkin's with their portion of siding and £30 for the connection on GER land. Wilkin subsequently financed their remaining portion. The siding was not, however, installed until the late summer of 1912, and then at a cost to the GER of £40, £10 above the amount estimated.

For the half year ending June 1910, traffic receipts of £1,462 exceeded working expenses by £50. The new station at Kelvedon and the light railway low level station received their first repairs and painting in July 1911, when the contract was awarded to R. Woollaston & Company who tendered at £213.

The rather remote location of the station at Tolleshunt D'Arcy caused minor inconveniences, as the porter in charge lived away from the railway, so in 1912 the GER Superintendent requested the provision of cottages for railway personnel to be built near the station. Because of the warning by the Board to keep costs of works on the branch to a minimum, the Way and Works Committee authorised the construction of only one cottage, at an estimated cost of £308. To achieve a 2½ per cent return on the outlay a rent of 5s 0d per week was requested but, at a meeting on 2nd May 1912, it was disclosed that the local authority had recently erected some cottages in the district and were charging tenants 3s 0d per week rent. The Traffic Superintendent was adamant that the man occupying the proposed house could not be charged any more, so after discussion, approval was given for the construction of the cottage adjacent to the station, on the east side of the railway and south of the road. The cost of construction was £308, with a weekly rent of 3s 0d giving a ¾ per cent return on the outlay. On 6th June 1912 the contract for building the cottage was awarded to M. Richards & Son of Witham who tendered at £225, and the cottage was completed the following year.

Earnings on the light railway continued to fluctuate and in the half year ending June 1912, the receipts of £1,349 were exceeded by working expenses of £1,418. Receipts from jam and fruit traffic to and from Wilkin's helped boost the receipts for the half year ending December 1912 to £1,810 which, after deduction of working expenses of £1,579 brought an operating surplus of £231. For the first half year of 1913, working results had almost evened out, with receipts of £1,415 being offset by expenses of £1,422. The Tollesbury line showed considerable improvement in traffic receipts during the six months ending 31st December 1913 and 30th June 1914, showing excess of receipts over working expenditure of £415 and £530 respectively. The figures were:

	Receipts	*Working Expenses*
Six months ending 31st December 1913	£1,929	£1,591
Six months ending 30th June 1914	£1,514	£1,061

A view of Tollesbury Station shortly after the line was opened in 1904. In addition to the low level platform and spartan facilities, the waterworks tower dominates the background.

KELVEDON AND TOLLESBURY LIGHT RAILWAY.—*Junction with Main Line at Kelvedon.*

Reference to other Tables	DOWN TRAINS.		WEEK DAYS. morn	morn	even.	even.	even.	even.
106 to 111	**LONDON (Liverpool St.)**	dep.	8 45	10 55	...	4 18	...	*6 20*
	Chelmsford	„	9 47	11 57	—	5 8	—	*7 18*
	Witham	„	10 3	12 15	...	5 27		*7 39*
	Kelvedon	arr.	10 11	12 23	—	5 35	Sats. only.	*7 46*
113 to 117	Ipswich	dep.	8 55	...	12 50	3 30		*6 12*
	Colchester	„	9 41	—	1 28	4 8	*4 51*	*7 10*
	Kelvedon	arr.	10 4	...	1 46	4 32	*5 10*	*7 37*
			Mxd					
106 111	**Kelvedon**	dep.	10 25	12 29	1 55	5 40		*7 50*
	Inworth	„	**C**	**C**	**C**	**C**		**C**
	Tiptree	„	10 45	12 44	2 11	5 56		*8 6*
	Tolleshunt D'Arcy	„	11 1	12 55	2 23	6 8		*8 18*
106 111	**Tollesbury**	arr.	11 6	1 0	2 28	6 13		*8 23*
		dep.	**A**	**A**	**A**	6 14		**A**
	Tollesbury (Pier Station)	arr.	...	...	...	6 20		...

(Last column: Wednesdays and Fridays only.)

Reference to other Tables	UP TRAINS.		WEEK DAYS. morn	Mxd morn	even.	Mxd even.	Mxd even.
	Tollesbury (Pier Station)	dep.	8**B**7	11**B**12	—	6 25	*8***B***23*
113 117	**Tollesbury**	arr.	8 13	11 18	...	6 31	*8 29*
		dep.	8 25	11 34	1 9	6 35	*8 42*
	Tolleshunt D'Arcy	„	8 32	11 44	1 15	6 46	*8 49*
	Tiptree	„	8 44	11 59	1 27	7 2	*9 5*
	Inworth	„	**C**	**C**	**C**	**C**	**C**
113 117	**Kelvedon**	arr.	8 59	12 14	1 41	7 17	*9 20*
106 to 111	Kelvedon	dep.	10 11	12 23	3 40	7 46	*10 32*
	Colchester	arr.	10 26	12 44	4 0	8 4	*10 52*
	Ipswich	„	10 58	1 25	4 40	9 16	*11 34*
113 to 117	Kelvedon	dep.	9 9	12 55	1 46	7 37	10 0
	Witham	arr.	9 19	1 7	1 56	7 49	—
	Chelmsford	„	9 41	1 26	2 15	8 12	10 21
	LONDON (Liverpool St.)	arr.	10 26	2 13	3 12	9 10	11 21

(Last column: Wednesdays and Fridays only.)

A These Trains will run through to Tollesbury Pier when necessary. **B** These Trains will only run from Tollesbury Pier when necessary.
C Calls when required to take up or set down Passengers.
ONLY ONE CLASS OF ACCOMMODATION WILL BE PROVIDED BETWEEN KELVEDON AND TOLLESBURY.

FARES:—

KELVEDON AND	d.
Inworth	3
Tiptree	4
Tolleshunt D'Arcy	7
Tollesbury	9
Tollesbury Pier	11

INWORTH AND	d.
Tiptree	1
Tolleshunt D'Arcy	4
Tollesbury	6
Tollesbury Pier	8

TIPTREE AND	d.
Tolleshunt D'Arcy	3
Tollesbury	5
Tollesbury Pier	7

TOLLESHUNT D'ARCY AND	d.
Tollesbury	2
Tollesbury Pier	4

TOLLESBURY AND
Tollesbury Pier ... ... 2d.

Tickets will be issued on the Train ...

The GER Passenger Timetable, 1910.

KELVEDON AND TOLLESBURY LIGHT RAILWAY.

See page			WEEK DAYS. morn	morn	morn	even.	even.	SUNDAYS.
30 to 32	**LONDON (L'pool St.)**	dep.	7 56	9 16	10 59	4 18	6**X**39	...
	Chelmsford	„	8 50	10 16	12 5	5 12	7 33	—
	Witham	„	9 5	10 34	12 23	5 29	7 51	...
	Kelvedon	arr.	9 13	10 42	12 31	5 37	7 59	—
33 to 35	**Ipswich**	dep.	7 55	10 22	12 39	3 27	5 50	...
	Colchester	„	8 44	11 1	1 28	4 55	7 11	—
	Kelvedon	arr.	9 10	11 24	1 49	5 15	7 36	...
			Mxd					
	KELVEDON	dep.	9 45	11 30	1 55	5 46	8 5	...
	Inworth	„	**C**	**C**	**C**	**C**	**C**	—
	Tiptree	„	10 0	11 46	2 11	6 2	8 21	...
	Tolleshunt Knights	„	**C**	**C**	**C**	**C**	**C**	—
	Tolleshunt D'Arcy	„	10 16	11 58	2 23	6 14	8 33	...
	TOLLESBURY	arr.	10 21	12 3	2 28	6 19	8 38	—
		dep.	...	**A**	**A**	**A**	...	...
	Tollesbury (Pier Station)	arr.	—	—	—	—	—	—

See page			WEEK DAYS. morn	Mxd morn	even.	Mxd even	even.	SUNDAYS.
	Tollesbury (Pier Station)	dep.	8**B**5	—	12**B**35	—	6**B**19	—
	TOLLESBURY	arr.	8 11	...	12 41	...	6 25	...
		dep.	8 26	10 32	1 3	3 15	6 39	—
	Tolleshunt D'Arcy	„	8 33	10 40	1 10	3 30	6 47	...
	Tolleshunt Knights	„	**C**	**C**	**C**	**C**	**C**	—
	Tiptree	„	8 45	10 56	1 22	4 7	7 0	...
	Inworth	„	**C**	**C**	**C**	**C**	**C**	—
	KELVEDON	arr.	9 0	11 12	1 37	4 20	7 15	...
30 to 32	**Kelvedon**	dep.	9 13	12 31	3**D**29	4 56	7 59	—
	Colchester	arr.	9 27	12 50	3**D**48	5 15	8 19	...
	Ipswich	„	10 0	1 31	4 30	5 59	9 30	—
33 to 35	**Kelvedon**	dep.	9 10	11 24	1 49	4 33	7 36	...
	Witham	arr.	9 19	11 31	1 59	4 44	7 46	—
	Chelmsford	„	9 28	11 52	2 18	5 4	8 6	...
	LONDON (L'pool St.)	„	10 20	12 39	3 13	5 45	9 5	—

A These trains will only run through to Tollesbury Pier when necessary.
B These trains will only run from Tollesbury Pier when necessary.
C Calls when required to take up or set down passengers.
D On Saturdays leaves Kelvedon at 2.55 p.m. and arrives Colchester at 3.14 p.m.
X On Saturdays leaves Liverpool Street at 6.8 p.m.

ONLY ONE CLASS OF ACCOMMODATION IS PROVIDED BETWEEN KELVEDON AND TOLLESBURY, AND SINGLE JOURNEY TICKETS ONLY ARE ISSUED.

SINGLE FARES:—

KELVEDON AND	
Inworth	3d.
Tiptree	4d.
Tolleshunt Knights	5d.
Tolleshunt D'Arcy	7d.
Tollesbury	9d.
Tollesbury Pier	11d.

INWORTH AND	
Tiptree	1d.
Tolleshunt Knights	2d.
Tolleshunt D'Arcy	4d.
Tollesbury	6d.
Tollesbury Pier	8d.

TIPTREE AND	
Tolleshunt Knights	1d.
Tolleshunt D'Arcy	3d.
Tollesbury	5d.
Tollesbury Pier	7d.

TOLLESHUNT KNIGHTS &	
Tolleshunt D'Arcy	2d.
Tollesbury	4d.
Tollesbury Pier	6d.

TOLLESHUNT D'ARCY AND	
Tollesbury	2d.
Tollesbury Pier	4d.

TOLLESBURY AND	
Tollesbury Pier	2d.

The GER Public Timetable, 1915.

KELVEDON, TIPTREE, AND TOLLESBURY LIGHT RAILWAY.

The Kelvedon, Tiptree, and Tollesbury Light Railway **(a Single Line)**, which is about 10 miles long, is provided with five Passenger and Goods Stations, viz. :—

Kelvedon (Low Level),
Tiptree,
Tolleshunt D'Arcy,
Tollesbury, and
Tollesbury Pier (not a Goods Station).

A Platform—called **"Inworth"**—is provided against the Level Crossing situate at about three miles from Kelvedon, and the trains are to call at Inworth to take up or set down Passengers when required.

A Platform—called **"Tolleshunt Knights"**—is provided against the Level Crossing situate at about ¾ mile from Tiptree, and the trains are to call at Tolleshunt Knights to take up or set down Passengers when required.

A Pier is provided at the end of the Railway, with access to and from Tollesbury Pier Station.

Intermediate Public and Private Goods Sidings are also provided as under:—

Brooklands Siding (Private),
between Kelvedon and Tiptree, about 1,100 yards from Kelvedon Station.

349

Kelvedon, Tiptree, and Tollesbury Light Railway—*continued.*

Heath Siding (Public),
between Kelvedon and Tiptree, 2¼ miles from Kelvedon Station.

Tudwick Road Siding (Public),
between Tiptree and Tolleshunt D'Arcy, about ½ mile from Tiptree Station.

Church Siding (Public),
between Tiptree and Tolleshunt D'Arcy, about 2¼ miles from Tiptree Station.

Old Hall Siding (Public),
between Tolleshunt D'Arcy and Tollesbury, about 1¼ miles from Tolleshunt D'Arcy Station.

The Points in the Single Line and the Catch Points in the Siding at the Intermediate Goods Sidings are worked by Ground Lever at each place, which is controlled by Annett's Lock, the Key being attached to the Kelvedon and Tollesbury Pier Train Staff. The Points leading to and from the Single Line at each of the Stations must always be kept padlocked, except when required to be used during the time a train is doing work at the Station, the Key (which is common to all the Points at each Station) being kept in the custody of the man in charge of the Station.

Whenever a train has work to do at an intermediate Goods Siding, the man in charge of the Station under whose supervision the Siding is, must arrange to meet the train at the Siding, or proceed with the train to the Siding, and assist with the shunting operations. On arrival of the train at the Siding, the man in charge must obtain the Train Staff from the Engine-driver to enable him to unlock the ground Lever and work the necessary Points. After the shunting operations are completed and the Points have been replaced in their normal position, he must hand the Train Staff back to the Driver.

The Light Railway is worked by Train Staff without Tickets, the Train Staff being round and painted green, and lettered "Kelvedon and Tollesbury Pier."

The Train Staff, when not in use, must be kept in the Station Master's Office at Kelvedon Station, the Station Master being the sole person authorised to deal with the Train Staff.

Only one engine in steam, or two or more engines coupled together, must be allowed on the Light Railway at one and the same time. The Light Railway is worked in accordance with the Train Staff Regulations contained in this "Appendix" for working Single Lines of Railway by only one engine in steam or two or more engines coupled together.

No train or engine must exceed a speed of **25 miles an hour**, and if a train should be worked by a Tender engine **running Tender first** the speed must not exceed **15 miles an hour.**

Where Gates are **not** provided at Public Road Level Crossings, a Board with the figure **10** on it is erected 300 yards on each side of the Level Crossing, and the speed of trains or engines must not exceed **10 miles an hour** when approaching within a distance of 200 yards of such Level Crossings.

Public Road Level Crossings, as under, are provided :—

Between Kelvedon (L.L.) and Tiptree Stations.

One, provided with Gates, about 600 yards from Kelvedon.
One, provided with Cattle Guards, 1¾ miles from Kelvedon.
One, provided with Cattle Guards, 2¼ miles from Kelvedon.
One, provided with Cattle Guards, at Heath Siding.
One, provided with Gates, about 3 miles from Kelvedon.
One, provided with Cattle Guards, at Kelvedon end of Tiptree Station.

Between Tiptree and Tolleshunt D'Arcy Stations.

One, provided with Cattle Guards, about ½ mile from Tiptree.
One, provided with Gates, about ¾ mile from Tiptree.
One, provided with Cattle Guards, about 1¼ miles from Tiptree.
One, provided with Gates, at Tiptree end of Tolleshunt D'Arcy Station.

(SEE NEXT PAGE.)

350

Kelvedon, Tiptree, and Tollesbury Light Railway—*continued.*

Between Tolleshunt D'Arcy and Tollesbury Stations.

One, provided with Cattle Guards, about ¾ mile from Tolleshunt D'Arcy.
One, provided with Cattle Guards, at Old Hall Siding.
One, provided with Cattle Guards, at Tollesbury Station.

Between Tollesbury and Tollesbury Pier Stations.

One, provided with Gates, about 600 yards from Tollesbury Station.
One, provided with Cattle Guards, about ¾ mile from Tollesbury Station.
One, provided with Cattle Guards, about 1 mile from Tollesbury Station.

At the five Public Level Crossings provided with Crossing Gates, the Gates are to stand normally across the Railway.

At each of the five Public Level Crossings (except the Level Crossing at Tolleshunt D'Arcy Station) the train must be brought to a stand well clear of the Gates. The Gates are to be opened for the passage of the train over the Crossing by the Fireman, and after the train has passed over the Crossing, the Guard of the train must close them across the Railway, the Driver taking care not to again proceed on his journey until he has received an "All-right" signal from the Guard. In the case of a Light engine, the Fireman must open and close the Gates.

At the Public Level Crossing at Tolleshunt D'Arcy Station, the man in charge of the Station must attend to the Gates, and take care that the Gates are closed across the Public Road in sufficient time to prevent delay to trains and engines.

Barriers are provided at the Public Level Crossing at Tiptree Station, and the man in charge of Tiptree Station must take care that the Barriers are placed, and securely fastened, across the Public Road during the time shunting operations are being carried out at that Station.

After dark, or in foggy weather or during falling snow, the Gate Lamp must be lighted and placed on the Gate at all the Public Road Level Crossings provided with Gates.

The responsibility for cleaning, trimming, lighting, and extinguishing the Lamps on the Gates of the Public Level Crossings is as under :—

Level Crossing about 600 yards from Kelvedon ...	Kelvedon Station Staff.
Level Crossing on each side of Tiptree Station ...	Man in charge of Tiptree Station, or his Assistant.
Level Crossing at Tolleshunt D'Arcy Station ...	Man in charge of Tolleshunt D'Arcy Station.
Level Crossing about 600 yards on Pier side of Tollesbury Station	Man in charge of Tollesbury Station.

In foggy weather or during falling snow, a Fogman (Platelayer) is to be provided about 300 yards from each of the five Public Level Crossings provided with Gates, and he must place two Detonators on the rail, 10 yards apart, in the direction from which a train will approach, in order to denote to the Enginemen the vicinity of the Level Crossing.

The Engine Whistle must be sounded on approaching all Public Road Level Crossings.

No engine, train, or vehicle must be allowed to stand foul of any of the Public Road Level Crossings.

At all Public Road Level Crossings, a Board lettered "Beware of the Trains," is placed in the Public Road about 50 yards on each side of the Crossing.

No shunting whatever must be allowed to take place on the Main Single Line at any of the Stations **unless the Branch engine is at the Station.**

The use of a Tow Rope is authorised, when necessary, at any Station on the Light Railway, and is to be carried in the Tollesbury Branch Goods Break Van.

351

Kelvedon, Tiptree, and Tollesbury Light Railway—*continued.*

After dark, or in foggy weather or during falling snow, the engine must carry a Red Head Light on the Chimney.

No engine, carriage, or truck (loaded or empty) having a greater weight than **14 tons** on any one pair of wheels must be run on the Light Railway.

The loads of **Goods** trains running over this Light Railway must not exceed **12** Trucks of Minerals, **17** Trucks of Goods, or **24 Empty Trucks.**

In the case of **Mixed** trains, **one** Passenger vehicle is to be considered equal to one loaded Truck of Goods.

Mixed trains running over the Light Railway are to be worked in accordance with the Mixed Train Regulations shewn in this "Appendix."

In foggy weather or during falling snow, the man appointed to work the Ground Locking Frame at Kelvedon Low Level Station must place two Detonators on the rail 10 yards apart, about 200 yards on the Tollesbury side of the Up Home Signal, for each approaching train.

The Engine Whistle for going to and from the Light Railway at Kelvedon Station is **3** distinct sounds.

Passenger train vehicles in use on the Light Railway are not to be allowed to come on to the Main Line at Kelvedon Station unless the Footboards of the vehicles have been removed.

Operating Instructions from the GER Appendix, 1910

The outbreak of World War I, on 4th August 1914, found the GER, with other British railway companies, under Government control. Train services continued to run to pre-war timetables, although by 1915 the public were warned that delays or cancellations could be caused by enemy action. Goods traffic flourished, as increased produce was dispatched from local farms and estates to London and other towns, to make up for the loss of imported food. Local railwaymen answered the call to arms and at least two men stationed on the light railway joined the colours. During the early part of World War I, the training of troops took place in the marshland near Tollesbury, and the branch train was often seen making additional runs between Kelvedon and the Pier Station with personnel, although horse traffic, goods and provisions required for the exercises were conveyed by special freight trains.

The strain of the war was taxing the resources of the railways, and in December 1916 the Railway Executive Committee issued an ultimatum to the effect that they would only carry on if drastic reductions were made to ordinary services, as locomotive power was short through lack of coal supplies. The Lloyd George Coalition Government thus agreed to the reduction of passenger services from 1st January 1917, but despite this edict, the Tollesbury branch services actually increased, except for a short period in 1918 when the service was reduced by one train in each direction.

From the opening of the line, footplate crews at Kelvedon had suffered considerable inconvenience, as no messroom had been provided. This meant that locomen had to eat their food, store their belongings and other equipment in the back of the draughty engine shed. On 30th June 1919, the Locomotive Superintendent requested that suitable accommodation be provided for enginemen and cleaners employed at the depot, and authority was duly given for a building to be provided adjacent to the engine shed at an estimated cost of £102.

From 26th September to 5th October 1919 there was a general railway strike with services on the Tollesbury Light Railway being suspended, and it was this industrial dispute and the General Strike of 1926 which contributed to the decline in railway freight. Farmers and growers realised, for the first time, that with improving roads, goods could be collected and delivered by lorry using, in many cases, vehicles purchased second-hand from the Army, thus motivating short haul journeys cheaper than the rates charged by the GER. This door-to-door service was more convenient than the double handling involved when loading and unloading into and out of railway wagons. The primitive commercial road vehicles of the day were, however, not capable of long-distance haulage, so middle and long-distance freight traffic remained safely in the hands of the GER. The same problem was not as acute with passenger traffic in the initial years after the war, as few local people owned cars and were, to some extent, reliant on the branch for journeys to Colchester or London and intermediate towns. The GER did not, however, have complete monopoly.

From the opening of the line, the local family firm of Osborne had trundled boxes of crabs, winkles, oysters and fish to Tollesbury Station for loading on the branch train. In 1919 they extended their sphere of activity and bought their first motor vehicle, a new Ford Model T chassis fitted with a horse-bus body. With a second bus, a Maxwell, the family initiated a one journey a day bus service to Colchester via Birch but were augmented, early in 1920, by the National Company who introduced a bus service connecting Maldon and Tiptree with Colchester. Further inroads were made in 1922 when Osborne's buses connected Tollesbury and Maldon, with National later extending their coverage with a bus service linking Witham to Kelvedon, Tiptree and Tollesbury, in direct competition with the light railway.

After World War I the railways were in a run-down state, and the economies of the Country were only improving slowly. Traffic to and from Tollesbury Pier was negligible, with trains only running when required between Tollesbury and the terminus, and often not at all. The desired development around the area of the pier failed to materialise and, therefore, sites for bungalows and yachting marinas remained as windswept grassland and mudflats, open to the swoops and cries of the sea and estuary birds. The Blackwater was slowly silting up and shipping stayed well out in the centre channel to sail to Maldon or Burnham-on-Crouch, leaving the pier solely in the hands of anglers and very infrequent day trippers. The GER, forever seeking savings in operating costs, quickly decided that the luxury of a train service on an 'as and when required' basis to such a desolate spot could no longer be justified. The necessary notices were posted and the passenger services between Tollesbury and Tollesbury Pier were withdrawn, from 17th July 1921, with the last train actually running the previous day and leaving the station to the ravages of the weather.

This was the position of the branch when the GER was absorbed, along with the Great Northern, Great Central and other minor railways, to form the London & North Eastern Railway from 1st January 1923.

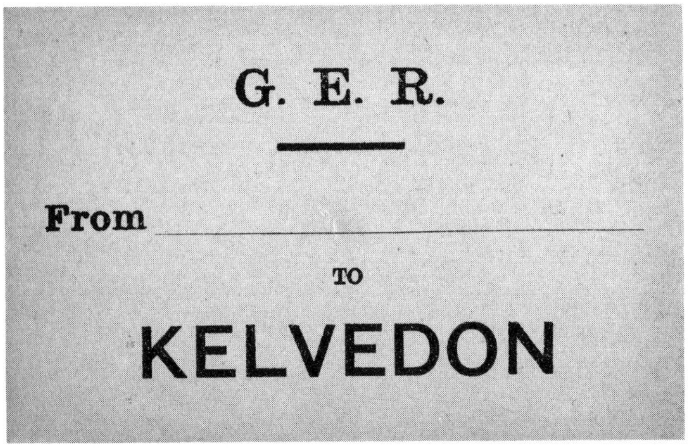

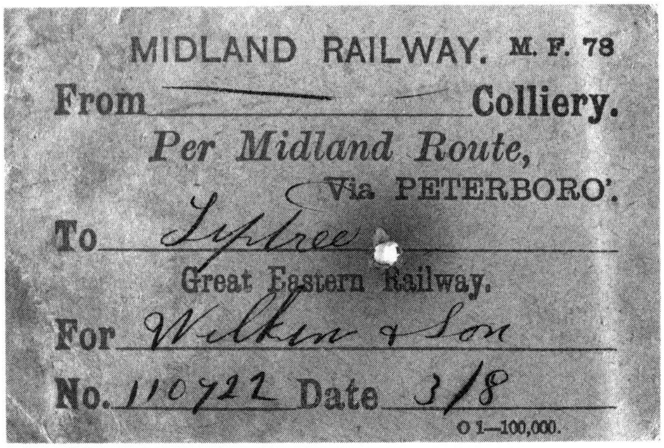

Chapter Three

Amalgamation and Nationalisation

The new ownership brought few changes to the branch but, within a year, industrial strife had changed matters. A seven day railway strike, from 20th January 1924, brought a further decline in the use of the light railway with prospective passengers turning to road transport, some travelling only short distances, but never again returning to the railway. The branch services were curtailed again, during the General Strike of 1926. The Kelvedon to Tollesbury line was no exception and as traffic decreased, the importance of increasing goods traffic to offset a loss on working expenses became more apparent for the survival of the line. Passenger receipts for the first six years of the LNER operation of the line proved the point:

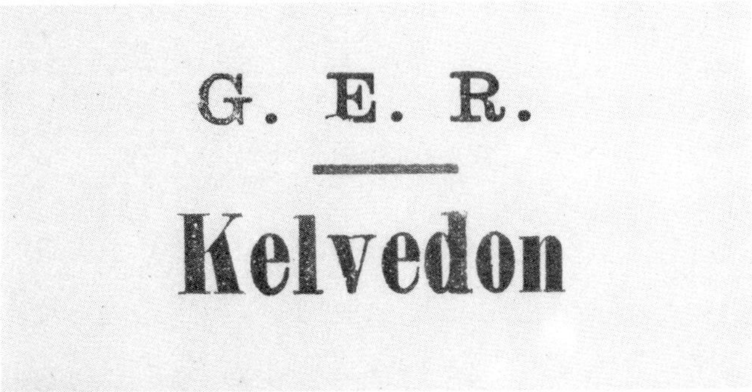

	Passengers	*Passenger Traffic Receipts*	*Parcels Traffic Receipts*		*Season Tickets Receipts*	*Total*
		£	£	No.	£	£
1923	28,598	1,233	1,679		84	2,996
1924	26,405	990	1,400		111	2,501
1925	26,321	1,099	1,620	10	94	2,813
1926	25,062	974	1,226	8	87	2,287
1927	28,217	1,192	801	7	87	2,080
1928	25,037	1,094	709	5	69	1,872

With a 12.45 per cent reduction in passengers carried, an 11.27 per cent reduction in passenger receipts, a massive 57.7 per cent reduction in parcels, a 17.8 per cent reduction in season tickets and an overall reduction in receipts of 37.5 per cent, the branch was lucky to survive the 1930s closures carried out by the LNER.

Fortunately passenger traffic receipts picked up in the mid-1930s, when holidays and rambles in the country became popular. Branch trains on Saturdays and bank holidays saw a welcome increase in passengers, as people took advantage of their free time in the countryside. Local bus services, however, also increased their hold on local traffic and in 1930, Osborne's buses began a service from Tollesbury to Tiptree, Kelvedon and Witham. Competition from Blue Bird Coaches of Tiptree ceased two years later when the firm sold out part of their stage services to Osborne's and part to Moore Brothers of Kelvedon, and as these bus services increased in frequency the number of passengers using the branch declined. An important factor for passengers travelling from Tollesbury and district to and from London was that the GER, and later the LNER, stopped a number of their faster trains at Witham, leaving only the slower services to call at Kelvedon. In consequence, by using the bus and changing at Witham on to the faster rail services, a quicker journey was possible to and from the Capital, especially when most rail travellers on the branch were subject to lengthy delays by mixed trains shunting at intermediate stations.

An amusing incident which occurred in the late 1920s, involved a derailment at Tollesbury when the 'Buck Jumper' 0-6-0T shunting wagons from the yard slipped on the greasy rails, slid forward and split the points, finishing up with the leading wheels off the track. A message was forwarded to the stationmaster at Kelvedon, who immediately sent for the Ipswich breakdown train but in the meantime, watched by inquisitive spectators, the driver, fireman, guard and porter-in-charge had used their ingenuity and obtained some sleepers to pack under the derailed wheels. After one or two attempts the driver succeeded in reversing and re-railing the locomotive and as no damage was evident, the train departed without further delay for Kelvedon. At the junction the stationmaster was rather concerned, as the breakdown train was later than scheduled. Unfortunately no one had bothered to advise him that all was well on the branch, and his relief at seeing the breakdown train arrive on the 'up' main line must have been quickly replaced by horror and foreboding as, with a cheery whistle and plumes of white smoke, the Tollesbury branch train pulled round the curve from Feering and into the low level station. Needless to say there were many red faces at subsequent enquiries into this lack of communication, and one or two staff suffered the inconvenience of loss of pay for a day.

In an effort to counteract the competition from road transport, and after several requests from the villagers of Feering, the LNER authorities agreed to site a halt adjacent to the level crossing to serve the locality. All trains stopped for the crews to open and close the level crossing gates on the A12 main road, and it was thought a halt could be provided adjacent to the crossing at minimal cost. The halt was subsequently erected with a low platform on the south of the crossing, on the 'up' or western side of the railway, and opened for traffic on 1st January 1934. The LNER evidently had exhausted their supply of ex-GER coach bodies, for the body of an ex-London General Omnibus Company 'B' type 'Old Bill', of World War I vintage, was provided as passenger waiting accommodation. The first Sunday passenger

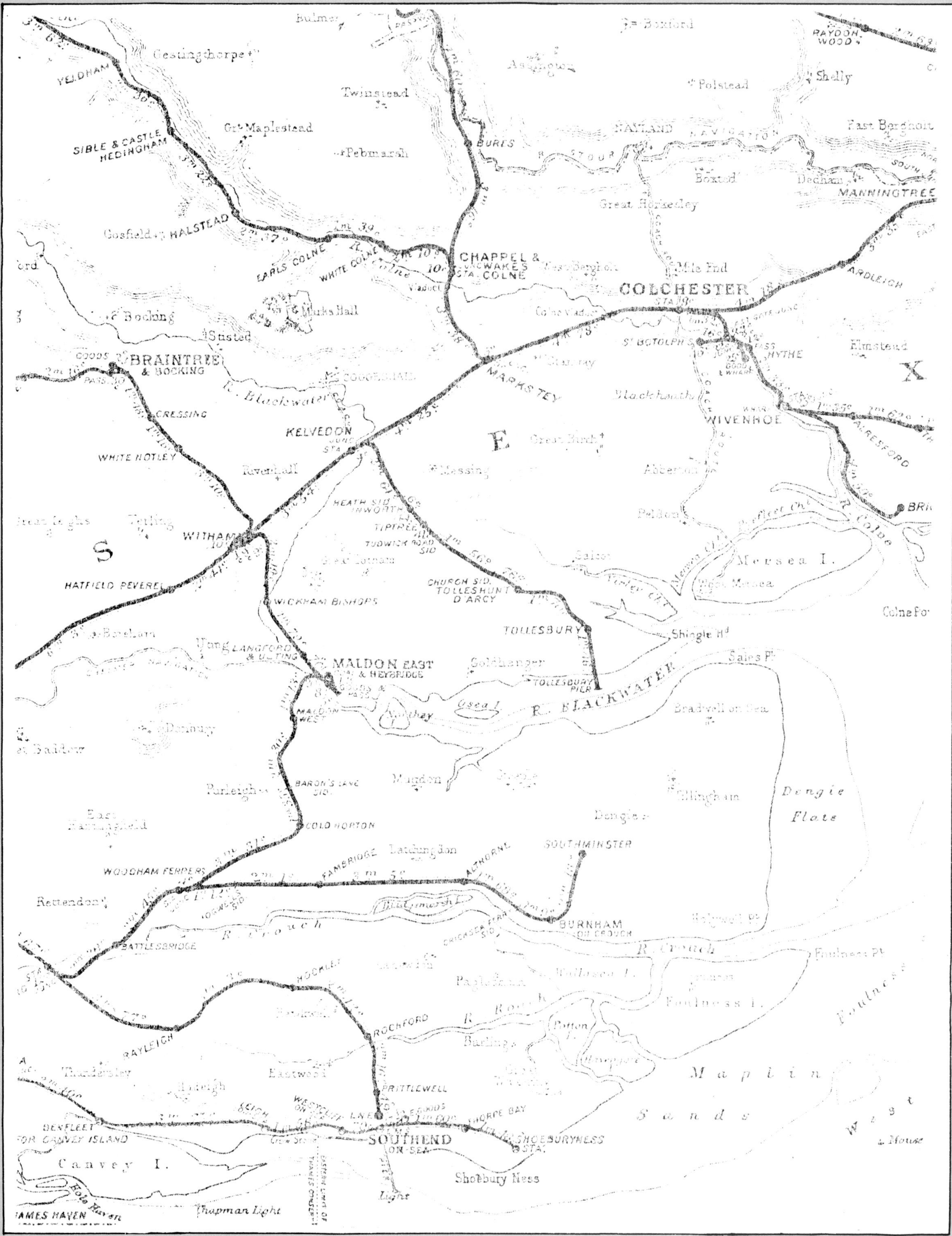

Railway Clearing House map; East of England, 1928, showing the Tollesbury branch and surrounding railways.

train ran on the light railway in September 1934 when 78 children, accompanied by 38 adults, travelled from Tollesbury on the branch train to Kelvedon, where they transferred to the main line train for the remainder of their journey to Walton-on-the-Naze. The excursion was repeated in subsequent years, until World War II curtailed such activities.

The outbreak of World War II saw the LNER merge with the other major railway companies under the Railway Executive Committee, from 1st September 1939. Within weeks the area south of Tollesbury was being transformed with the track south of Tollesbury being cleared of empty wagons awaiting repairs or scrapping while overgrowing brambles and weeds were removed to enable trains to again work through to the shores of the Blackwater Estuary.

Two buildings were erected during the war in the vicinity of Tollesbury Pier, the first being a pillbox constructed of thick reinforced concrete at the landward end of the pier, whilst the other was a control tower for electrically-controlled mines, which were laid in the Blackwater Estuary to safeguard against enemy seaborne attack. This building was three quarters of a mile inland, on the seaward side of the line. Also, as a precaution against enemy landing, a large portion of the shore end of the decaying and decrepit Tollesbury Pier was also removed, in 1940, as anti-invasion arrangements. To safeguard against air raids, especially at night, station oil lamps remained dimmed, and staff utilised shielded hand lamps to attend to train and shunting duties. As a precaution against enemy attacks, station nameboards were also removed and stored in station buildings, leaving the guard or porter in charge to call out the station names.

Within months of the outbreak of hostilities, the service pattern on the light railway was reduced to one goods and two passenger trains in the 'down' direction and two mixed and one passenger on the 'up' road, a feature which remained until after the war years. The agricultural nature of freight handled on the light railway, however, was of the utmost importance, as the vital provisions of home-grown food, grain, vegetables and fruit traffics were dispatched to the markets, with the freight and mixed trains often running with a full complement of wagons. If circumstances permitted, additional freight trains ran to handle the produce.

Although the branch had no strategic importance for troop movements other than a few manoeuvres, it assumed considerable importance in the defence of the Blackwater Estuary, as at one time or another four War Department locomotives were located on the Tollesbury Pier extension with flat wagons, on which were mounted anti-aircraft guns. In addition, a few special freight trains conveyed arms and ammunition to the shore batteries located round Tollesbury Wick Marshes, although most of the equipment went by road. As it was, the branch remained remarkably free of trouble except for a raid by a Luftwaffe fighter bomber on a train near Feering. Fortunately, the aim of the German crew was off target.

After the war the railways resumed peacetime services but with run-down rolling stock and equipment, and with stations in need of maintenance. The severe weather in 1947, which saw heavy snowfalls, brought delays to services and, early in February, the 'Crab & Winkle Flyer' was forced to abandon its journey and return to Kelvedon when the cutting near Blind Lane was partly blocked by snow. Ser-

The afternoon sunshine highlights the drab condition of Class J15 0-6-0 No. 65470, trundling along with the branch freight near Kelvedon, in August 1958.

Dr I. C. Allen

vices were reinstated the following day.

The easing of petrol rationing brought the buses back on the local roads, much to the detriment of the branch traffic. By 1947 only 33 passenger journeys were being made daily on the 'Crab & Winkle', and the LNER Divisional General Manager commenced enquiries into the future viability of the service, although events the following year delayed a decision.

The nationalisation of the railways, from 1st January 1948, brought little change to the branch, which retained its GER atmosphere to the end although gradually, however, new posters, paperwork and uniforms appeared. Although stocks of LNER tickets remained in use until 1951, those in demand were replaced by tickets bearing the legend British Railways. The 'Buck Jumper' Class J67 and J69 tank locomotives and the Class J15 0-6-0 tender locomotives remained in their dull black livery, but soon lost their NE or LNER identity in favour of British Railways and the later lion and wheel emblems. The varnished teak or brown paint remained on the coaching stock until closure of the line to passenger traffic.

In the immediate post-war years, the Tollesbury Pier extension appeared as a decaying, decrepit and redundant asset. An old four wheel coach body and a red brick hut was all that was left of the former terminal station. The track was again overgrown, and rapidly disappearing under an almost impenetrable undergrowth. The section of line near Tollesbury became a dumping ground for old wooden-bodied wagons which remained for months rotting and rusting away before being taken elsewhere for scrapping. Following the trend of passenger services, freight traffic showed a further decline in the later 1940s and early 1950s as a result of the curtailment of fuel rationing, with farmers and traders increasing the dispatch and receipts of produce and goods by motor lorry. Livestock traffic was negligible compared with pre-war years, and cattle for markets in the surrounding area went exclusively by road.

Soon after taking office, the cost conscious Railway Executive advised the railway regions of the need for further investigations into unremunerative services. Accordingly Eastern Region headquarters resurrected and dusted the papers on the Tollesbury branch left by their LNER predecessors, and enquiries were resumed into the viability of the service. In the two years since their report, the number of passenger journeys on the light railway had dropped to between eight and ten daily. Efforts had been made to increase the number of trains on the line, but with such depressing figures there was no argument save that of withdrawing the passenger services. Another factor in the case for closure was the ancient rolling stock which was considered life-expired, the cost of modifying existing main line stock for duties on the line being prohibitive when compared with probable receipts.

In the spring of 1950, rumours of the threatened closure were rife, only to be confirmed in June of the same year when the Railway Management officially informed members of the staff and NUR and ASLEF branches in the Colchester area that such proposals were actively in hand. The Railway Executive duly informed the public, in July 1950, of the proposals to close the line to passenger traffic, subject to further investigation. Despite the edict the branch train continued to wend its way three times daily (weekdays only) from Kelvedon to Tollesbury and back, its meagre number of passengers often augmented by railway enthusiasts seeking a nostalgic ride on the 'Crab & Winkle'. On 19th January 1951, the Railway Executive caused further alarm when they announced the contemplated closure of Kelvedon main line station if the light railway closed.

Despite the additional journeys made by enthusiasts, passenger numbers and receipts continued to fall and often trains ran without a passenger on board. The inevitable announcement came from the Railway Executive, early in April 1951, of the withdrawal of passenger services from the branch on and from 7th May 1951. After the announcement, Tom Driberg, MP for Maldon, made a plea in Parliament on Monday 16th April for the line to be reprieved for four months, as it was thought that as an authentic Edwardian curiosity, it might attract a number of summer visitors. A strong appeal was made for the overhaul of branch railways, and where this was not practicable, no closure would take place until as good an alternative was offered by road transport.

Kelvedon (Low Level) Station, photographed facing the buffer stops, with the branch train being unloaded after arriving from Tollesbury. Passenger traffic must have been poor on this day, for only 24 seats were provided in brake third No. 62261, the other vehicle being a four wheel Gresley passenger brake van.

G. Pember Collection

Class J67/1 No. 68608 takes water from the column adjacent to Kelvedon Shed, on 30th September 1950. The locomotive is standing on the main branch line, with the shed road in the background. The handrails of the footpath, connecting the high and low level stations, can be seen to the left of the picture.

LCGB/Ken Nunn Collection

An eight vehicle mixed train stretches almost to the buffer stops, above the River Blackwater, on 12th August 1950. Awaiting departure at 10.10 a.m. from Kelvedon (Low Level) is Class J67/1 0-6-0T No. 68616, hauling bogie tram No. E60461, brake thirds Nos. E62262 and E62261, a van, two open wagons, the parcels brake and the branch goods brake van. In the foreground is the run-round loop.

I. H. Meredith

Class J67/1 No. 7169 stands at Kelvedon (Low Level) with the two coach branch train on 27th March 1937.

W. A. Camwell

Class J69/1 No. 7165 (later No. 8612) awaits departure from Kelvedon (Low Level), in 1939. Its train is formed of an ex-Wisbech & Upwell four wheel third tramcar, built by the GER in 1890 and transferred to the Tollesbury Light Railway in 1928, followed by the two Stoke Ferry brake thirds and Wisbech & Upwell bogie tram third.

A Rail Enthusiasts' Club special train of two brake vans and three open wagons, stands at Tiptree, on 6th April 1957, hauled by Class J15 0-6-0 No. 65443.

R. C. Riley

Class J69/1 No. 8636 pauses at Tolleshunt D' Arcy with the 6.37p.m. Tollesbury to Kelvedon train on 16th April 1949.

W. A. Camwell

The decrepit and worse for wear ex-GER four wheel five compartment third class coach body, of 1872 vintage, serves as a waiting-room at Tolleshunt Knights. It is almost dwarfed by the normal-sized station nameboard.

G. Pember Collection

Tolleshunt D'Arcy Station in 1950, facing Kelvedon, with the branch train leaving the platform. The comparative size of the main line vehicle, on the rear of the train, and the station buildings is interesting.

L&GRP

Kelvedon (Low Level) Station, facing the engine shed and buffer stops, on 11th July 1950. The three way points leading to the shed and run-round loop are in front of the branch 'Buck Jumper', which is being prepared for another round trip to Tollesbury and back. The path leading to the main line station climbs the embankment beyond the station buildings.

P. N. Williams

Class J67/1 No. 68616 pulls away from Kelvedon, past the 'up' home signal, with the 10.10a.m. mixed train to Tollesbury, on 29th July 1950. In the foreground is the short siding used to stable the branch coaching stock.

LCGB/Ken Nunn Collection

Class J69/1 0-6-0T No. 68607 stands by the run-round loop at Tollesbury, before pulling over the level crossing and into the station with a train formed of ex-Stoke Ferry six wheel brake third, a Wisbech & Upwell bogie tram and an LNER four wheel full brake. Note the comparison in height between the standard brake and the light railway vehicles.

Dr I. C. Allen

Class J67/1 No. 68616 pulls away from Tollesbury with a mixed train, on 19th September 1950.

Ian L. Wright

Enthusiasts crowd into and on top of the last train at Kelvedon, on 5th May 1951. Needless to say, those on the roof had taken up safer positions before the train commenced its journey.

J. Watling Collection

J67/1 No. 68616 awaits departure at Kelvedon (Low Level) with the 10.10a.m. mixed train to Tollesbury, on 11th July 1950. The passenger vehicles are composed of the two ex-Stoke Ferry 6 wheel brake thirds and an ex-Wisbech & Upwell bogie third.

P. N. Williams

Unfortunately, the plea fell on deaf ears. Arthur Barnes, Minister of Transport, fully understood the case for modernisation but advised Driberg that such modernisation was not possible as, over the whole country, the Railway Executive had many such lines needing an essential amount of maintenance, following the nominal attention received in the war years. Barnes advised that the Tollesbury branch only carried an average of six to seven passengers daily so no stay of execution was granted and the Minister summed up: 'The public have more or less deserted these lines for road services and it is not an economic proposition to keep them open'. So sparse was passenger traffic, even at the end, that the *Essex County Standard* reporter advised readers that he made a trip on the line, on Friday 4th May 1951, 'In splendid isolation'.

On the last day of passenger services, Saturday 5th May 1951, Class J69/1 0-6-0T No. 68578 worked the branch with the two ex-Stoke Ferry six wheel tramcars, and a Wisbech & Upwell bogie tramcar between them. No. 68578 was adorned with the chalk inscription 'Crab & Winkle, sorry to say you died because you did not pay' on the bunker side. Most trains were well-filled with local people and railway enthusiasts paying their last respects to the light railway.

The last 'down' train departed from Kelvedon (Low Level) at 5.35p.m. hauled by Class J69/1 0-6-0T No. 68578, with Driver Jim Gardner in charge. On the footplate, as honorary fireman, was Tom Driberg, the Maldon MP, and detonators were exploded as people waved football rattles and cheered the train on its way. In charge of the three coach train, which was decorated with streamers, was Conductor Guard M. Petchey. At various points along the line people waved and cheered, while at each station more passengers joined. At Tiptree a black coffin covered with wreaths, one of which was shaped in the letters BR, was borne solemnly along the platform and loaded into the brake compartment of tramcar No. E62262. The locomotive, bearing the chalk inscription 'Born 1902 Died 1951' on the smokebox door, pitched and swayed its way along the track, hauling the ancient carriages into the late spring evening. More people joined for the final 'down' journey and, by the time the cavalcade arrived at Tollesbury, over 450 passengers disgorged themselves on to the platform.

For the return working, the bunker of No. 68578 was adorned with the chalk inscription 'There will be many a poor soul who will have to walk' and so great was the crowd that there was no room for the coffin. Amongst the 450 passengers on the return journey was the District Commercial Superintendent for Ipswich.

The last ride on the branch was especially tinged with sadness for two of the passengers, the first of which was 76 years old Peter Warne of Kelvedon who, before retirement, had been a guard on the branch for 36 years. The second person, sitting in the front coach, was Mrs C. Deal who, as a girl, had made a first ride on the line in a wagon and had a hole burnt in her dress by a spark from the locomotive.

On return to Kelvedon the crowd dispersed after watching No. 68578 return light engine to Colchester Shed, the coaching stock remaining at Kelvedon. On the Monday following the withdrawal of the passenger service, civil engineering staff commenced removing station nameboards, platform seats and other redundant assets, loading them on to the daily goods trains for further use elsewhere.

The ex-Stoke Ferry six wheel tramcars, Nos. E62261 and E62262, remained at Kelvedon for some considerable time after closure of the branch. One vehicle was stored in the former engine shed whilst the other, along with eight-wheeled Nos. E60461 and E60462, was standing in the siding adjacent to the building. They were finally dispatched, after the removal of side steps, to Stratford for scrapping.

In 1950 Ealing Studios were planning a comedy film, based on the fight by local people to save their local branch railway, and during the course of their search for a suitable branch railway the Kelvedon to Tollesbury line was inspected, but was found unsuitable. One of the former Wisbech & Upwell tram coaches, No. E60461, was thought suitable and was later purchased. During subsequent filming in 1952, on the former Great Western Railway's Camerton to Limpley Stoke branch, it became one of the star attractions. Fortunately , at the conclusion of filming, the coach was again sold and is now preserved.

After withdrawal of the passenger services, freight traffic beyond Tiptree declined rapidly to such an extent that British Railways announced, in August 1951, the proposal to withdraw all freight facilities beyond Tudwick Road Siding on and from 29th October 1951. After closure, the branch formation gradually succumbed to the ravages of nature before the track was removed. The contract for the removal of the track, between Tudwick Road and Tollesbury, was placed late in 1951 and work on the removal of the assets began early the following year, commencing at Tollesbury and working back towards Tudwick Road. To facilitate the loading of scrap by contractors, a supply of wagons was propelled from Kelvedon but as the gradients of the branch were severe, and to stop runaway wagons, the Class J15 locomotive was in attendance during loading operations. Rails were cut into 20ft. lengths and, together with recovered chairs and fishplates, were dispatched to Sheffield. The work was completed remarkably quickly, and culminated in a pair of buffer stops being erected 200 yards south of Tudwick Road Siding entrance points. The former trackbed was offered to farmers and landowners with most of the offers being accepted and, where possible, the new owners quickly transferred the former railway land as extensions to fields for arable or grazing. Other sections remained as farm tracks.

The truncated section of Tollesbury Pier was further damaged during floods which eroded much of East Anglia's coastline in February 1953, when water swept inland for almost half a mile across Tollesbury Wick Marshes. Even so, the former pierhead remained a danger to shipping and, until the late 1950s, British Railways employed the services of a man to row out in a boat and attend to the red light. After 1951 most inward goods traffic, totalling up to 2,000 tons annually, was conveyed to the coal merchants Frosts & Garwood, whereas outgoing freight was almost exclusively forwarded from the Tiptree jam factory siding. Freight trains ran daily during the winter, but were booked to run on Mondays, Wednesdays and Fridays only, during the summer when the Witham pilot locomotive, a Class J69 0-6-0T or Class J15 0-6-0, and latterly a 204hp diesel-mechanical shunting locomotive, was employed.

Two railtours ran across the branch after closure to passenger traffic. On 6th April 1957, the Railway Enthusiasts' Club ran a brake van special hauled by Class J15 0-6-0 No. 65443. A second brake van special, organised by the Railway Club, was hauled across the branch on 27th September 1958 by Class E4 2-4-0 No. 62785, which now resides in the National Railway Museum at York as GER Class T26 No. 490.

In 1961 it was announced that BR was losing £600 annu-

BRITISH RAILWAYS

KELVEDON AND TOLLESBURY BRANCH LINE

WITHDRAWAL OF PASSENGER TRAIN SERVICE

The Railway Executive hereby give notice that on and from Monday, 7th May, 1951 the passenger train service will be withdrawn from the undermentioned stations and halt on the Kelvedon–Tollesbury branch:–

FEERING HALT
INWORTH
TIPTREE
TOLLESHUNT KNIGHTS
TOLLESHUNT D'ARCY
TOLLESBURY

Parcels traffic will continue to be dealt with at Tiptree, Tolleshunt D'Arcy and Tollesbury stations until further notice

An omnibus service operated by Messrs. Osborne & Sons is available between Tollesbury, Tiptree, Kelvedon and Witham

A notice announcing the withdrawal of passenger train services, on and from 7th May 1951.

M. Brooks Collection

Kelvedon (Low Level) Station, pictured from the approach path on 26th June 1946. Class J69/1 No. 8636 waits at the platform before shunting the stock. The branch goods brake is in the run-round loop.

H. C. Casserley

Kelvedon (Low Level) Station, on the last day of passenger services. The three coach train waits to depart for Tollesbury, with two of the three passenger vehicles off the platform. Ex-Stoke Ferry No. E62262 is the last vehicle on the train, as passengers wait to board.

J. J. Smith/R. C. Riley

Class J69/1 0-6-0T No. 68578 waits at Tollesbury with a Railway Club special train, in 1949.

R. C. Riley

A Railway Enthusiasts' Club special to Tiptree, hauled by Class J15 0-6-0 No. 65443, stands at Inworth on 6th April 1957. Behind the train is Heath Siding.

R. C. Riley

Class E4 2-4-0 No. 62785 leaves Tiptree with the Railway Club brake van railtour on 27th September 1958.
Dr I. C. Allen

On 6th April 1957, Class J15 0-6-0 No. 65443 stands south of the crossing at Inworth while waiting for the enthusiasts to rejoin the special train to Tiptree.
R. C. Riley

Members of the Railway Enthusiasts' Club and their friends take advantage of the stop at Inworth, to photograph Class J15 0-6-0 No. 65443 and it special train on 6th April 1957. The gates at Inworth Crossing are being opened to allow the train to continue to Tiptree.
R. C. Riley

A Class E4 2-4-0. No. 62785, leaves Tiptree for Kelvedon, on 27th September 1958, with the Railway Club brake van railtour of the branch.
Dr I. C. Allen

Class J67/1 0-6-0T No. 68616 leaves Tolleshunt D'Arcy with a mixed train from Tollesbury to Kelvedon in 1950. The goods siding, with points released by a key attached to the train staff, is in the foreground.
Dr I. C. Allen

ally by keeping the Kelvedon to Tudwick Road section open for goods traffic. In their modernisation programme it was the intention to concentrate freight traffic for this area of Essex at Maldon East, whilst parcels and full loads were to be centralised at Witham, with road delivery to the Tiptree and Tollesbury area. British Railways then submitted their plans to the Transport Users' Consultative Committee for East Anglia at Norwich, who subsequently approved of the programme, and passed it to the Central Transport Users' Consultative Committee who agreed to the closure of the line on and from 1st October 1962.

The final train, hauled by Hunslet diesel shunting locomotive No. D2571, ran across the branch to Tiptree on Friday, 28th September 1962. Watched by a couple of spectators the train, formed of locomotive, brake van and eight 16 ton all-steel mineral wagons, departed with the last revenue-earning traffic from Wilkin's jam factory, and made an uneventful run back to the junction.

The contract for the removal of the track from Tudwick Road to Kelvedon was awarded early in 1963 and, as before, wagons were propelled from the junction to the works site to enable scrap rails, chairs and fishplates to be loaded and forwarded to Sheffield. Again the rails were cut into 24ft. lengths, to facilitate easy loading. Gradients on the branch were also a problem, so the Hunslet 204hp shunting locomotive remained with the wagons during loading.

Most of the former trackbed and railway land has since been sold, and much of the branch obliterated. At Kelvedon (Low Level), the station area has been levelled, as the coal stage was demolished in April 1978, but the base of the engine shed is still visible and the trackbed of the steeply-graded connection to the main line, and of the branch, are evident for 200 yards beyond the lower junction, before disappearing under a housing estate. The built-up area continues to Feering, where the trackbed is again visible on either side of the former A12 (new B1024) level crossing. Beyond the site of Feering Halt, the former light railway has been swallowed up as farmland and a farm track. The new A12 Kelvedon bypass breaches the trackbed, before farmland again conceals the route to Inworth, where the site of the station and siding has been grassed over to form a lawn. The trackbed south of the station is occupied by buildings, a factory yard and allotments. At Tiptree, allotments also conceal the former railway north of the level crossing, whilst the station site is covered by a telephone exchange, built in 1969. The trackbed continues through the premises of Wilkin's jam factory to the junction of the siding to Tudwick Road, but no trace remains of the siding. At Tolleshunt Knights the trackbed is built over on either side of the B1023 level crossing, whilst the route to Blind Lane overbridge, which still spans the cutting, is used as pasture. South of the overbridge, the cutting is overgrown, but beyond the earthworks the trackbed has reverted to farmland as far as Church Siding. From the site of Church Siding there is now an open area located on the east side of the former railway, the route of the line forming a farm track to Tolleshunt D'Arcy where the former station area is levelled. The farm track continues on to the site of Old Hall Siding, but beyond the site of the former yard the trackbed is overgrown for a distance, before being reclaimed as arable land. Some 200 yards north of Tollesbury Station a house is built on the trackbed, and the drive from the main road follows the site of the railway. There is no trace of Tollesbury Station, where the site is now wasteland.

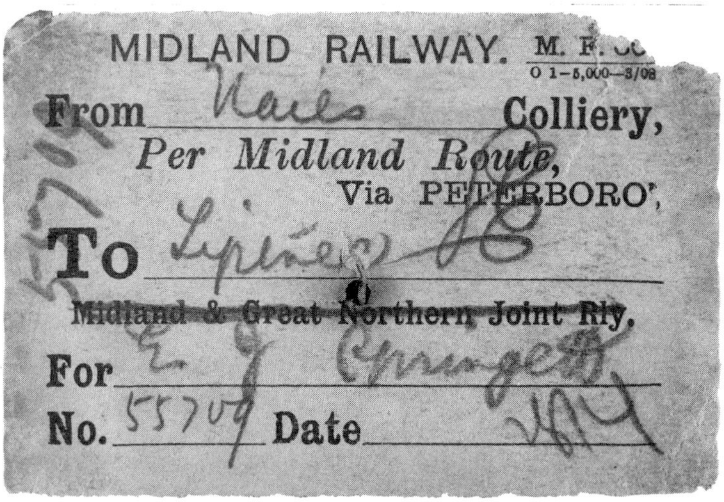

Beyond the Tollesbury terminus the trackbed is overgrown. Woodrolfe Road level crossing can be identified by a mound in the road, whilst adjacent to Woodrolfe Farm Lane level crossing a new housing estate has been developed. South of the new estate the trackbed of the extension is used as a footpath for a short distance, before disappearing under the plough. A farm track then continues along the route to the pier, where the former trackbed has been bisected by the new sea wall, but nothing now remains of Tollesbury Pier Station, the site of which has now been levelled. The pier has been largely demolished, leaving only a few rotting timbers in the muddy waters of the Blackwater as evidence of former grandeur.

Public transport facilities in this area of Essex are maintained by G. W. Osborne & Sons, who continue to operate five local bus routes. Two routes link Tollesbury with Colchester, one provides a service along the route of the old railway from Tollesbury to Kelvedon and thence to Witham, the fourth connects Tollesbury and Maldon, whilst the fifth, co-ordinated with Colchester Borough Transport, operates from Colchester to Great Wigborough. Few now remember the light railway ever existed.

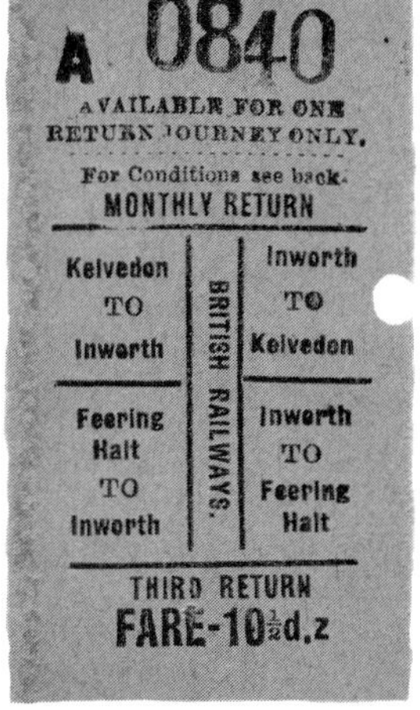

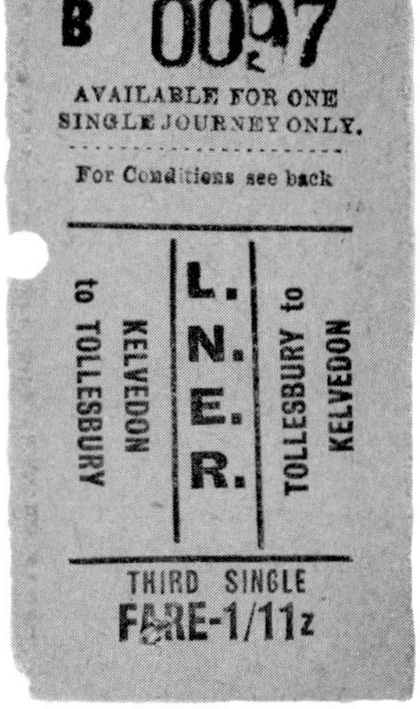

Chapter Four

The Route Described

Kelvedon main line station, 42 miles and 19 chains from Liverpool Street on the ex-GER London and Norwich main line, had two facing platforms serving 'up' and 'down' directions. The main station buildings included booking office, waiting-rooms, staff accommodation and toilets and were located on the 'up' or south side platform, whilst a separate waiting-room and exit was available on the 'down' or north side platform. The station was extensively modernised when the Chelmsford to Colchester section of the main line was electrified. The original wrought and cast-iron footbridge, which connected the platforms, was replaced by a pre-cast concrete structure raised to a greater height than the original to span the overhead wires. At the same time, the platforms were lengthened to accommodate longer trains.

To the west of the station, a small goods yard served the requirements of the local merchants. The 'up' side was served by three sidings, with access to cattle pens at the east end of the inner siding, whilst the 'down' side yard consisted of a long siding running parallel to the 'down' main line, with facing and trailing points affording access to a long siding which served a granary at the east end and a coal ground at the west end. The long siding also gave access to two reception sidings at the London end of the yard, with the goods shed being located at the back of the 'down' platform.

At the Colchester end of the station, the 'down' platform extended over the brick-built bridge which carried the railway over the Kelvedon to Coggeshall Road, and the infant River Blackwater, which flowed parallel with the road. On the 'up' side, the platform was shorter in length and was restricted by the connecting spur from Kelvedon (Low Level), on the Tollesbury Light Railway, which joined the 'up' main line by a trailing connection. The spur descended, at a gradient of 1 in 50 from the main line to the junction points east of the light railway terminus. Passenger access from the main line station to the independent light railway station was by way of a partially-covered footpath, which ran from the east end of the 'up' main platform across the road/river bridge parallel with the main line, and then down to the low level station.

Kelvedon (Low Level), formed solely of a low platform 100ft. in length, 6ft. wide and 15in. above rail level, was host to a small wooden waiting shelter, with a gents' toilet attached, and surrounded by evergreen shrubs and a privet hedge. A large nameboard, post and wall oil lamps and two platform seats completed the amenities. The track layout consisted of the through platform line, which continued past the platform to terminate at buffer stops located above the eastern bank of the river. Facing points on the 'down' side, west of the platform, gave access to the corrugated iron, wooden-framed engine shed, just large enough to

The GER's wooden station nameboard at Kelvedon main line station, advising passengers to alight for Coggeshall and the Tollesbury Light Railway.
R. C. Riley Collection

Class J69/1 0-6-0T No. 68578, garlanded with a wreath around the top smokebox lamp bracket, prepares to depart from Kelvedon (Low Level) with the last train to Tollesbury on 5th May 1951, the last day of passenger services.
J. J. Smith/R. C. Riley

The view facing west from Kelvedon main line station 'up' platform. In the foreground is the signal box which controlled entry to the connecting line, between the main line and the Tollesbury Light Railway, while to the right is the 'down' side goods yard.

J. Watling Collection

Kelvedon main line station, facing Colchester, pictured in 1911. To the left is the goods shed and yard crane, in the 'down' side yard, and behind the 'up' platform, on the right, is the cattle pen. The main station buildings were also on the 'up' side, and on the opposite side of the approach road is the stationmaster's house.

D. Taylor Collection

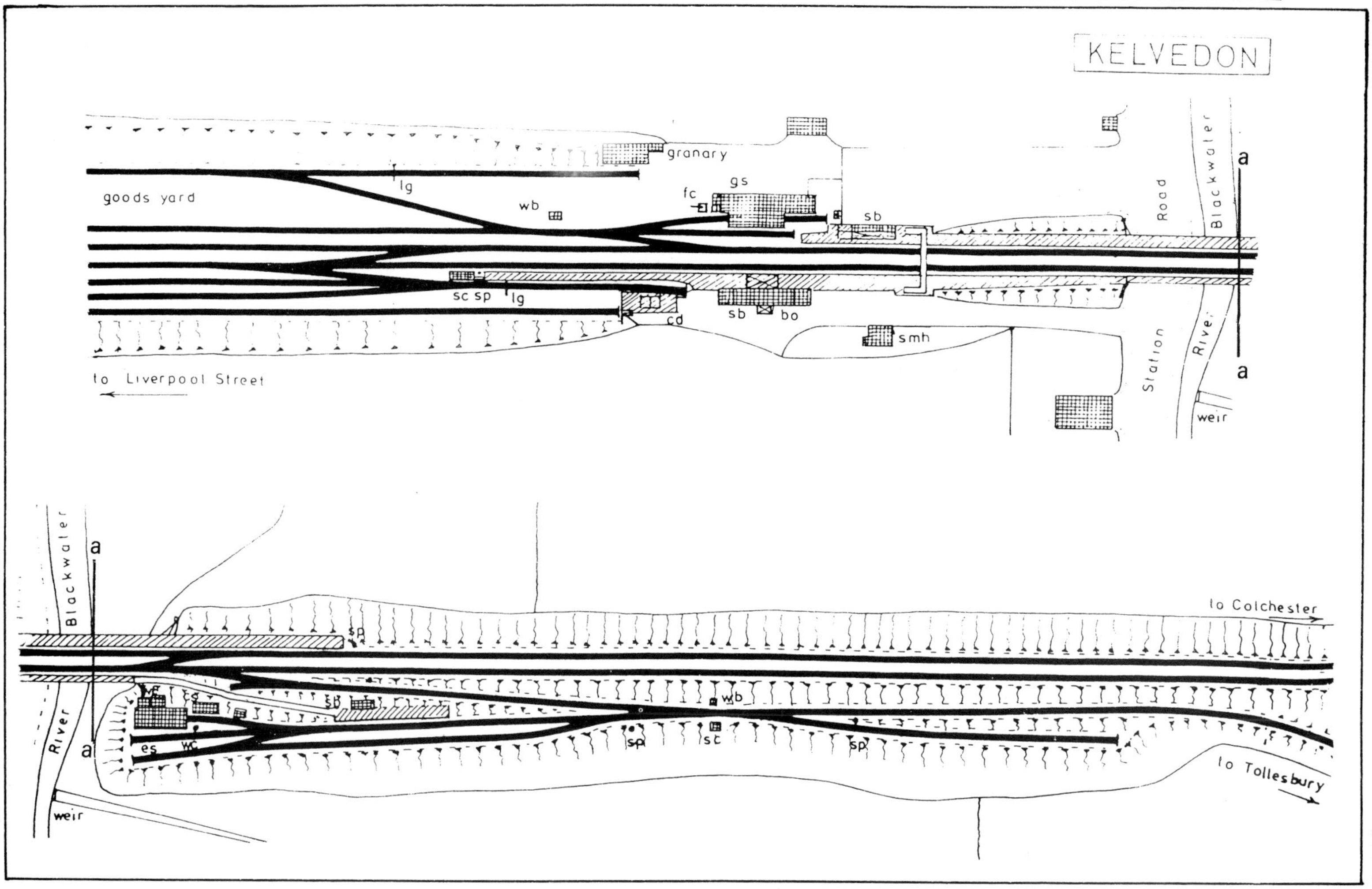

A view from Kelvedon Station footbridge, in 1911, facing Colchester. The 'down' platform, on the left, is carried on the underbridge over the Coggeshall to Kelvedon road and the infant River Blackwater. At the east end of the 'up' platform, the covered walkway leads to the low level platform and the Tollesbury branch train. Beyond the walkway the connecting spur from the 'up' main line, descending at a gradient of 1 in 50 to the Tollesbury branch, can be seen. The points in the 'up' main line were operated from Kelvedon signal box, while those at the low level were worked from the nine lever ground frame by the light railway station. The engine shed and water tank can be seen behind the covered walkway.

A view from the top of Kelvedon (Low level) 'up' home signal, showing the relationship of the light railway terminus (left) to the main line station (right), with the connecting spur rising at 1 in 50 (centre). Crowds are gathered round the branch train in the low level station, as Class J69/1 No. 68578 prepares to depart with the last 'down' train on Saturday, 5th May 1951.

J.J. Smith/R. C. Riley

Kelvedon (Low Level) Junction, showing the connecting spur from the main line. The 'down' starter signal in the foreground, complete with decorative finial, dwarfs the controlling ground level signal box. Beyond this structure is the small holding siding which was used to stable coaching stock and wagons, and the branch 'up' home signal. The branch goods brake stands on the main single line, in this view taken on 28th August 1950.

LCGB/Ken Nunn Collection

The small hut which housed the former eleven lever ground frame in Kelvedon main line 'up' yard.

J. Watling

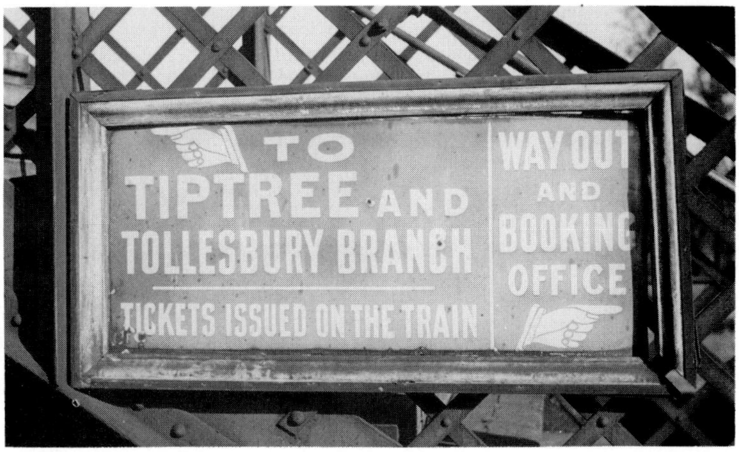

Above: The GER stove enamelled notice on Kelvedon Station footbridge directing passengers to the Tiptree and Tollesbury branch.
R. C. Riley Collection

Left: The GER station nameboard, with cast-iron letters, on the 'down' platform at Kelvedon main line station.
D. Trevor Rowe

A view from the footbridge at Kelvedon main line station, in 1958, looking towards Liverpool Street. The main station buildings are located on the 'up' platform, with the 42 lever signal box positioned at the west end. Behind the signal box is the 'up' side yard, whilst beyond the goods shed (right) is the 'down' side yard, with coal ground at the west end.
G. Pember

Kelvedon (Low Level) Station, facing the buffer stops, with the branch freight brake van standing in the run-round loop. In the background is the engine shed and water tank.

Class J69/1 No. 68578 and a brake van, take the connecting incline at Kelvedon while shunting between working trains on 28th April 1951.

G. R. Mortimer

Class J69/1 No. 68578 takes water at Kelvedon after arriving with a train from Tollesbury on 28th April 1951.

G. R. Mortimer

The granary, located at the back of the east end of the 'down' side goods yard at Kelvedon.

J. Watling

The minute Kelvedon (Low Level) terminus, facing towards the junction of the connecting spur from the high level main line and Tollesbury, on 29th July 1950.

LCGB/Ken Nunn Collection

Kelvedon (Low Level) Engine Shed in 1937, with Class J68 No. 7045 stabled within. To the right is the water tank and coal stage, while the ornate gas lamp provided illumination during the hours of darkness.

G. Pember Collection

Class J67/1 0-6-0T No. 7169 stands outside Kelvedon Shed on 27th March 1937.

W. A. Camwell

The junction between the connecting spur from the 'up' main line and the main single branch line at Kelvedon (Low Level). This view, looking towards the low level platform, shows the small signal box equipped with a nine lever frame which controlled signals and points at the light railway terminus (left) and the small hut which housed the weighbridge (right).

M. Brooks Collection

Class J69/1 0-6-0T No. 68578 storms away from Kelvedon (Low Level) up the 1 in 63 gradient towards Feering with a mixed train, on 23rd April 1951. One ex-Stoke Ferry brake third and one ex-Wisbech & Upwell bogie tram form the passenger stock on the train, whilst sister vehicles stand in the adjacent siding.

A. R. Goult

A view from the platform of Kelvedon (Low Level) Station, looking towards Feering, showing the considerable difference in height between a main line vehicle, behind the locomotive, and a coach adapted for working on the light railway. The latter was fitted with side steps, to enable passengers to board and alight at the low station platforms. These steps had to be removed before the vehicles ran on the main line, as they would foul the loading gauge dimension.

D. Taylor Collection

accommodate one of the Class J67/69 'Buck Jumper' 0-6-0 tank locomotives. On the north side of the engine shed road, adjacent to the shed, was the coal stage, and behind the engine shed the water tank was fixed on cast-iron columns. Between the shed road and main single line, was the water-column.

Alongside the platform road on the 'up' side was the run-round loop, which was served by points forming a facing connection for 'up' branch trains. A shunt spur, at the west end of the loop, also terminated at buffer stops by the river. Leaving the platform, the main single branch line continued in a north-easterly direction to the junction points with the connecting spur from the main line. The points and signals at the light railway terminus were controlled from a small nine lever ground frame located on the south side of the line. Opposite the ground frame, on the north side of the line, were the instruments of the weighbridge, the latter being installed to ensure that no vehicle with a greater axle weight than 14 tons (imposed by the Light Railway Order) ran on the branch. The three-way points by the ground frame also gave access to a short siding on the south side of the branch. Because of the steep 1 in 50 gradient, only freight trains, empty coaching stock trains or light engines were permitted to use the connecting spur.

Leaving Kelvedon, the branch curved sharply away on a 20 chain radius right-hand curve through fields belonging to Feering Hall Farm, climbing at 1 in 63 over the first occupational level crossing. Beyond the quarter mile post the line levelled out then fell at 1 in 50, entering a shallow cutting and passing Kelvedon 'up' fixed distant signal which was located on the 'down' side of the line, before crossing the former London to Colchester (A12) main road. The level crossing was protected by gates which were opened and closed by the train crew, an operation that frequently caused considerable delays to road traffic as, initially, the fireman opened the gates for the train to be driven across the crossing, where it was halted for the guard to descend and close the gates across the railway.

Immediately south of the crossing was Feering Halt, 33 chains from Kelvedon and opened by the LNER on 1st January 1934 to serve the village of Feering three quarters of a mile east of the railway, although the halt was much nearer Kelvedon. The platform, like others on the branch was 100ft. in length and was constructed of clinker and ashes with timber facing to a height of 15in. above rail level. It was sited on the 'up' side of the line and was host to an ex-London General Omnibus Company B Type bus body, which served as a waiting shelter and parcels office. The usual notice-boards were attached to the fencing alongside the crossing or on the bus body, whilst lighting was afforded by a single post oil lamp illuminated and extinguished during the hours of darkness by the guard.

Away from Feering Halt the light railway passed near to the site of Gore Pit, reputedly the site of the burial ground of Queen Boadicea's warriors. The railway then descended the 1 in 50 gradient to level out at Brooklands Siding, 50 chains from Kelvedon and situated on the 'down' side of the line, with entry being afforded by facing and trailing points forming a loop siding, with shunt spurs at each end. The siding served Threshfords Farm, crossing a field and the Feering to Tiptree road before gaining access to the farm. It saw little traffic after the initial years and soon became overgrown, before being removed in the mid-1930s. The branch then climbed at 1 in 50 on straight track over a shallow embankment, and through an equally shallow cutting, to a minor summit, with a view on the 'up' side of

Feering level crossing gates and Kelvedon 'up' distant signal in 1957. The passage of a train over the level crossing often caused considerable delays to road traffic, as the fireman had first to open the gates to let the train over the crossing, before the guard closed the gates back across the line; an exercise which often took up to five minutes.

Hugh Davies

Class J69/1 0-6-0T No. 8636 stands at Feering Halt with the two coach 6.37p.m. Tollesbury to Kelvedon train on 16th April 1949. In the foreground is the level crossing over the main A12 road.

W. A. Camwell

Feering Halt, adjacent to the A12 trunk road level crossing, looking towards Kelvedon with the ex-GER 'up' fixed distant signal beyond the gates. Note the old bus body provided as a waiting-room, and the single post oil lamp for night-time illumination.

LCGB/Ken Nunn Collection

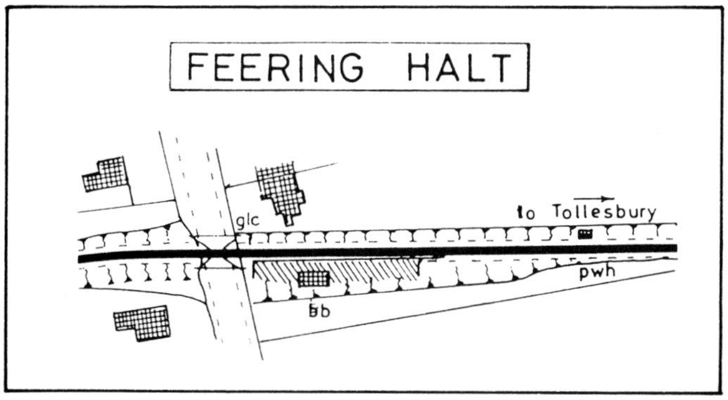

Feering Halt, facing Tollesbury, pictured on 28th August 1950. Brooklands Siding left the single line branch some 17 chains beyond Feering Halt, on the 'down' side of the line in the dip, where the gradient levelled out and ran across the adjacent field to serve a farm. It was removed in the 1930s. The undulating nature of the light railway can be seen in this photograph, as the line descends and ascends with the rolling landscape.
LCGB/Ken Nunn Collection

A view looking towards Kelvedon, down the 1 in 50 gradient to the site of Brooklands Siding and Feering Halt. The permanent way on the Tollesbury Light Railway was laid on a clinker and ash foundation, whilst the width of the formation taken by the railway was generally 16ft.
Dr I. C. Allen

The branch train, formed of Class J67/1 'Buck Jumper' No. 68616 and coaches Nos. E62262 and E60461, waits at Feering Halt, on 12th August 1950, for the gates to be opened across the A12 main road before continuing the short journey to Kelvedon.

John H. Meredith

GER Class R24 0-6-0T No. 391, with front coupling rods removed and running as a 2-4-0T, passes Kelvedon 'up' distant, on the approach to Feering Crossing, with the 12.30p.m. Kelvedon to Tollesbury train on 31st March 1910. The train is formed of a five compartment four wheel third and a two compartment four wheel brake third, modified from main line stock in 1904 for use on the line conversion. This included the fitting of 2ft. 9in. diameter wheels and the modification of headstock, drawbar and buffers.

LCGB/Ken Nunn Collection

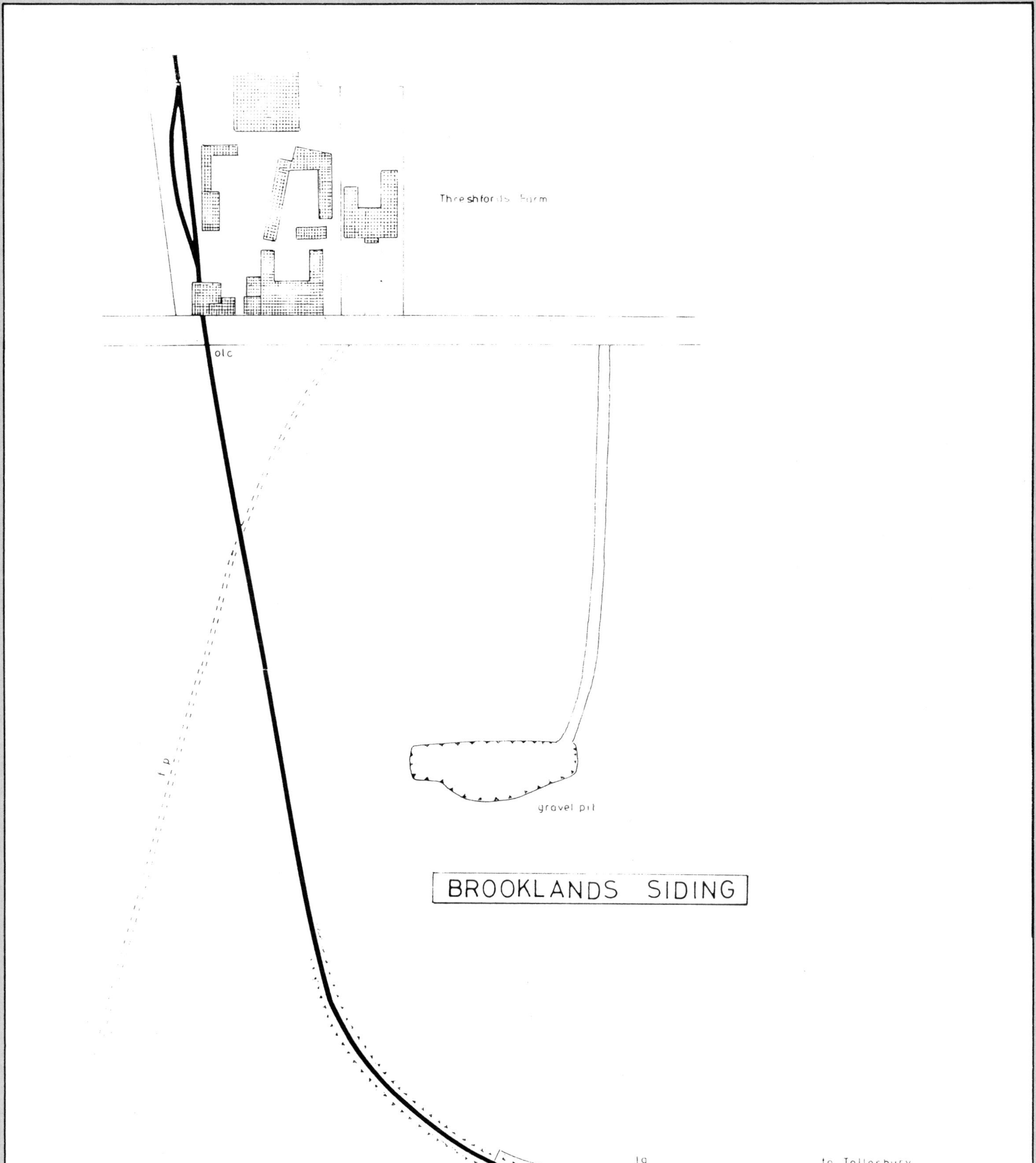
Threshfords Farm
o/c
f p
gravel pit
BROOKLANDS SIDING
lg
to Tollesbury

the Totham Hills. From the summit, near the 2 mile post, the branch levelled out and curved slightly on a 40 chain curve, before climbing again at 1 in 50 to the ungated level crossing which carried the road from Tiptree Heath across the line. Like other ungated crossings on the branch, it was protected by cattle guards. On the railway approach to the crossing 'Whistle' boards were erected 300 yards in advance of the crossing, together with black-painted boards with white lettering advising the driver of the speed limit of 10m.p.h. Beyond the crossing the light railway descended at 1 in 70 over a further five occupational crossings and two ungated level crossings to Heath Siding (2 miles and 62 chains from Kelvedon), situated in the Parish of Tiptree.

The goods yard, sited on the 'down' or east side of the main single line, consisted of a single siding with access by facing and trailing points, allowing shunting to be performed from either direction. At the end of the loop siding were shunting necks. The facilities were completed by a loading gauge, a loading dock at the south end of the shunting neck and a cart road. Immediately beyond Heath Siding the branch entered Inworth Station (2 miles and 69 chains from Kelvedon) where the customary 100ft. long low platform, on the 'down' side of the line, was host to an old four wheel coach body which served as a waiting shelter and parcels store. When the halt was opened in 1905 no accommodation was provided, but the GER made amends a few years later by placing the coach body at the back of the platform, after receiving complaints from local travellers. The station was illuminated, during the hours of darkness, by two post type oil lamps while two platform seats were provided for intending passengers. At the Tiptree end of the station the branch crossed the road which connected Inworth Village, over two miles distant, with Tiptree, Tolleshunt D'Arcy and Tollesbury. The level crossing was protected by gates which were opened and closed by trainmen.

Beyond Inworth the railway continued at a descent of 1 in 70 and then eased to a short gradient of 1 in 150 across the edge of Inworth Heath, reputedly the battlefield where local tribesmen fought Caesar's Army. Later the open land became the haunt of smugglers, gypsies, highwaymen and footpads as well as a resident band of squatters who lived in mud huts. Half a mile across the heath the branch entered a residential area and crossed an open level crossing protected by cattle guards, entering Tiptree Station (3 miles and 31 chains from Kelvedon) on a 1 in 260 falling gradient. The low timber-fronted clinker platform, 100ft. in length, was located on the 'up' side of the line a few yards south of the crossing. Passenger facilities were afforded by a wooden station building which housed the waiting-room and parcels office, this initially being supplemented by a small wooden hut which was used as a staff and lamp room. Later, a second wooden shed was erected and used for parcels storage, eventually becoming a general store. Two platform seats were provided for passengers, while two post type and one wall oil lamp were provided for illumination at night, with a further post type oil lamp being installed by the level crossing. After closure of the branch to passenger traffic, the main station building was converted for use as a goods office.

On the 'down' side of the main single line, opposite the platform, was the goods yard, served by a loop siding with access by facing and trailing points. This loop, together with the north end headshunt, was used as the goods siding, whilst the south end spur led to the two sidings serving Wilkin's jam factory. The factory was the major employer in the area, and Tiptree Station was sited on land donated by the firm. When initially opened this company also financed the upkeep of Tiptree Station gardens, which were laid out with flowers and shrubs. From Tiptree Station the falling gradient sharpened to 1 in 50 as the main single branch continued past the factory and residential area, round a slight left-hand curve, and over two ungated occupational level crossings to Tudwick Road, where there was a further ungated level crossing protected by cattle guards. At this point Tudwick Road Siding (3 miles and 72 chains from Kelvedon) branched off on the 'down' side of the line from points forming a trailing connection for 'down' trains. A short shunt spur ran parallel to the main single line. Tudwick Road Siding was the terminal point on the branch soon after withdrawal of passenger traffic in 1951, when buffer stops were located 200 yards to the south of the points on the main single line, after complete closure of the remainder of the line to Tollesbury on 29th October 1951.

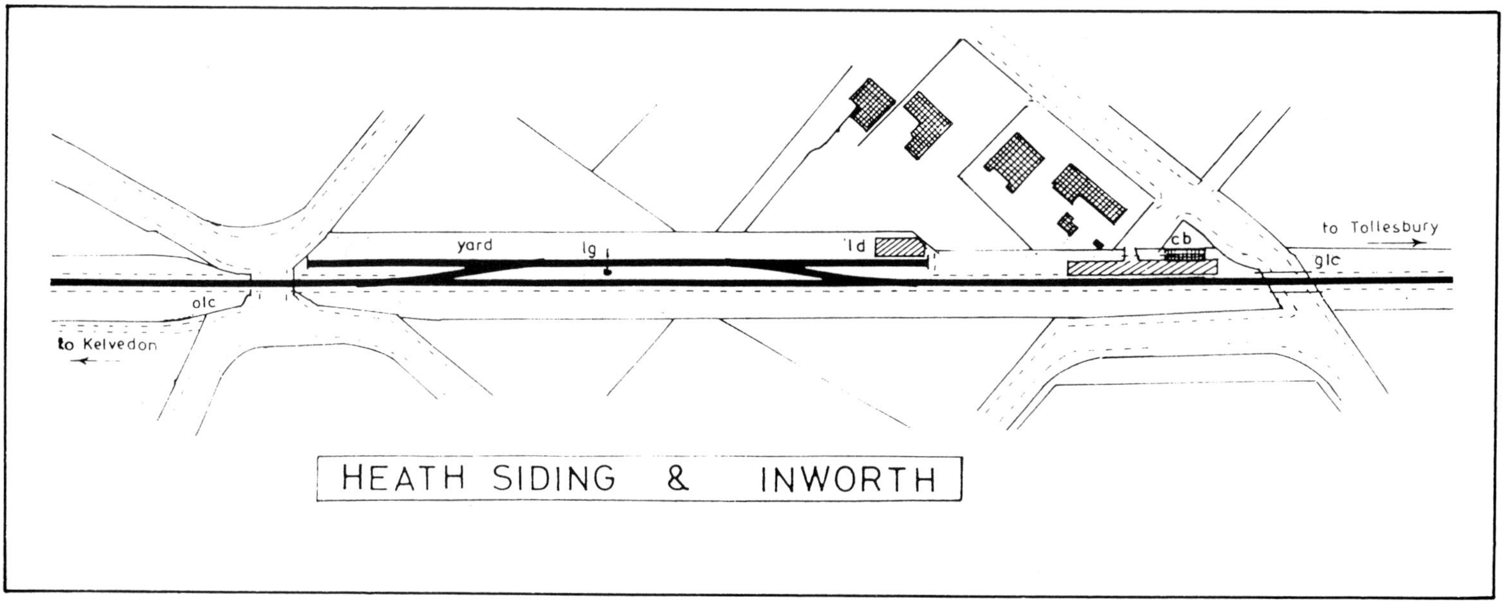

Above: Class J69/1 No. 8636 pulls over the level crossing into Inworth with the 6.37p.m. Tollesbury to Kelvedon train on 16th April 1949.

W. A. Camwell

Inworth Station, opened on 1st May 1905 by the GER. The coach body was added a few years later for use as a waiting-room. This view is facing Kelvedon, and beyond the halt is Heath Siding.

M. Brooks Collection

In August 1958, Class J15 0-6-0 No. 65470 pulls off the main single branch line into Heath Siding. Beyond the siding is the site of Inworth Station and its adjacent level crossing, which was opened and closed by trainmen.

Dr I. C. Allen

Class J15 0-6-0 No. 65470, pictured shunting the sidings to Wilkin's jam factory at Tiptree in August 1958. The main single branch line descends on a falling gradient, to the right of the picture.

Dr I. C. Allen

At the south end of the goods loop siding at Tiptree, two sidings served Wilkin's jam factory. Previously known as Britannia Fruit Farms, the firm provided considerable traffic for the railway company and after the withdrawal of passenger traffic, the branch remained open until 1962, almost wholly to serve the needs of the factory at Tiptree and Tudwick Road. In this view, Class J15 0-6-0 No. 65470 shunts into Wilkin's No. 2 siding, with vans, during August 1958. Two further vans stand in No. 1 siding whilst the brake van is standing on the main single branch line. In the foreground is the 3 ½ milepost.

Dr I. C. Allen

Tiptree Station and goods siding in 1950, facing Kelvedon, with an 'up' train at the platform. Beyond the station is the open level crossing and of note, in the foreground, is the points lever, which was released and locked by a key attached to the train staff.

Real Photographs

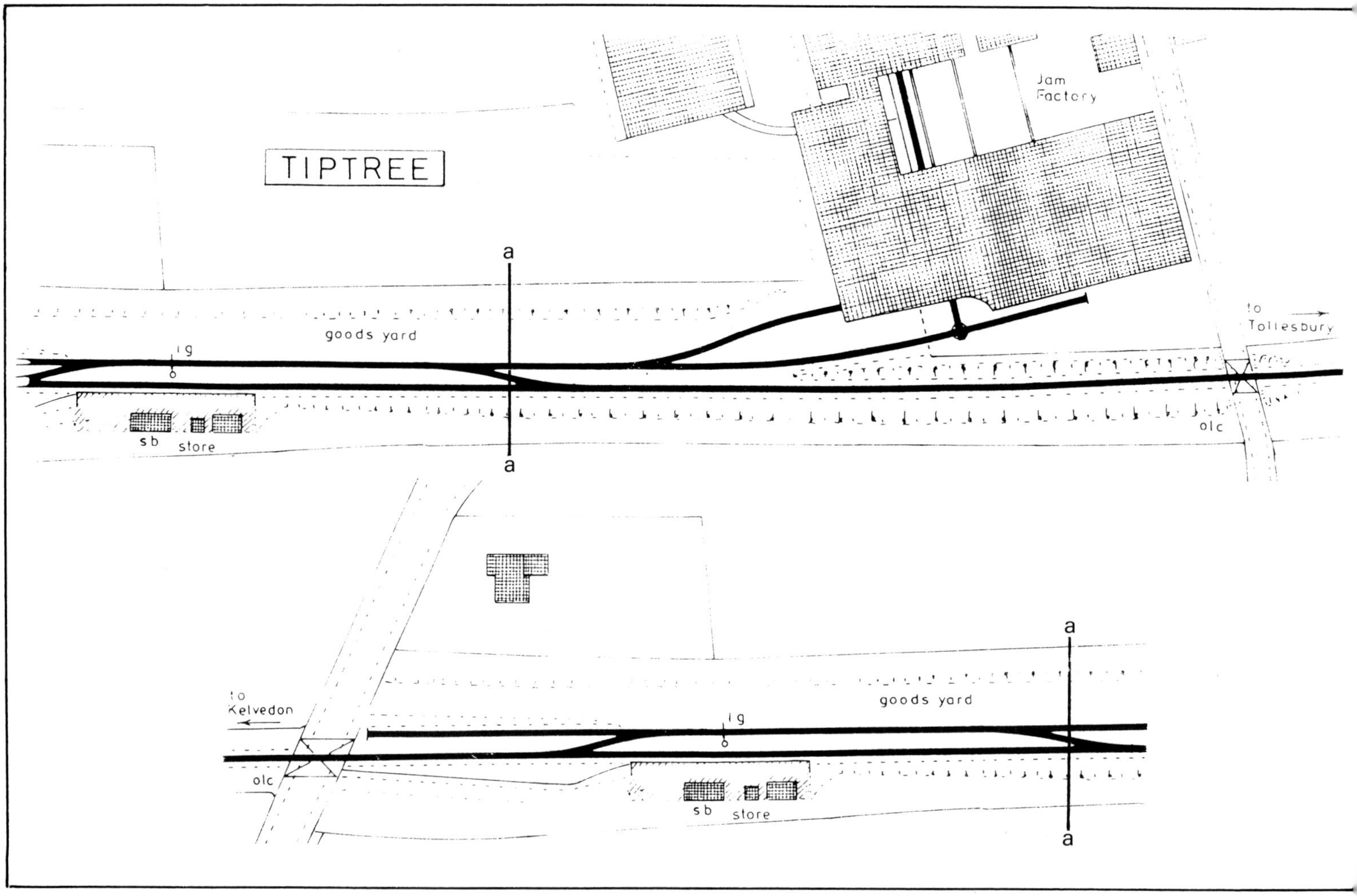

Tiptree Station (3 miles and 31 chains from Kelvedon) facing north. The low platform, which was 15in. above rail level, was host to two substantial wooden huts which served as a waiting-room, parcels office and store, as well as staff accommodation. The smaller hut was utilised, in later years, as a lamp room and store. The station was built on land donated by Wilkin's, the jam manufacturers and fruit growers.

M. Brooks Collection

The ornate garden, hedges and shrubs at Tiptree, viewed from the access path linking the road with the platform. Here Class J69/1 0-6-0T No. 8636, still bearing LNER on the side tanks, pauses with a Tollesbury to Kelvedon train on 26th June 1948.

H. C. Casserley

Class J69/1 0-6-0T No. 8636 enters Tolleshunt Knights with the 6.37p.m. Tollesbury to Kelvedon train on 16th April 1949.

W. A. Camwell

Class J67/1 No. 68616 ambles through the Essex countryside, near Tolleshunt D'Arcy, with a mixed train in 1950.

Dr I. C. Allen

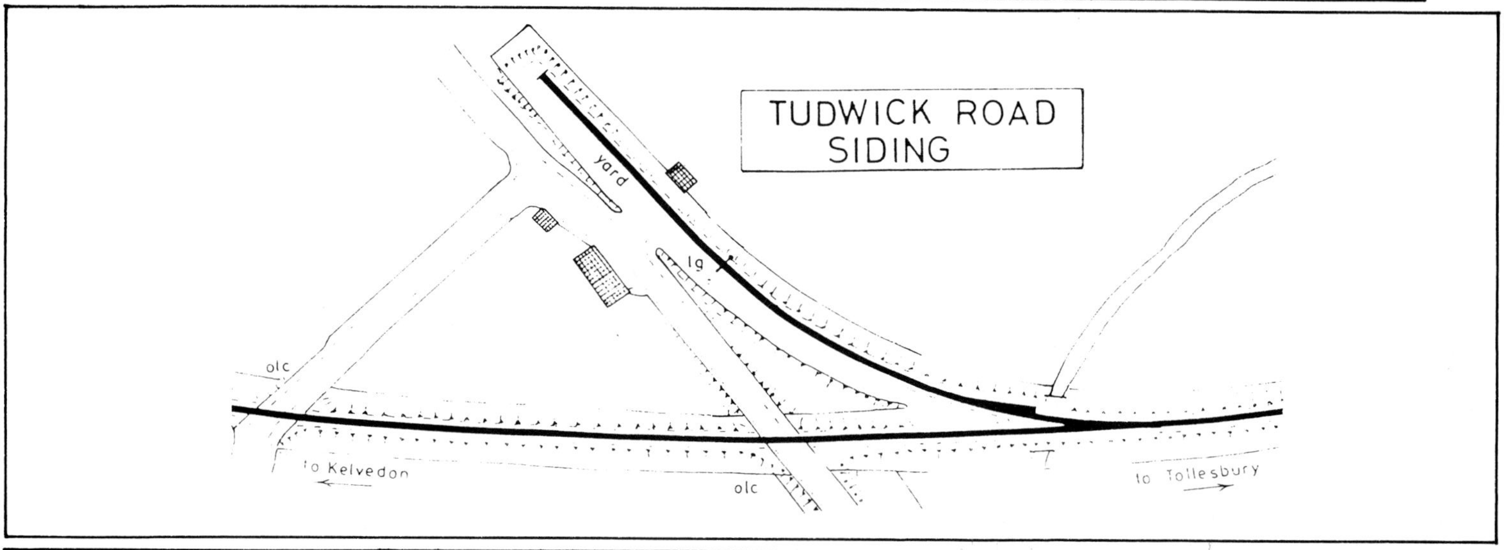
TUDWICK ROAD SIDING
yard
lg
olc
to Kelvedon
olc
to Tollesbury

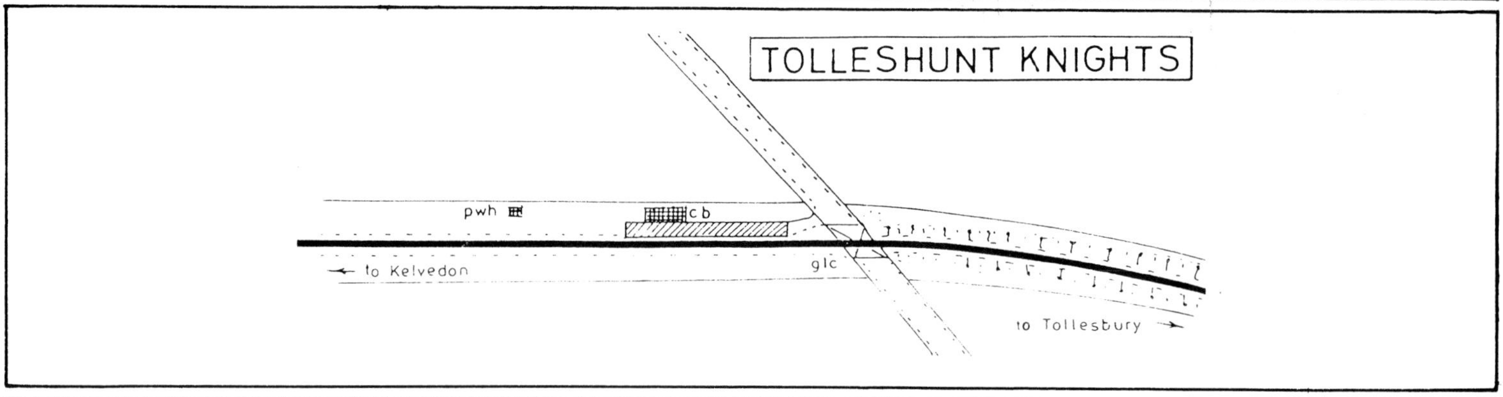
TOLLESHUNT KNIGHTS
pwh
cb
to Kelvedon
glc
to Tollesbury

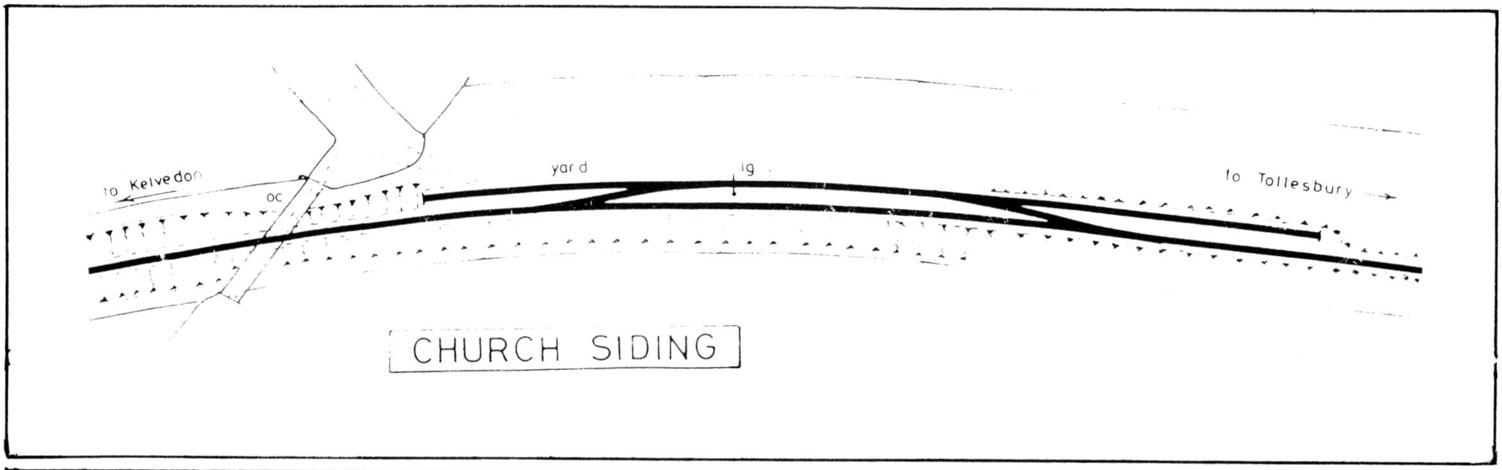
to Kelvedon
oc
yard
lg
to Tollesbury
CHURCH SIDING

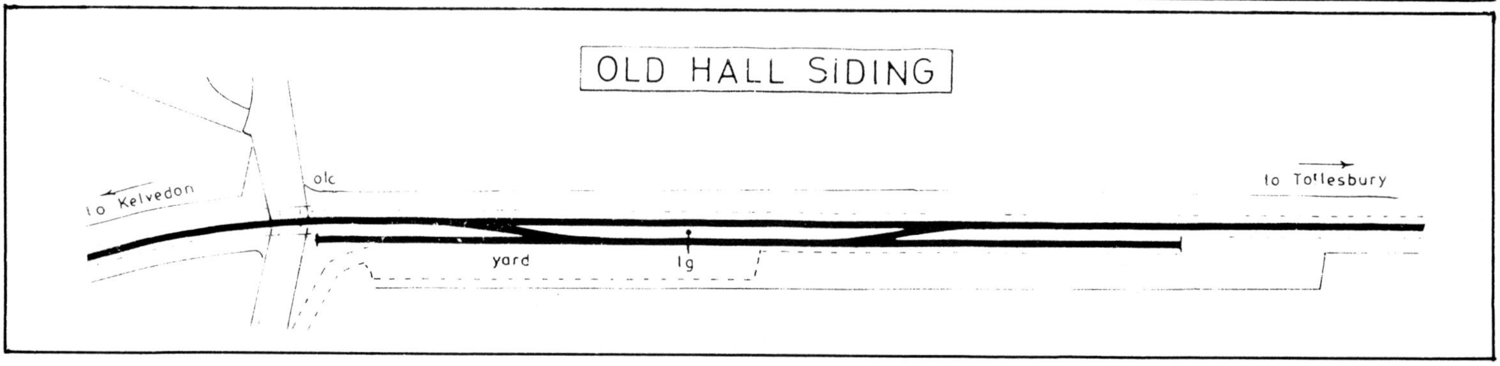
OLD HALL SIDING
to Kelvedon
olc
to Tollesbury
yard
lg

From Tudwick Road the branch crossed Paternoster Heath, with its locally-known King John's Hunting Box or Priory. After a short level section, rising gradients of 1 in 50/level/1 in 50/level took the line past Brook Hall, an Elizabethan Manor House and one time home of Sir John Spenser, (Lord Mayor of London in 1594) and on to Tolleshunt Knights Station (4 miles and 6 chains from Kelvedon), opened by the GER on 12thDecember 1910 to serve the large scattered area. The 100ft. long low platform on the 'down' side of the branch was host to a four wheel coach body which served as a waiting-room, passenger accommodation being completed by a platform seat and two post type oil lamps. The platform was backed by a tubular iron railway fence supported by rail posts, and the exit was via a wooden gate leading to the road connecting Tiptree and Tolleshunt D'Arcy, the latter bisecting the railway immediately south of the station. The crossing was protected by gates which were opened and closed by the train crew.

Beyond the 4¼ mile post the branch negotiated an undulating course, following the contours of the land and rising at 1 in 50 before levelling out and then falling at 1 in 50 through a lengthy cutting. Here the railway reached a depth of 19ft. below the surface of the surrounding land, before passing under Blind Lane Overbridge (No. 875), at 4 miles and 71 chains, which carried a narrow road across the railway. Beyond the bridge the line left the cutting and levelled out for a few yards, before falling again at 1 in 50 for half a mile past Manifold Wick Farm to the adjacent Church Siding (5 miles and 48 chains from Kelvedon), the latter being named after the local church of Tolleshunt Knights, located over a mile from the village and near the siding. In the early years the loop siding, with shunting necks at each end, which was located on the 'down' side of the line with access via facing and trailing points from the main single line, handled considerable loads of seasonal pea and fruit traffic from local farms but, in later years, very little was handled.

The area of fruit trees and farmland gave way to alluvial soil and cattle grazing land, as the branch followed easier falling gradients of 1 in 260/100 across an area well-known during smuggling days for illegal rum trafficking, the contraband being offloaded at the nearby Salcott Creek and transferred to a barn sited near the railway. After a short level section, undulating gradients of 1 in 80 falling/level/50 rising level/100 falling/level and 1 in 70 rising, brought the light railway to the gated level crossing where the Tolleshunt D'Arcy to Great Wigborough and Colchester Road bisected the line. A few yards south of the crossing was Tolleshunt D'Arcy Station (6 miles and 45 chains from Kelvedon), located over a mile from the village. The waiting accommodation on the 100ft. long low platform, sited on the 'down' side of the line, was provided by a wooden shed similar to that at Tiptree. An ex-GER third class four wheel carriage body, with the station nameboard located on the roof of the vehicle, served as a parcel store, with a small brick building at the south end of the platform as an oil store. Two post type oil lamps and a station seat completed the amenities, with a further post type oil lamp being situated by the level crossing. On the 'up' side of the line a loop siding, with facing and trailing points from the main single line, served the small goods yard, with road access to the yard being via a gate off the public road which led to a cart road. A loading gauge was also provided. Tolleshunt D'Arcy Station, like Tiptree, was staffed by a porter who, in addition to his normal station duties, was responsible for shunting and the opening and closing of the level crossing gates. In the mid-1930s the porter's post was abolished, after which trainmen opened and closed the gates.

Beyond Tolleshunt D'Arcy the branch curved sharply to the left on a 25 chain radius curve, falling at 1 in 260 before rising again at 1 in 80 to a level section near the 7 mile post. Here the railway passed an ungated crossing protected by cattle guards where the lane known as Salcott Stone, leading from Tollesbury to the Maldon to Colchester Road, bisected the line. From the crossing the railway descended at 1 in 100 to a short level section and then continued, falling at 1 in 50, past Bouchiers Hall as the low-lying land near the River Blackwater was approached. At 7 miles and 62 chains from Kelvedon, Old Hall Siding was located on the 'up' side of the main single line, with access via facing and trailing points. The loop siding, with shunting necks at each end served local farms and, during the early years of the line, oysters, shrimp and fish traffic, brought by small boats up the navigable Old Hall Creek, was loaded and forwarded to local and London markets from the siding.

From Old Hall Siding the line climbed at 1 in 100 followed by a short level section, before climbing at 1 in 50 past Carrington Farm. On the 'down' side of the branch a short siding, equipped with a loading gauge and serving a loading dock, was entered by facing and trailing points in the 'down' direction and heralded the approach to Tollesbury Station (8 miles and 35 chains from Kelvedon) as the line approached on a 40 chain radius left-hand curve. The usual 100ft. long low timber-fronted clinker platform was host to a wooden station building similar to the building provided at Tiptree. This was used as a waiting-room and parcels office, whilst an old four wheel coach body supplemented as a general store, with a nameboard, two post type oil lamps and a platform seat completing the fixed assets.

The track was single through the station, and immediately beyond the platform the light railway crossed Station Road, originally called North Lane, adjacent to an ungated level crossing protected by cattle guards. To the south of the crossing a loop line was located on the 'up' or west side of the main single branch, to enable the locomotive to run round the train. Beyond the run-round loop, the single line continued on a 1 in 50 falling gradient, curving in a south-easterly direction on a 40 and then 25 chain radius right-hand curves to skirt Tollesbury Village. The branch then levelled out before falling at 1 in 100, following a fairly straight course over three minor roads. Two were open crossings protected by cattle guards and one, at Tollesbury Wick, was protected by gates which were opened and closed by the train crew. A short level section, followed by an equally short 1 in 50 falling gradient, brought the branch on to the level across Tollesbury Wick Marshes to the remote Tollesbury Pier Station (9 miles and 77 chains from Kelvedon) and the terminus of the light railway. Passengers waiting on the 100ft. long platform, located on the 'down' side of the line, were offered protection in this windswept locality by a wooden station building which served as a waiting-room as well as staff accommodation. An old four wheel coach body was sited by the buffer stops as a store while the station was located some 40 yards north of the landward end of the pier, the main single line continuing

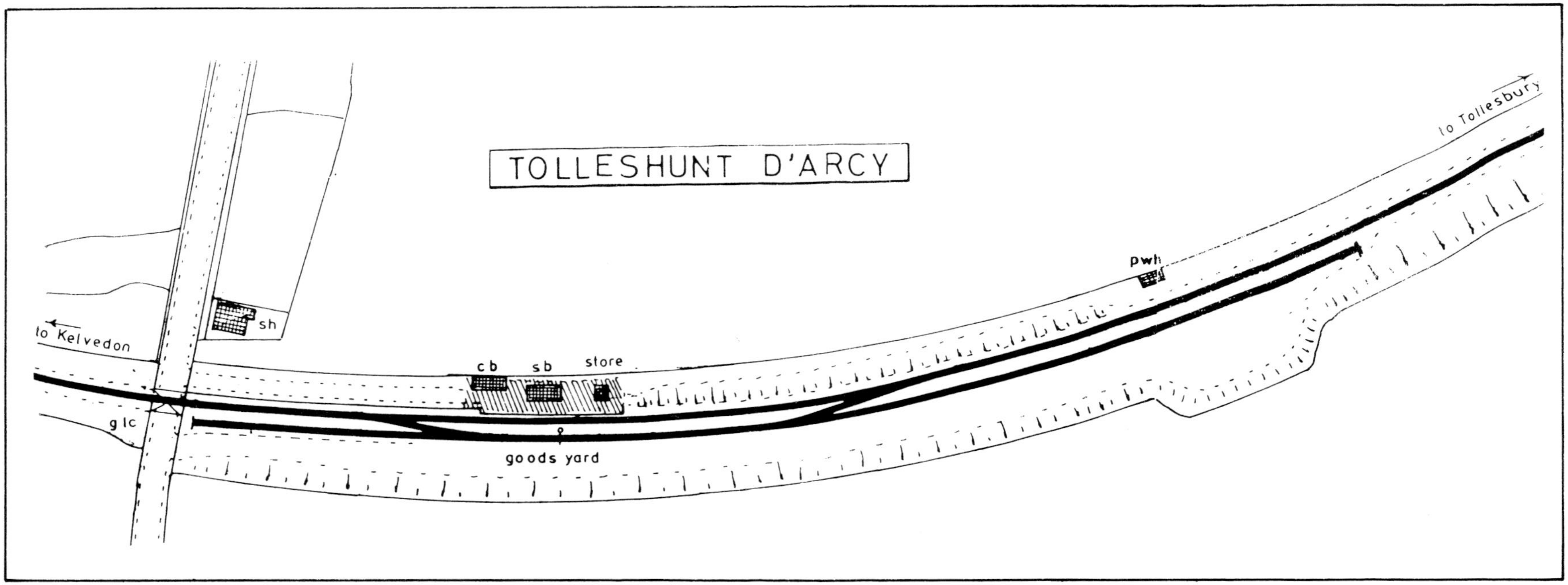

An ex-GER four wheel third saloon coach body, originally dating from the Eastern Counties Railway, and withdrawn in the 1880s, is pictured here, at Tolleshunt D'Arcy Station, serving as a lock-up store.

A. G. Ellis/R. C.Riley & Lens of Sutton/G. Pember

until it terminated at buffer stops. No sidings were provided, but a loop was located on the 'up' side to enable the locomotive to run round its train. Because of the lack of facilities the GER issued instructions that no wagons were to be stabled or held on the run-round loop.

Tollesbury Pier was 1,770ft. in length and was mainly of timber construction, with earthworks at the shore end. During spring tides the depth of water at the pierhead was 25ft. at high tide and 10ft. at low tide The shallow nature of water round the rest of the structure can be gauged by the fact that where steps to water level were provided alongside the pier, at 1,500ft. from the station, the depth of water was only 8ft. at high tide and 66ft. from the station where the depth was 5 ft. at high tide. The pier was 8ft. 10in wide along its length, whilst the promenade at the pierhead was 50ft. wide by 18ft. deep. Wood fencing to a height of 6ft. 6in. protected the public alongside the whole length of the structure, although the pierhead was unprotected.

By virtue of its status as a light railway, the maximum permissible speed on the Tollesbury branch was 25m.p.h., with 10m.p.h. being worked within a distance of 200 yards approaching and over all ungated level crossings. Tender locomotives working tender first were restricted to a speed limit of 15m.p.h. Mileposts measuring zero from Kelvedon (Low Level) were erected on the 'down' side of the line, whilst gradient posts were located on the 'up' side of the track.

Permanent Way

The initial permanent way provided for the light railway was formed of second-hand bullhead track, originally weighing 80lb. per yard but reduced by wear to 70lb. per yard, laid in 24ft. lengths and connected by fishplates weighing 40lb. per pair. The rails were laid in chairs weighing 43lb. each, each chair being secured to sleepers by two wrought-iron spikes and two oak trenails. Nine of

Tolleshunt D'Arcy Station (6 miles and 45 chains from Kelvedon), in a view facing Kelvedon soon after the opening of the line. The main wooden station building, similar to those at Tiptree and Tollesbury, is supplemented by an ex-ECR coach body. The goods loop siding is in the foreground, whilst to the left the gated level crossing, which carried the road from Tolleshunt D'Arcy to Great Wigborough across the line can be seen. The fence alongside the footpath, linking the road to the station, was later replaced by an ornate hedgerow.

The winding nature of the Kelvedon to Tollesbury Light Railway, and the sparse flat terrain traversed by the branch, are evident in this photograph taken near Church Siding.

D. Trevor Rowe

Tolleshunt D'Arcy Station, facing Kelvedon. The wooden station building (centre) is augmented by a brick-built lamp store (foreground) and an ECR wooden coach body, the latter provided as a parcels store.

J. Watling Collection

Tolleshunt D'Arcy Station (6 miles and 45 chains from Kelvedon) and goods siding, soon after the light railway opened to traffic. This view, facing Tollesbury, shows the main timber station building, used by the porter in charge and as a waiting-room. Adjacent to this, and used as the parcels and general store, is the old GER coach body. Three post type oil lamps provided illumination during the hours of darkness.

Lens of Sutton

Class J67/1 No. 68616 darkens the neighbourhood as she pulls away from Tollesbury, past the deserted goods yard, with a mixed train, on 19th September 1950.

Ian L. Wright

Passengers crowd off the branch train, hauled by Class J69/1 No. 7364, at Tollesbury in 1929. This locomotive was one of the earliest to be withdrawn, in January 1931.

J. E. Kite

After passengers alighted at Tollesbury, it was necessary for the train to run forward across Station Road open level crossing to the run-round loop, to enable the locomotive to run round its train. Here, Class J69/1 No. 7364 pulls across Station Road in 1929. The vehicle behind the engine is brake third No. E62261 (ex-GER No. 337), built in 1877 and converted for use on the light railway in 1904. The vehicle was withdrawn in 1931 and replaced by an ex-Stoke Ferry branch vehicle, which took the same number.

J. E. Kite

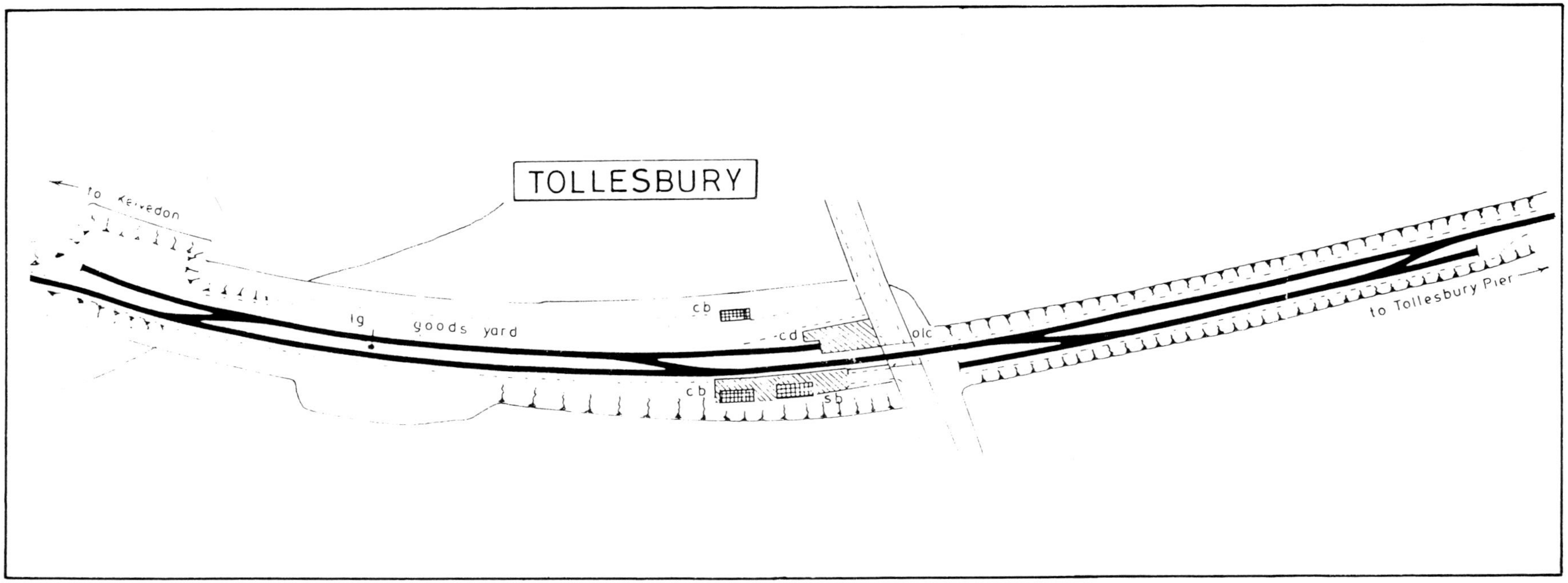

Awaiting departure from Tollesbury, Class J67/1 0-6-0T No. 68608 simmers in the sunshine with a two coach train.

Lens of Sutton

A mixed train formed of bogie tram No. E60461, six wheel brake third No. E62262 and the branch goods brake, hauled by Class J69/1 0-6-0T No. 8636, approaching Tollesbury in 1948.

Dr I. C. Allen

Tollesbury Station, in the early 1930s. The branch train has just arrived from Kelvedon, hauled by a Class J68 0-6-0T and formed of ex-Wisbech & Upwell tram No. 60462 and ex-Stoke Ferry six wheel brake third No. 62262. On the left is the cattle and loading pen and the yard siding.

A 1934 view of Tollesbury Station, facing Tollesbury Pier. The entry points to the goods yard siding are in the foreground and the cattle dock siding is on the left, whilst beyond the platform is Station Road open level crossing. Compared with earlier views, the coach body has been added as a parcels store and lamp room. *L&GRP*

On 26th June 1948, Class J69/1 0-6-0T No. 8636 stands by the run-round loop at Tollesbury and is ready to pull into the station with its three coach train.

H. C. Casserley

A study of ex-Stoke Ferry brake third No. 62262 and ex-Wisbech & Upwell bogie tramcar No. 60462, together with a van to normal main line loading gauge, at Tollesbury, on 26th June 1948. No. 62262, built to GER diagram No. 609, had 3ft. diameter wheels, whilst No. 60462 had wheels of 2ft. 9in. diameter, which partly accounts for the difference in height of the vehicles.

H. C. Casserley

Class J69/1 No. 7053 poses at Tollesbury, in the early 1930s, with a mixed train for Kelvedon. No. 7053 was later renumbered 8619, and gained fame as the highly-polished East Side pilot at Liverpool Street in the 1950s and early 1960s. Note the old style headcode disc in the incorrect position.

Class J69/1 0-6-0T No. 68578 pulls into Tollesbury Station, from the run-round loop, with a train composed of the two ex-Stoke Ferry six wheel brake thirds.
R. C. Riley

Tollesbury Station, facing Kelvedon, with the branch train waiting at the low platform. The station presents a neat appearance but, by this time (1950), traffic was light and passengers few. Despite nationalisation, the noticeboards still proclaim LNER.
Real Photographs

No. 68578 at Tollesbury, with a Railway Club special formed of the two ex-Stoke Ferry six wheel coaches.

R. C. Riley

Crowds gather round the last 'up' departure at Tollesbury, on 5th May 1951. Class J69/1 0-6-0T No. 68578, adorned with wreaths and with 'RIP Born 1904 Died 1951' written on the tank sides, and with 'There be many a poor soul have to walk' scrawled on the bunker, waits for the 'right away' for the last time. Leaning out of the cab is 'honorary fireman' Tom Driberg (MP for Maldon), who made last minute attempts in Parliament to reprieve the line.

D. Trevor Rowe

Class J69/1 0-6-0T No. 68578, adorned with a wreath and the message 'RIP Born 1904 Died 1951', pulls slowly through Tollesbury Station on the last day of passenger services on the light railway, 5th May 1951.

D. Trevor Rowe

the creosoted sleepers, measuring 8ft. 6in. by 10in. by 5in. were laid under each length of track. The track rested on gravel ballast laid to a depth of 1ft. below sleeper level. The width of the formation of the railway along the whole length of the line was 16ft., except at stations where there were slight variations.

As rails became life-expired they were replaced by further second-hand lengths, but by the outbreak of World War I, 85lb. per yard second-hand track in 24ft. lengths had replaced the lighter track. From 1923 the LNER began replacing the shorter lengths of rail with lengths 30 and 45ft., weighing up to 90lb. per yard. These rails remained in use with odd lengths of 87 and 93lb. per yard, until the line was closed and the track lifted.

The original gravel ballast used when the line opened was found suitable for the light traffic but, within a few years, the GER introduced ashes and clinker to the formation. The GER found ashes adequate for ballasting many of their branch lines, and supplies were readily available from the motive power depots on the system. When supplies of ashes or clinker were not available from locomotive sheds, wagon loads were obtained from Tate & Lyle's sugar refinery at Silvertown and, after the mid-1920s, from the British Sugar Corporation factories at Felstead, Bury St. Edmunds, Ipswich and Ely.

Maintenance of the permanent way from the opening of the line was covered by an augmented permanent way gang based at Kelvedon, consisting of a ganger and four platelayers, who also spent some of their time on main line maintenance. In addition to attending to day-to-day track maintenance, the permanent way gang was responsible for cleaning the toilets at stations, maintenance of fencing and gates and unmanned crossings. On hot and dry summer days they were also required to patrol the line, acting as beaters to extinguish fires caused by stray sparks deposited along the lineside by the branch locomotive, to stop fire spreading to local farmers' crops.

Signalling

Signalling on the Tollesbury Light Railway was minimal, and was concentrated at the Kelvedon end of the line. Points and signals at Kelvedon main line station, including the connection from the 'up' main line to the branch, were controlled from Kelvedon Station signal box, situated at the London end of the 'up' platform, which contained a 42 lever Saxby & Farmer frame with 38 working and four spare levers. At Kelvedon (Low Level) a nine lever ground frame with seven working and two spare levers was provided adjacent to the points, from the main single branch line leading to the connecting spur, on the south or 'up' side of the line, east of the low level station. Signalling consisted of a lower quadrant 'up' home signal and a 'down' starter with pitch pine posts, cedar arms, and cast and wrought-iron fittings. Adjacent to the former A12 main road crossing, near Feering Halt, the 'up' branch fixed distant of similar manufacture was located on the 'down' side of the line, north of the crossing, in advance of the 'up' home signal. This distant signal was painted the same red as stop signals, in GER days, but with a 'V'. It also showed to drivers at night the same red and green aspect. To avoid confusion with the home signal, it was fitted with a Coligny-Welch lamp, which showed an additional white 'V' at night. In common with GER practice each wooden signal arm was stamped on the back 'Kelvedon LL', this being the controlling ground frame. With the advent of the LNER the distant signal was painted the familiar yellow with a black 'V', the Coligny-Welch lamp being modified to serve as an ordinary lamp.

The light railway was worked under the 'one engine in steam or two or more engines coupled together' principle using train staff without tickets, the train staff being round in shape, painted green and lettered 'Kelvedon and Tollesbury Pier'. When not in use, the train staff was kept in the custody of the stationmaster at Kelvedon, who was the sole person authorised to deal with it.

Points on the main single line, and catch points in the sidings at the intermediate goods sidings, were worked by a ground frame at each place, locked and released by Annetts' lock, with the key attached to the Kelvedon and Tollesbury Pier train staff. The points leading to and from the main single line at each station were kept padlocked for the main single line, except when required to be used for the train shunting at the station, the key for these points being kept in the custody of the porter in charge of the station.

Whenever a train required to shunt at the intermediate sidings, the man in charge of the station controlling the siding was instructed either to meet the train at the siding or travel with the train to the siding, and then assist with shunting operations. On arrival of the train at the siding the man in charge obtained the train staff from the engine driver, unlocked the ground frame, and worked the points during shunting operations. After shunting was complete and the points replaced in the normal position for the main single line, the man in charge returned the train staff to the engine driver.

Initially, no shunting was permitted on the main single line, without the branch engine being at the station, but later instructions regarding Tollesbury amended this. These allowed shunting on the main single line in an emergency without the branch engine being at the station but, in order to protect the line, the porter in charge arranged for a man with flags and detonators to be sent about 1,000 yards in the direction of Kelvedon, to stop any approaching train before vehicles were allowed to foul the main single line. Once shunting was under way any vehicles detained on the main line were secured by handbrake and scotches, to prevent them running away on the falling gradient. Before shunting commenced, the porter in charge at Tollesbury also advised the porter in charge at Tolleshunt D'Arcy Station of the shunting movement, so that the latter could detain the train at his station. The train was not permitted to depart from Tolleshunt D'Arcy until the porter in charge had ascertained from Tollesbury that shunting was complete, and that the main single line was clear.

Of the sixteen public level crossings on the light railway, eleven were open crossings protected by cattle guards while the remaining five were provided with crossing gates which, in the normal position, were open for road traffic and closed across the main single line. At four of the gated level crossings (Feering, Inworth, Tolleshunt Knights and Tolleshunt Wick) the gates were opened and closed by the train crew. After the train was brought to a stand well clear of the crossing, the fireman opened the gates for the passage of the train over the crossing. Once the train had been brought to a halt clear of the gates, the guard closed them across the railway. Before proceeding, the driver was required to take care that he had received the 'all right' signal from the guard. In the event of a light engine traversing the branch, the fireman was responsible for opening and closing the gates. At the remaining gated crossing, at Tolleshunt

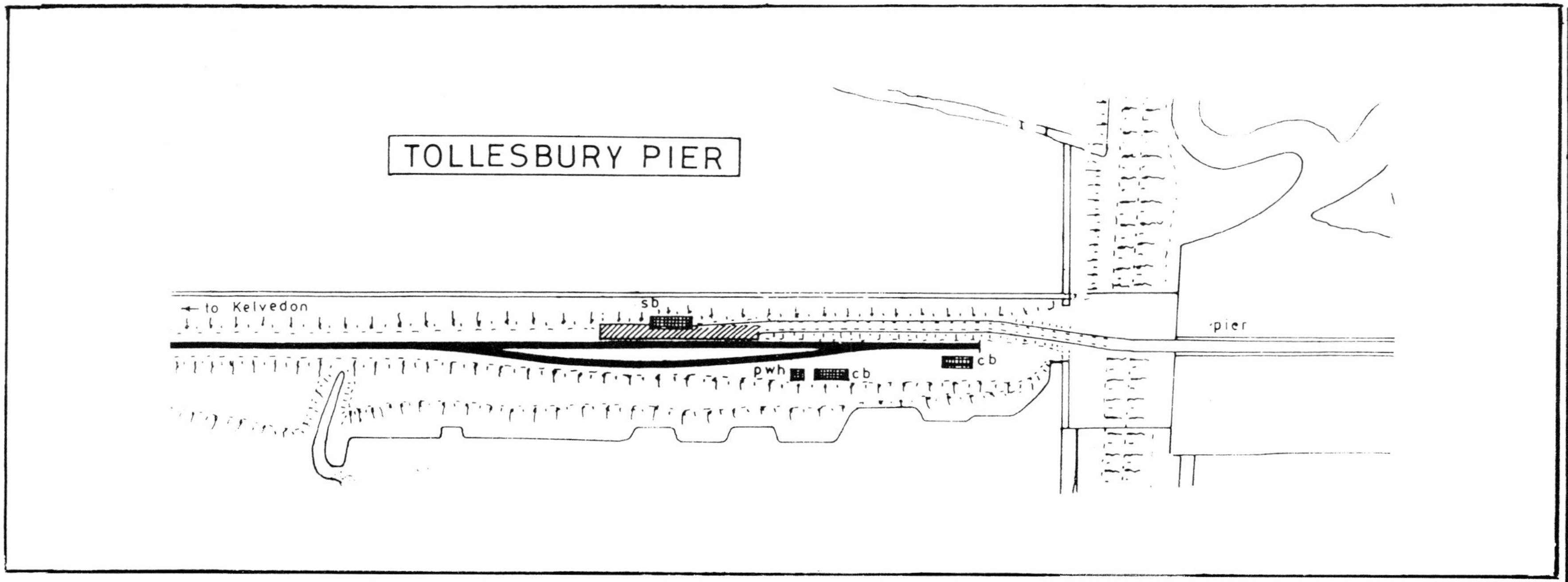

Tollesbury Station looking towards Tollesbury Pier. After the closure of the Tollesbury Pier section in 1921, the track beyond the run-round loop was used for the storage of wagons.

M. Brooks Collection

The remains of Tollesbury Pier, derelict and with a section removed as an anti-invasion precaution during World War II, photographed on 8th January 1949. Most of the structure was later destroyed, during the floods which inundated most of the East Anglian coast in 1953.

John H. Meredith

D'Arcy Station, the porter in charge was responsible for opening and closing the gates, taking care to open them in sufficient time to prevent delays to rail traffic. In later years, after the abolition of the porter in charge post at Tolleshunt D'Arcy, the train crew opened and closed the gates.

The open crossing near Tiptree Station was also provided with barriers, which were placed across the road by the porter in charge, or his assistant, during shunting operations at the station. The barriers were not lowered however, for the passage of a booked passenger, mixed or goods train. The use of these barriers was suspended in 1937 after which time the driver had to give 3 blasts on the whistle to warn the public that shunting was taking place.

After dark, and during fog or falling snow, the gate lamps were required to be illuminated and placed on all gated crossings. The responsibility for cleaning, trimming, lighting and extinguishing the lamps on the gates being placed with Kelvedon Station staff, for Feering Crossing, the porter in charge at Tiptree, or his assistant; for Inworth and Tolleshunt Knights crossings, the porter in charge; for Tolleshunt D'Arcy Crossing, and for Tollesbury Wick Crossing, the porter in charge at Tollesbury. In foggy weather, or during falling snow, a platelayer, acting as fogman, placed two detonators 10 yards apart, about 300 yards on the approach to each of the five gated level crossings, to warn enginemen of approaching trains and of the whereabouts of the crossing. In 1937, this instruction reduced the number of detonators to one. In addition, during adverse weather, the man appointed to work the ground frame at Kelvedon (Low Level) Station placed two detonators on the rails 10 yards apart, about 200 yards on the Tollesbury side of the 'up' home signal, for each approaching train.

The desolate Tollesbury Pier Station, soon after opening in 1907, with a GER Class R24 0-6-0T running with front coupling rods removed as a 2-4-0T, hauling three of the original coaches supplied to the light railway, two thirds and a brake third, approaching the low platform. In contrast to later years, a few passengers are seen waiting for the branch train. Tollesbury Pier was only a passenger station with a run-round loop, to enable the engine to run round its train. There were no sidings.

The isolated Tollesbury Pier Station, facing the buffer stops, with the pier disappeariing in the haze beyond. The wooden building was provided for the needs of staff and passenger comfort, and was opened on 15th May 1907. The station was later served on an 'as and when required basis', after the area failed to attract developers to turn this part of the Blackwater Estuary into a yachting centre on a par with Brightlingsea and Burnham-on-Crouch. Traffic was so sparse that services were withdrawn on and from 17th July 1921.

Courtesy National Railway Museum

Tollesbury Pier, on the shores of the Blackwater, 1,770ft. in length and mainly of timber construction. It is shown at low tide. During spring tides the depth of water at the pierhead was 25ft. at high tide, and 10ft. at low tide. Unfortunately, the area never developed, and the structure became a 'white elephant', gradually decaying until sections were removed during World War II. Most of it was later washed away in the floods of 1953.

L&GRP/Courtesy David & Charles

The remains of the once impressive Tollesbury Pier viewed from the shore in 1949. The walkway planks and intermediate section of the pier were removed as anti-invasion precautions in 1940. Note also the silted up foreshore of the Blackwater. This was a far cry from the developers' dreams of 1907.

D. Trevor Rowe

A gated level crossing on the light railway.

D. Trevor Rowe

The site of Tollesbury Pier Station, facing the buffer stops, viewed in the late 1930s. The run-round loop is still extant, but is covered in undergrowth.

L&GRP/Courtesy David & Charles

The site of Tollesbury Pier Station, facing inland, in the late 1930s. Only the track, the decaying coach body and the brick hut remain in this desolate spot.

L&GRP

310

KELVEDON, TIPTREE, AND TOLLESBURY LIGHT RAILWAY.

The Kelvedon, Tiptree, and Tollesbury Light Railway (**a Single Line**), which is about 10 miles long, is provided with five Passenger and Goods Stations, viz.:—

Kelvedon (Low Level)	**Tollesbury**
Tiptree	**Tollesbury Pier** (not a Goods Station).
Tolleshunt D'Arcy	

A Platform—called "**Inworth**"—is provided against the Level Crossing situate at about three miles from Kelvedon, and the trains are to call at Inworth to take up or set down Passengers when required.

A Platform—called "**Tolleshunt Knights**"—is provided against the Level Crossing situate at about ¾ mile from Tiptree, and the trains are to call at Tolleshunt Knights to take up or set down Passengers when required.

A Pier is provided at the end of the Railway, with access to and from Tollesbury Pier Station.

Intermediate Public and Private Goods Sidings are also provided as under:—

Brooklands Siding (Private),
between Kelvedon and Tiptree, about 1,100 yards from Kelvedon Station.

Heath Siding (Public),
between Kelvedon and Tiptree, 2¼ miles from Kelvedon Station.

Tudwick Road Siding (Public),
between Tiptree and Tolleshunt D'Arcy, about ½ mile from Tiptree Station.

Church Siding (Public),
between Tiptree and Tolleshunt D'Arcy, about 2¼ miles from Tiptree Station.

Old Hall Siding (Public),
between Tolleshunt D'Arcy and Tollesbury, about 1¼ miles from Tolleshunt D'Arcy Station.

The Points in the Single Line and the Catch Points in the Siding at the Intermediate Goods Sidings are worked by Ground Lever at each place, which is controlled by Annett's Lock, the Key being attached to the Kelvedon and Tollesbury Pier Train Staff. The Points leading to and from the Single Line at each of the Stations must always be kept padlocked, except when required to be used during the time a train is doing work at the Station, the Key (which is common to all the Points at each Station) being kept in the custody of the man in charge of the Station.

Whenever a train has work to do at an intermediate Goods Siding, the man in charge of the Station under whose supervision the Siding is, must arrange to meet the train at the Siding, or proceed with the train to the Siding, and assist with the shunting operations. On arrival of the train at the Siding, the man in charge must obtain the Train Staff from Engine-driver to enable him to unlock the ground Lever and work the necessary Points. After the shunting operations are completed and the Points have been replaced in their normal position, he must hand the Train Staff back to the Driver.

The Light Railway is worked by Train Staff without Tickets, the Train Staff being round and painted green, and lettered "Kelvedon and Tollesbury Pier."

The Train Staff, when not in use, must be kept in the Station Master's Office at Kelvedon Station, the Station Master being the sole person authorised to deal with the Train Staff.

Only one engine in steam, or two or more engines coupled together, must be allowed on the Light Railway at one and the same time. The Light Railway is worked in accordance with the Train Staff Regulations contained in this "Appendix" for working Single Lines of Railway by only one engine in steam or two or more engines coupled together.

No train or engine must exceed a speed of **25 miles an hour,** and if a train should be worked by a Tender engine **running Tender first** the speed must not exceed **15 miles an hour.**

Where Gates are **not** provided at Public Road Level Crossings, a Board with the figure 10 on it is erected 300 yards on each side of the Level Crossing, and the speed of trains or engines must not exceed **10 miles an hour** when approaching within a distance of 200 yards of such Level Crossings.

Public Road Level Crossings, as under, are provided:—

Between Kelvedon (L.L.) and Tiptree Stations.

One, provided with Gates, about 600 yards from Kelvedon.
One, provided with Cattle Guards, 1¾ miles from Kelvedon.
One, provided with Cattle Guards, 2¼ miles from Kelvedon.
One, provided with Cattle Guards, at Heath Siding.
One, provided with Gates, about 3 miles from Kelvedon.
One, provided with Cattle Guards, at Kelvedon end of Tiptree Station.

Between Tiptree and Tolleshunt D'Arcy Stations.

One, provided with Cattle Guards, about ½ mile from Tiptree.
One, provided with Gates, about ¾ mile from Tiptree.
One, provided with Cattle Guards, about 1¼ miles from Tiptree.
One, provided with Gates, at Tiptree end of Tolleshunt D'Arcy Station.

The GER Appendix to the Working Timetable, 1919

311

Kelvedon, Tiptree, and Tollesbury Light Railway—*contd.*

Between Tolleshunt D'Arcy and Tollesbury Stations.

One, provided with Cattle Guards, about ¾ mile from Tolleshunt D'Arcy.
One, provided with Cattle Guards, at Old Hall Siding.
One, provided with Cattle Guards, at Tollesbury Station.

Between Tollesbury and Tollesbury Pier Stations.

One, provided with Gates, about 600 yards from Tollesbury Station.
One, provided with Cattle Guards, about ¾ mile from Tollesbury Station.
One, provided with Cattle Guards, about 1 mile from Tollesbury Station.

At the five Public Level Crossings provided with Crossing Gates, the Gates are to stand normally across the Railway.

At each of the five Public Level Crossings (except the Level Crossing at Tolleshunt D'Arcy Station) the train must be brought to a stand well clear of the Gates. The Gates are to be opened for the passage of the train over the Crossing by the Fireman, and after the train has passed over the Crossing, the Guard of the train must close them across the Railway, the Driver taking care not to again proceed on his journey until he has received an "All-right" signal from the Guard. In the case of a Light engine, the Fireman must open and close the Gates.

At the Public Level Crossing at Tolleshunt D'Arcy Station, the man in charge of the Station must attend to the Gates, and take care that the Gates are closed across the Public Road in sufficient time to prevent delay to trains and engines.

Barriers are provided at the Public Level Crossing at Tiptree Station, and the man in charge of Tiptree Station must take care that the Barriers are placed, and securely fastened, across the Public Road during the time shunting operations are being carried out at that Station.

After dark, or in foggy weather or during falling snow, the Gate Lamp must be lighted and placed on the Gate at all the Public Road Level Crossings provided with Gates.

The responsibility for cleaning, trimming, lighting, and extinguishing the Lamps on the Gates of the Public Level Crossings is as under:—

Level Crossing about 600 yards from Kelvedon ...	Kelvedon Station Staff.
Level Crossing on each side of Tiptree Station ...	Man in charge of Tiptree Station, or his Assistant.
Level Crossing at Tolleshunt D'Arcy Station ...	Man in charge of Tolleshunt D'Arcy Station.
Level Crossing about 600 yards on Pier side of Tollesbury Station	Man in charge of Tollesbury Station.

In foggy weather or during falling snow, a Fogman (Platelayer) is to be provided about 300 yards from each of the five Public Level Crossings provided with Gates, and he must place two Detonators on the rail, 10 yards apart, in the direction from which a train will approach, in order to denote to the Enginemen the vicinity of the Level Crossing.

The Engine Whistle must be sounded on approaching all Public Road Level Crossings.

No engine, train, or vehicle must be allowed to stand foul of any of the Public Road Level Crossings.

At all Public Road Level Crossings, a Board lettered "Beware of the Trains," is placed in the Public Road about 50 yards on each side of the Crossing.

No shunting whatever must be allowed to take place on the Main Single Line at any of the Stations except Tollesbury (see special instructions on next page), **unless the Branch engine is at the Station.**

The use of a Tow Rope is authorised, when necessary, at any Station on the Light Railway, and is to be carried in the Tollesbury Branch Goods Break Van.

After dark, or in foggy weather or during falling snow, the engine must carry a Red Head Light on the Chimney.

No engine, carriage, or truck (loaded or empty) having a greater weight than **14 tons** on any one pair of wheels must be run on the Light Railway.

The loads of **Goods** trains running over this Light Railway must not exceed 12 Trucks of Minerals, 17 Trucks of Goods, or **24 Empty Trucks.**

In the case of **Mixed** trains, **one** Passenger vehicle is to be considered equal to one loaded Truck of Goods.

Mixed trains running over the Light Railway are to be worked in accordance with the Mixed Train Regulations shown in this "Appendix."

In foggy weather or during falling snow, the man appointed to work the Ground Locking Frame at Kelvedon Low Level Station must place two Detonators on the rail 10 yards apart, about 200 yards on the Tollesbury-side of the Up Home Signal, for each approaching train.

The Engine Whistle for going to and from the Light Railway at Kelvedon Station is 3 distinct sounds.

Passenger train vehicles in use on the Light Railway are not to be allowed to come on to the Main Line at Kelvedon Station unless the Footboards of the vehicles have been removed.

Line No. 100—KELVEDON TO TOLLESBURY

KELVEDON, TIPTREE AND TOLLESBURY LIGHT RAILWAY

Where gates are not provided at public road level crossings, a board with the figure **10** on it is erected 300 yards on each side of the level crossing, and the speed of trains or engines must not exceed 10 miles an hour when approaching within a distance of 200 yards of such level crossings.

The points leading to and from the Single Line at each of the stations and intermediate sidings must always be kept padlocked, except when required to be used during the time a train is doing work at the station, the key, which is common to all the points at each station, being kept in the custody of the man in charge of the station.

Whenever a train has work to do at an intermediate goods siding, the man in charge of the station under whose supervision the siding is, must either arrange to meet the train at the siding, or proceed with it to the siding, and assist with the shunting operations.

Public road level crossings are situated as under :—

Between Kelvedon (L.L.) and Tiptree Stations.

One, provided with gates, about 600 yards from Kelvedon.
One, provided with cattle guards, 1¾ miles from Kelvedon.
One, provided with cattle guards, 2½ miles from Kelvedon.
One, provided with cattle guards, at Heath Siding.
One, provided with gates, about 3 miles from Kelvedon.
One, provided with cattle guards, at Kelvedon end of Tiptree Station.

Between Tiptree and Tolleshunt D'Arcy Stations.

One, provided with cattle guards, about ½ mile from Tiptree.
One, provided with gates, about ¾ mile from Tiptree.
One, provided with cattle guards, about 1¼ miles from Tiptree.
One, provided with gates, at Tiptree end of Tolleshunt D'Arcy Station.

Between Tolleshunt D'Arcy and Tollesbury Stations.

One, provided with cattle guards, about ¾ mile from Tolleshunt D'Arcy.
One, provided with cattle guards, at Old Hall Siding.
One, provided with cattle guards, at Tollesbury Station.

During fog or falling snow, a Fogman is to be provided about 300 yards from each of the public level crossings provided with gates, and he must place one detonator on the rail in the direction from which a train will approach, in order to denote to the Enginemen the vicinity of the level crossing.

The engine whistle must be sounded on approaching all public road level crossings.

An engine, train, or vehicle must not be allowed to stand foul of any of the public road level crossings.

The use of a tow rope is authorised, when necessary, at any station on the Light Railway and is to be carried in the Tollesbury Branch goods brake van.

An engine or vehicle, loaded or empty, having a greater weight than 14 tons on any one pair of wheels must not be run on the Light Railway.

In the case of Mixed trains, one passenger vehicle is to be considered equal to one loaded wagon of goods.

During fog or falling snow, the man appointed to work the ground frame at Kelvedon Low Level Station must place one detonator on the rail about 200 yards on the Tollesbury side of the Up Home Signal, for each approaching train.

Passenger train vehicles in use on the Light Railway are not to be allowed to come on to the Main line at Kelvedon Station unless the footboards of the vehicles have been removed.

Special Instructions for working on the branch. LNER Sectional Appendix, 1947.

3.—Kelvedon and Tollesbury.

Week Days.							
LONDON (Liverpool St.) dep.	8 55	10 55	....	4 18	....	....	....
KELVEDON — — — "	10 45	12 30	2 45	5 40	—	—	—
TIPTREE .... "	11 3	12 44	2 59	5 54	....	....	....
TOLLESHUNT D'ARCY "	11 15	12 56	3 11	6 6	—	—	—
TOLLESBURY .... arr.	11 25	1 [illegible]	3 17	6 12	....	....	....
Week Days.							
TOLLESBURY .... dep.	8 25	11 40	2 0	6 20	....	....	....
TOLLESHUNT D'ARCY "	8 34	11 47	2 7	6 31	—	—	—
TIPTREE .... "	8 44	11 59	2 19	6 47	....	....	....
KELVEDON — — — arr.	8 57	12 [illegible]	2 32	7 0	—	—	—
LONDON (Liverpool St.) "	10 20	2 25	4 20	9 6	....	....	....

No Trains on Sundays.

Fares for the Single Journey:—

KELVEDON AND	d.	TIPTREE AND	d.	TOLLESHUNT D'ARCY AND	d.
Tiptree	4	Tolleshunt D'Arcy	3	Tollesbury..........	2
Tolleshunt D'Arcy	7	Tollesbury..........	5		
Tollesbury........	9				

Tickets will be issued on the Train.

Passenger Timetable, April 1905.

KELVEDON DEPOT.

WEEK DAYS.

No. 1.

arr. a.m.		dep. a.m.
	On Duty	3 45‡
	Loco'	4 30 L
	Kelvedon	6 40 G
8 5	Tollesbury	8 24
9 0	Kelvedon	9 25†
10 6 / 10 26	Tollesbury	9 45* / 10 36
		p.m.
11 16	Kelvedon	12 29
p.m.		
1 10	Tollesbury	3 15
4 20	Kelvedon	5 54
6 27	Tollesbury	6 42
7 27	Kelvedon Loco'	L

‡ For water raising.

Men change Kelvedon.

Second set on duty driver 12.0 noon, fireman 12.10 p.m.

† Commencing September 14th, runs daily.

* Not after 12th September.

Locomotivemen's diagram, July 1925.

88

Stations and Signal Boxes. — Stations.	Signal Boxes.	Distance from Signal Box next above. — Miles.	Chains.	Refuge Sidings. — Down.	Up.	Opening and Closing.
KELVEDON and TOLLESBURY Light Railway.						
Kelvedon L.L.	.... ●	...	...	...	...	Closed at Night, and on Sundays.
Inworth Station*	....	2	68	...	...	No Signals or Signal Boxes are provided at these places, and the distances given are from Station to Station.
Tiptree ,,	.... ●	...	44	...	...	
Tolleshunt D'Arcy ,,	.... ●	3	13	...	...	The special Regulations for working this Light Railway are contained in this Appendix.
Tollesbury ,,	.... ●	1	7	...	...	* Trains call only when required to take up or set down Passengers.
Tollesbury Pier ,,	.... ●	1	43	...	...	

Staff only.

An extract from the GER Appendix to the Working Timetable, 1910.

Chapter Five

Timetables and Traffic

After years of petitioning for a railway to serve the area south of Kelvedon, towards the banks of the Blackwater, the developers' hopes regarding passenger traffic were hardly justifiable. The branch made only a minor contribution towards the increase in population in the area in the early years and, throughout its existence, the line was almost totally reliant on goods traffic for the greater part of its revenue. By the time the population of Kelvedon and Tiptree had increased substantially, after World War II, the railway was already closed to passenger traffic.

Most of the land served by the Tollesbury Light Railway formed part of large agricultural estates and, consequently, the majority of the populace was employed locally on the land. With the exception of Wilkin's jam factory, a small brewery and a printing establishment at Tiptree, industry here was almost non-existent and because of the sparse service offered, rail travel to and from work was negligible. The branch carried the majority of its local passengers on Colchester market day (Saturday), other traffic being generally long-distance and spasmodic. This 10 mile line supported a daily service of between two and five trains in each direction for its 47 year passenger carrying history, when the population of the villages served, excluding Kelvedon, was around the 5,000 mark as the figures quoted below show:

Class J15 0-6-0 No. 65443 pauses near the site of Feering Halt, with the Railway Enthusiasts' Club special train from Kelvedon on 6th April 1957.

R. C. Riley

	1901	*1911*	*1921*	*1931*	*1951*	*1961*
Kelvedon	1,569	1,597	1,547	1,695	2,954	2,391
Inworth	667	806	804	847	712	363
Tiptree	731	770	824	929	2,453	3,018
Tolleshunt D'Arcy	753	852	861	827	758	864
Tolleshunt Knights	431	591	765	1,128	405	326
Tollesbury	1,720	1,858	1,721	1,694	1,594	1,577
	5,871	6,474	6,522	7,120	8,876	8,539

The initial service provided by the GER on the new light railway showed three passenger and one mixed trains in each direction, and allowed 32 minutes for passenger trains and 40 minutes for mixed trains on the 8 mile 35 chains journey.

'Down'

		mixed *a.m.*	*p.m.*	*p.m.*	*p.m.*
Kelvedon	(dep)	10.45	12.30	2.45	5.40
Tiptree	(dep)	11.08	12.44	2.58	5.54
Tolleshunt D'Arcy	(dep)	11.19	12.56	3.11	6.06
Tollesbury	(arr)	11.25	1.02	3.17	6.12

'Up'

		a.m.	*a.m.*	*p.m.*	*mixed* *p.m.*
Tollesbury	(dep)	8.25	11.40	2.00	6.20
Tolleshunt D'Arcy	(dep)	8.32	11.47	2.07	6.31
Tiptree	(dep)	8.44	11.59	2.19	6.47
Kelvedon	(arr)	8.57	12.12	2.32	7.00

The fastest journey time from London to Tollesbury, 1 hour 54 minutes, was available by the 4.18p.m. ex-Liverpool Street train which connected with the 5.40p.m. ex-Kelvedon service, whilst the slowest 'down' journey was 2 hours 30 minutes, on the 8.55a.m. ex-Liverpool Street working which connected with the 10.45a.m. branch train from Kelvedon. In the 'up' direction, passengers departing from Tollesbury on the 8.25a.m. train were afforded the fastest timing to Liverpool Street of 2 hours 1 minute, arriving there at 10.26a.m. The slowest timing to the Capital was by the 11.40a.m. with connection ex-Kelvedon arriving in Liverpool Street at 2.25p.m. giving an overall 2 hours 45 minutes for the 50¾ mile journey. Four months later, the branch service was reduced to three trains daily in each direction, but this rather spartan offering by the GER was quickly altered as traffic increased.

In April 1905 the passenger service was provided by four trains in each direction, departing from Kelvedon at 10.45 a.m., 12.30p.m., 2.45p.m. and 5.40p.m In the 'up' direction departures from Tollesbury were at 8.25a.m., 11.40 a.m., 2.00p.m. and 6.20p.m. The stock for the first 'up' service was conveyed on the morning goods train which departed from Kelvedon at 6.50a.m. whilst the afternoon goods, the 3.50p.m. ex-Tollesbury service, also conveyed the coaching stock for the 5.40p.m. 'down' passenger working. Both freight services served all sidings as required. Passenger trains were allowed 32 minutes and mixed trains 40 to 45 minutes for the journey between Kelvedon and Tollesbury.

The working timetable for 1907 showed a service of four passenger, one mixed and one goods trains in the 'down' direction and three passenger, two mixed and one goods train on the 'up' road. In the 'down' direction the goods train departed from Kelvedon at 6.56a.m. and made mandatory stops at Tiptree and Tolleshunt D'Arcy calling, if required, at Old Hall Siding and Church Siding. The train also conveyed the coaching stock for the first 'up' service and, after shunting at Tollesbury, ran e.c.s. at 8a.m. to the Pier Station for the 8.16a.m. 'up' departure. The mixed train, departing from Kelvedon at 10.25a.m., ran through to Tollesbury Pier as did three of the four 'down' passenger services. The 10.25a.m. mixed and 5.40p.m. 'down' passenger trains were permitted to take horse and carriage traffic from Kelvedon to Tollesbury only. When required, a special goods train was also authorised to run between Kelvedon and Tiptree, calling at Brooklands Siding and Heath Siding worked by the branch engine, running between the 'up' arrival at Kelvedon at 8.55a.m. and before departure of the 10.25a.m. mixed ex-Kelvedon train. In the 'up' direction the 8.16a.m. mixed and 6.25p.m. passenger (ex-Tollesbury Pier) trains were authorised to convey horse and carriage traffic from Tollesbury only, whilst the goods train departed from Tollesbury at 3.30 p.m. and called at all stations and sidings (except Inworth) as and when required.

Three years later four passenger carrying trains ran in each direction, departing from Kelvedon at 10.25a.m. mixed, 12.29p.m., 1.55p.m. and 5.40p.m., the first three running through to Tollesbury Pier as and when required, whilst the 5.40p.m. service was a booked through train. In addition a Wednesdays and Fridays only train also departed from Kelvedon at 7.50p.m. for Tollesbury, being extended if required to Tollesbury Pier. In the 'up' direction trains departed from Tollesbury at 8.25a.m., 11.34a.m.

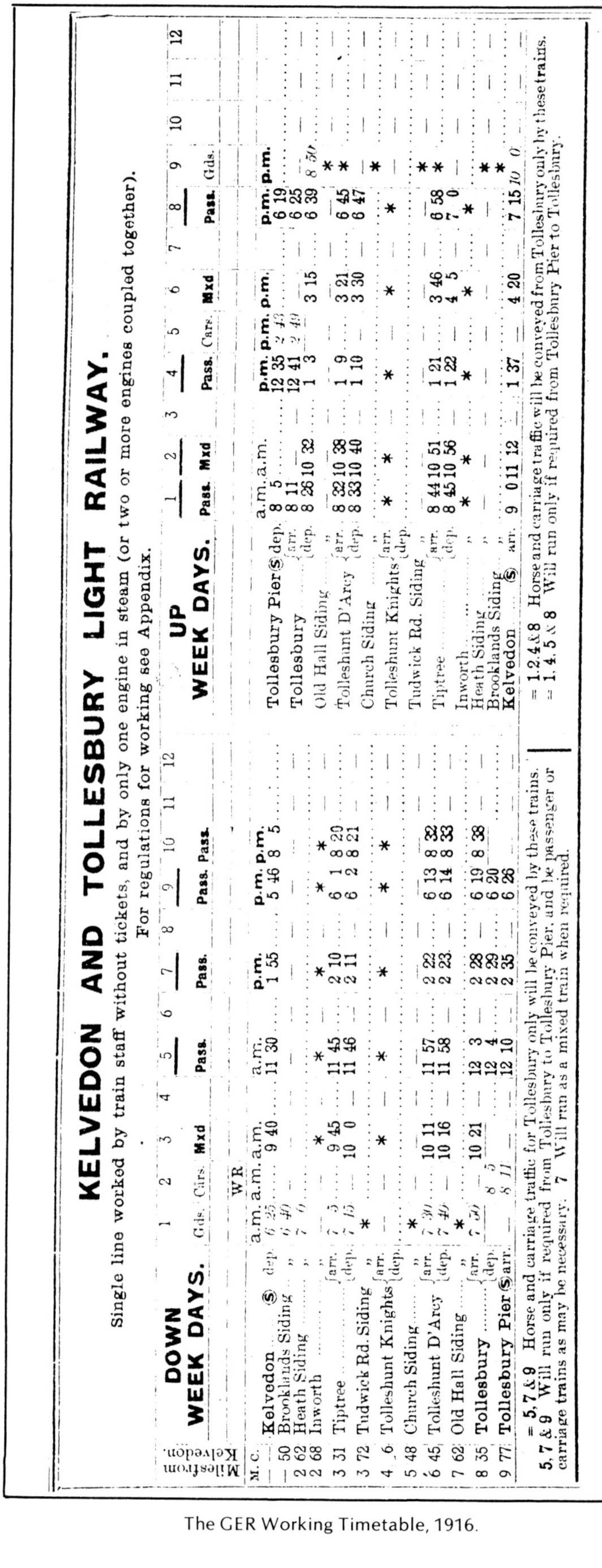

KELVEDON AND TOLLESBURY LIGHT RAILWAY.

Single line worked by train staff without tickets, and by only one engine in steam (or two or more engines coupled together).

For regulations for working see Appendix.

Miles from Kelvedon. M. C.	DOWN WEEK DAYS.		1 Gds.	2 Cars.	3 Mxd	4	5 Pass.	6	7 Pass.	8	9 Pass.	10 Pass.	11	12
				WR										
			a.m.	a.m.	a.m.		a.m.		p.m.		p.m.	p.m.		
— —	Kelvedon Ⓢ	dep.	6 25		9 40		11 30		1 55		5 46	8 5		
— 50	Brooklands Siding	"	6 40	—	—	—	—	—	—	—	—	—	—	—
2 62	Heath Siding	"	7 0											
2 68	Inworth	"	—	—	*	—	*	—	*	—	*	*	—	—
3 31	Tiptree	arr.	7 5		9 45		11 45		2 10		6 1	8 20		
		dep.	7 15	—	10 0	—	11 46	—	2 11	—	6 2	8 21	—	—
3 72	Tudwick Rd. Siding	"	*											
4 6	Tolleshunt Knights	arr. dep.	—	—	*	—	*	—	*	—	*	*	—	—
5 48	Church Siding	"	*	—	—	—	—	—	—	—	—	—	—	—
6 45	Tolleshunt D'Arcy	arr.	7 30		10 11		11 57		2 22		6 13	8 32		
		dep.	7 40	—	10 16	—	11 58	—	2 23	—	6 14	8 33	—	—
7 62	Old Hall Siding	"	*											
8 35	Tollesbury	arr.	7 50	—	10 21	—	12 3	—	2 28	—	6 19	8 38	—	—
		dep.		8 5			12 4		2 29		6 20			
9 77	Tollesbury Pier Ⓢ	arr.	—	8 11	—	—	12 10	—	2 35	—	6 26	—	—	—

= 5, 7 & 9 Horse and carriage traffic for Tollesbury only will be conveyed by these trains.
5, 7 & 9 Will run only if required from Tollesbury to Tollesbury Pier, and be passenger or carriage trains as may be necessary. 7 Will run as a mixed train when required.

UP WEEK DAYS.		1 Pass.	2 Mxd	3	4 Pass.	5 Cars.	6 Mxd	7	8 Pass.	9 Gds.	10	11	12
		a.m.	a.m.		p.m.	p.m.	p.m.		p.m.	p.m.			
Tollesbury Pier Ⓢ	dep.	8 5			12 35	2 43			6 19				
Tollesbury	arr.	8 11	—	—	12 41	2 49	—	—	6 25	—	—	—	—
	dep.	8 26	10 32		1 3		3 15		6 39	8 50			
Old Hall Siding	"	—	—	—	—	—	—	—	—	*	—	—	—
Tolleshunt D'Arcy	arr.	8 32	10 38		1 9		3 21		6 45	*			
	dep.	8 33	10 40	—	1 10	—	3 30	—	6 47	—	—	—	—
Church Siding	"									*			
Tolleshunt Knights	arr. dep.	*	*	—	*	—	*	—	*	—	—	—	—
Tudwick Rd. Siding	"	—	—	—	—	—	—	—	—	*	—	—	—
Tiptree	arr.	8 44	10 51		1 21		3 46		6 58	*			
	dep.	8 45	10 56	—	1 22	—	4 5	—	7 0	—	—	—	—
Inworth	"	*	*		*		*		*				
Heath Siding	"	—	—	—	—	—	—	—	—	*	—	—	—
Brooklands Siding	"									*			
Kelvedon Ⓢ	arr.	9 0	11 12	—	1 37	—	4 20	—	7 15	10 0	—	—	—

= 1, 2, 4 & 8 Horse and carriage traffic will be conveyed from Tollesbury only by these trains.
= 1, 4, 5 & 8 Will run only if required from Tollesbury Pier to Tollesbury.

The GER Working Timetable, 1916.

312

TOLLESBURY STATION.

Shunting on Main Single Line.

The Main Single Line at **Tollesbury Station** may be fouled by shunting operations in cases of emergency **although the Branch Engine is not at the Station.** In such cases, however, the man in charge at Tollesbury Station **must arrange for a Flagman—with Hand and Detonating Signals—to be sent out about 1,000 yards in the direction of Kelvedon to stop any** approaching train before a vehicle or vehicles are **allowed to foul** the Main Single Line. The man in charge must also take special care to properly secure the vehicle or vehicles on the Main Single Line by means of the Hand brake and Scotches in order no prevent their running away. Before allowing the Main Single Line to be fouled, the man in charge at Tollesbury Station must advise the man in charge at Tolleshunt D'Arcy Station what is about to be done, and the latter must not allow a train or engine to leave his Station until he has ascertained from the man in charge at Tollesbury Station that the Main Single Line at that Station is again clear.

Instruction regarding shunting at Tollesbury Station from GER Appendix to Working Timetable.

mixed, 1.09p.m. and 6.35p.m., the first two and the last one starting back from Tollesbury Pier if required. An additional train also ran on Wednesdays and Fridays, departing from Tollesbury at 8.42p.m. and running from the Pier Station if required. The fastest 'down' journey from Liverpool Street to Tollesbury was available on the 8.45a.m. departure from the Capital, which connected at Kelvedon with the 10.25a.m. branch departure due at 11.06a.m. The slowest journey was 2 hours 5 minutes by the 10.55 a.m. train from Liverpool Street, which connected with the 12.29p.m. branch train due in Tollesbury at 1p.m. In the 'up' direction the best timing available was 2 hours 1 minute, on the 8.25a.m. departure from Tollesbury, which connected with a main line train due at Liverpool Street at 10.26 a.m., whilst the slowest journey was 2 hours 39 minutes, on the 11.34a.m. mixed ex-Tollesbury working.

The outbreak of World War I in 1914 made no difference to the service, and four trains continued to run each way, with the additional evening service running on Wednesday and Fridays only. The GER public timetable during the war

The 'Crab & Winkle' Flyer waits to depart from Kelvedon (Low Level) Station, with a 'Buck Jumper' at the head of the two coach train formed of bogie tram No. E60461 and brake third No. E62262. The branch brake and Gresley four wheel van are not being taken on this trip, and stand on the run-round loop.

J. H. Aston/G. Pember

KELVEDON AND TOLLESBURY LIGHT RAILWAY.

Single line worked by train staff without tickets, and by only one engine in steam (or two or more engines coupled together).
For regulations for working see Appendix.

Miles from Kelvedon. M.	C.	DOWN WEEK DAYS.		1	2	3	4	5	6	7	8	9	10	11	12
				Gds.	Cars.	Mxd		Pass.		Pass.		Pass.	Pass.		
					WR										
				a.m.	a.m.	a.m.		a.m.		p.m.		p.m.	p.m.		
—	—	Kelvedon ⓢ	dep.	6 25		9 30		11 30		1 50		5 46	8 5		
—	50	Brooklands Siding	„	6 40	—	—	—	—	—	—	—	—	—	—	—
2	62	Heath Siding	„	7 0											
2	68	Inworth	„	—	—	*	—	*	—	*	—	*	*	—	—
3	31	Tiptree	arr.	7 5		9 45		11 45		2 5		6 1	8 20		
			dep.	7 15	—	9 50	—	11 46	—	2 6	—	6 2	8 21	—	—
3	72	Tudwick Rd. Siding	„	*											
4	6	Tolleshunt Knights	arr.	—	—	*	—	*	—	*	—	*	*	—	—
			dep.												
5	48	Church Siding	„	*	—	—	—	—	—	—	—	—	—	—	—
6	45	Tolleshunt D'Arcy	arr.	7 30		10 1		11 57		2 17		6 13	8 32		
			dep.	7 40	—	10 6	—	11 58	—	2 18	—	6 14	8 33	—	—
7	62	Old Hall Siding	„	*											
8	35	Tollesbury	arr.	7 50	—	10 11	—	12 3	—	2 23	—	6 19	8 38	—	—
			dep.		8 5			12 4		2 24		6 20			
9	77	Tollesbury Pier ⓢ	arr.	—	8 11	—	—	12 10	—	2 30	—	6 26	—	—	—

= 5, 7 & 9 Horse and carriage traffic for Tollesbury only will be conveyed by these trains. 5, 7 & 9 Will run only if required from Tollesbury to Tollesbury Pier, and be passenger or carriage trains as may be necessary. 7 Will run as a mixed train when required.

UP WEEK DAYS.		1	2	3	4	5	6	7	8	9	10	11	12
		Pass.	Mxd		Pass.	Cars.	Mxd		Pass.	Gds.			
		a.m.	a.m.		p.m.	p.m.	p.m.		p.m.	p.m.			
Tollesbury Pier ⓢ	dep.	8 5			12 35	2 43			6 19				
Tollesbury	arr.	8 11	—	—	12 41	2 49	—	—	6 25	—	—	—	—
	dep.	8 26	10 32		12 56		3 15		6 39	8 50			
Old Hall Siding	„	—	—	—	—	—	—	—	—	*	—	—	—
Tolleshunt D'Arcy	arr.	8 32	10 38		1 2		3 21		6 45	*			
	dep.	8 33	10 40	—	1 3	—	3 30	—	6 47	—	—	—	—
Church Siding	„									*			
Tolleshunt Knights	arr.	*	*	—	*	—	*	—	*	—	—	—	—
	dep.												
Tudwick Rd. Siding	„	—	—	—	—	—	—	—	—	*	—	—	—
Tiptree	arr.	8 44	10 51		1 14		3 46		6 58	*			
	dep.	8 45	10 56	—	1 15	—	4 5	—	7 0	—	—	—	—
Inworth	„	*	*		*		*		*				
Heath Siding	„	—	—	—	—	—	—	—	—	*	—	—	—
Brooklands Siding	„									*			
Kelvedon ⓢ	arr.	9 0	11 12	—	1 30	—	4 20	—	7 15	10 0	—	—	—

= 1, 2, 4 & 8 Horse and carriage traffic will be conveyed from Tollesbury only by these trains.
= 1, 4, 5 & 8 Will run only if required from Tollesbury Pier to Tollesbury.

The GER Working Timetable, 1917

KELVEDON AND TOLLESBURY LIGHT RAILWAY.

Single line worked by train staff without tickets, and by only one engine in steam (or two or more engines coupled together).
For regulations for working see Appendix.

Miles from Kelvedon. M.	C.	DOWN WEEK DAYS.		1	2	3	4	5	6	7	8	9	10	11	12
				Gds.		Mxd		Pass.		Mxd		Pass.			
				a.m.		a.m.		a.m.		p.m.		p.m.			
—	—	Kelvedon ⓢ	dep	6 40		9 30		11 30		1 45		5 44			
—	50	Brooklands Siding	„	6 55	—	—	—	—	—	—	—	—	—	—	—
2	62	Heath Siding	„	7 15											
2	68	Inworth	„	—	—	*	—	*	—	*	—	*	—	—	—
3	31	Tiptree	arr.	7 20		9 45		11 45		2 0		5 59			
			dep.	7 30	—	9 50	—	11 46	—	2 5	—	6 0	—	—	—
3	72	Tudwick Rd. Siding	„	*											
4	6	Tolleshunt Knights	arr.	—	—	*	—	*	—	*	—	*	—	—	—
			dep.												
5	48	Church Siding	„	*	—	—	—	—	—	—	—	—	—	—	—
6	45	Tolleshunt D'Arcy	arr.	7 45		10 1		11 57		2 16		6 11			
			dep.	7 55	—	10 6	—	11 58	—	2 21	—	6 12	—	—	—
7	62	Old Hall Siding	„	*											
8	35	Tollesbury	arr.	8 5	—	10 11	—	12 3	—	2 26	—	6 17	—	—	—
			dep.					12 4		2 27					
9	77	Tollesbury Pier ⓢ	arr.	—	—	—	—	12 10	—	2 32	—	—	—	—	—

= 7 Will run as a mixed train when required. Horse and carriage traffic for Tollesbury only will be conveyed by this train.
= 5 & 7 Run only if required from Tollesbury to Tollesbury Pier.

UP WEEK DAYS.		1	2	3	4	5	6	7	8	9	10	11	12
		Pass.	Mxd		Pass.	Cars.	Mxd		Mxd				
						WR							
		a.m.	a.m.		p.m.	p.m.	p.m.		p.m.				
Tollesbury Pier ⓢ	dep.				12 20	2 43							
Tollesbury	arr.	—	—	—	12 26	2 49	—	—	—	—	—	—	—
	dep.	8 26	10 32		12 36		3 15		6 32				
Old Hall Siding	„	—	—	—	—	—	*	—	—	—	—	—	—
Tolleshunt D'Arcy	arr.	8 32	10 38		12 42		3 21		6 38				
	dep.	8 33	10 40	—	12 43	—	3 30	—	6 45	—	—	—	—
Church Siding	„						*						
Tolleshunt Knights	arr.	*	*	—	*	—	*	—	*	—	—	—	—
	dep.												
Tudwick Rd. Siding	„	—	—	—	—	—	*	—	—	—	—	—	—
Tiptree	arr.	8 44	10 51		12 54		3 46		6 56				
	dep.	8 45	10 56	—	12 55	—	4 5	—	7 2	—	—	—	—
Inworth	„	*	*		*		*		*				
Heath Siding	„	—	—	—	—	—	*	—	—	—	—	—	—
Brooklands Siding	„						*						
Kelvedon ⓢ	arr.	9 0	11 12	—	1 10	—	4 20	—	7 17	—	—	—	—

= 1, 4 & 8 Horse and carriage traffic will be conveyed from Tollesbury only by these trains.
= 4 Runs only if required from Tollesbury Pier to Tollesbury.
= 6 To call at Old Hall, Church Sdg., Tudwick Rd., Heath & Brooklands Sdgs., if required, to attach important traffic. Other traffic to be worked on 6.40 a.m. goods train ex Kelvedon.

The GER Working Timetable, 1920

years advised 'During the continuance of the war the train service is liable to be altered or cancelled without prior notice and the Great Eastern Railway Company thereby give notice that they will not be responsible for any loss, damage or delay in consequence thereof.' Despite this warning, the branch service actually increased to five trains each way in 1915 with 'down' trains departing from Kelvedon at 9.40a.m. mixed, 11.30a.m., 1.55p.m., 5.46p.m. and 8.05p.m., while departures from Tollesbury were at 8.26a.m., 10.32a.m. mixed, 1.03p.m., 3.15p.m. and 6.39p.m. Three trains in each direction worked to or from Tollesbury Pier if required.

By 1916 the 'down' service had increased to four passenger, one mixed and one goods train, together with an empty stock train from Tollesbury to Tollesbury Pier, which ran as required. The morning goods train, which departed from Kelvedon at 6.25a.m., also conveyed the passenger stock for the first 'up' working and served all sidings, although Tudwick Road, Church Siding and Old Hall Siding were only served if there was traffic for collection. The 11.30a.m., 1.55p.m. and 5.46p.m. passenger trains were permitted to convey horse and carriage traffic for Tollesbury, but only continued to Tollesbury Pier when required. The 1.55 p.m. working was also permitted to run as a mixed train, if any urgent goods traffic was required to be forwarded from Kelvedon.

In the 'up' direction the working timetable provided for three passenger, two mixed and one goods train, with an additional empty stock train from Tollesbury Pier to Tollesbury which only ran if required. The three passenger trains at 8.05a.m., 12.35p.m. and 6.19p.m. ex-Tollesbury Pier ran only if required between the Pier Station and Tollesbury. All 'up' passenger and mixed trains, with the exception of the 3.15p.m. ex-Tollesbury service, were permitted to convey horse and carriage traffic from Tollesbury through to Kelvedon. The 'up' goods working departed from Tollesbury at 8.50p.m., and served all sidings as required to clear traffic. All 'up' and 'down' passenger and mixed trains called only if required at Inworth and Tolleshunt Knights to pick up or set down passengers.

The working timetable for 1917 showed four passenger, one mixed and one goods train in the 'down' direction, with the goods train departing from Kelvedon at 6.25a.m. and serving all sidings. After shunting at Tollesbury for fifteen minutes, the locomotive continued on to Tollesbury Pier with the empty coaching stock for the 8.05a.m. 'up' train only if required. Three passenger trains were also booked to run to Tollesbury Pier if required, but the mixed 9.30a.m. departure from Kelvedon and the final train of the day, the 8.05p.m. working, terminated at Tollesbury. Horse and carriage traffic for Tollesbury was permitted to be conveyed on the 11.30a.m., 1.50p.m. and 5.46p.m. passenger trains from Kelvedon, whilst in the 'up' direction three passenger, two mixed and one goods train were provided. The three passenger trains started back from Tollesbury Pier only if required, and the two mixed trains commenced their journey from Tollesbury. The goods train departed from Tollesbury at 8.50p.m., providing an evening pick-up service from all sidings on the line, with an allowed seventy minutes for the run to Kelvedon.

By 1920 the working timetable showed two passenger, two mixed and one goods train in the 'down' direction. The goods train departed from Kelvedon at 6.40a.m. and ran as far as Tollesbury, conveying the passenger cars for the first 'up' working. The train served all yards en route, although Tudwick Road, Old Hall Siding and Church Siding were shunted only if required. The 11.30a.m. passenger and 1.45p.m. mixed working only ran between Tollesbury and Tollesbury Pier if required, whilst the latter was also permitted to convey horse and carriage traffic. In the 'up' direction two passenger and three mixed trains were provided, with a set of empty cars departing from Tollesbury Pier for Tollesbury at 2.43p.m. when required, as a back working of the 1.45p.m. 'down' train. Horse and carriage traffic was permitted on the 8.26a.m. passenger, 12.20 p.m. ex-Tollesbury Pier passenger and 6.32p.m. mixed trains between Tollesbury and Kelvedon only. The 3.15 p.m. mixed train called at Church, Old Hall, Tudwick Road and Brooklands sidings, if required, to attach important traffic. Other less important wagon loads were picked up by the 6.40a.m. 'down' goods service. All trains at this time called at Inworth and Tolleshunt Knights only if required, to pick up or set down passengers.

The 1925 LNER timetable continued to show four trains in each direction over the light railway, with the first 'down' train being a goods, this conveying the coaching stock for the first 'up' working. Other 'down' departures from Kelvedon were at 9.25a.m., 12.29p.m. and 5.54 p.m., with timings of between 33 and 41 minutes. In the 'up' direction trains departed from Tollesbury at 8.24a.m., 10.36a.m., 3.15p.m. and 6.42p.m., the timing for the 8 mile 35 chain journey varying between 36 minutes for passenger and 65 minutes for the mixed trains, the additional time being allowed for shunting at stations and intermediate sidings. The fastest journey time to Tollesbury from Liverpool Street was 2 hours 9 minutes, this being by the 4.18p.m. departure which connected with the 5.54 p.m. ex-Kelvedon service. In contrast, passengers catching the 6.05a.m. ex-Liverpool Street train connected with the 9.25a.m. ex-Kelvedon working, which gave the slowest time of 3 hours 16 minutes to Tollesbury. In the 'up' direction the fastest timing between Tollesbury and London was 1 hour 59 minutes, this being by the 8.24a.m. service, which connected with the 10.23a.m. arrival at Liverpool Street. The final 'up' train of the day, the 6.42p.m. ex-Kelvedon service, afforded passengers an extended 2 hours 35 minutes timing to Liverpool Street.

During the General Strike in 1926 services were withdrawn whilst from 31st May a reduced number of trains were reinstated departing Kelvedon at 9.25a.m., 12.29p.m. and 5.54p.m.; and Tollesbury at 8.24a.m., 10.38a.m., 3.15p.m and 6.42p.m.

In 1930 the LNER working timetable allowed for one passenger, two mixed and one goods train in the 'down' direction, and one passenger and three mixed workings on the 'up' road. The goods train still departed from Kelvedon at 6.40a.m. conveying the passenger coaching stock for the first 'up' train, and called at Tudwick Road Siding, Church Siding and Old Hall Siding if required. All other stations or sidings were mandatory calls, except for Inworth and Tolleshunt Knights. In the 'up' direction, the 8.24a.m. passenger and 6.42p.m. mixed trains were permitted to convey horse and carriage traffic from Tollesbury to Kelvedon. The 3.15p.m. mixed ex-Tollesbury train called at Old Hall, Church, Tudwick Road, Heath and Brooklands sidings, if required, to attach important traffic. Empties and other unimportant items continued to be collected by the 6.40a.m. ex-Kelvedon goods working the following morning.

The level crossing at Feering, where the A12 main road crossed the Tollesbury branch. This is a view facing Kelvedon from Feering Halt, with Kelvedon 'up' fixed distant beyond the gates.

D. Taylor Collection

KELVEDON AND TOLLESBURY LIGHT RAILWAY.

Single line worked by train staff without tickets, and by only one engine in steam (or two or more engines coupled together).

For regulations for working see Appendix.

Miles from Kelvedon. M	C.	DOWN WEEK DAYS.		1	2	3	4	5	6	7	8	9	10	11	12
				Gds.		Mxd.	Mxd.			Mxd.		Pass.			
						TWTh	MFS								
				a.m.		a.m.	a.m.			p.m.		p.m.			
—	—	Kelvedon Ⓢ	dep.	6 40		9 25	9 45			12 29		5 54			
—	50	Brooklands Siding	„	6 55	—	—	—	—	—	—	—	—	—	—	—
2	62	Heath Siding	„	7 15											
2	68	Inworth	„	—	—	9 35	9 55	—	—	12 39	—	6 4	—	—	—
3	31	Tiptree	arr.	7 20		9 40	10 0			12 44		6 9			
			dep.	7 30	—	9 45	10 5	—	—	12 49	—	6 10	—	—	—
3	72	Tudwick Rd. Siding	„	*											
4	6	Tolleshunt Knights	„	—	—	9 48	10 8	—	—	12 52	—	6 13	—	—	—
5	48	Church Siding	„	*											
6	45	Tolleshunt D'Arcy	arr.	7 45	—	9 56	10 16	—	—	1 0	—	6 21	—	—	—
			dep.	7 55		10 1	10 21			1 5		6 22			
7	62	Old Hall Siding	„	*	—	—	—	—	—	—	—	—	—	—	—
8	35	Tollesbury	arr.	8 5		10 6	10 26			1 10		6 27			
			dep.		—			—	—		—		—	—	—
9	77	Tollesbury Pier Ⓢ	arr.												

=3 Commencing 15th September, runs daily.
—4 Will not run after 13th September.

UP WEEK DAYS.		1	2	3	4	5	6	7	8	9	10	11	12
		Pass.		Mxd.			Mxd		Mxd.				
		a.m.		a.m.			p.m.		p.m.				
Tollesbury Pier Ⓢ	dep.												
Tollesbury	arr.	—	—	—	—	—	—	—	—	—	—	—	—
	dep.	8 24		10 36			3 15		6 42				
Old Hall Siding	„	—	—	—	—	—	—	—	—	—	—	—	—
Tolleshunt D'Arcy	arr.	8 30		10 42			3 21		6 48				
	dep.	8 32	—	10 44	—	—	3 30	—	6 55	—	—	—	—
Church Siding	„						*						
Tolleshunt Knights	„	8 38	—	10 50	—	—	3 36	—	7 1	—	—	—	—
Tudwick Rd. Siding	„												
Tiptree	arr.	8 43	—	10 55	—	—	3 46	—	7 6	—	—	—	—
	dep.	8 45		11 0			4 5		7 12				
Inworth	„	8 48	—	11 3	—	—	4 8	—	7 15	—	—	—	—
Heath Siding	„						*						
Brooklands Siding	„	—	—	—	—	—	*	—	—	—	—	—	—
Kelvedon Ⓢ	arr.	9 0		11 16			4 20		7 27				

=1 & 8 Horse and carriage traffic will be conveyed from Tollesbury only by these trains.
=6 To call at Old Hall, Church Sdg., Tudwick Rd., Heath & Brookland Sdgs., if required, to attach important traffic. Other traffic to be worked on 6.40 a.m. goods train ex Kelvedon.

Passenger trains are worked on the "Conductor Guard" principle.

JLY. 7

The LNER Working Timetable, summer 1924.

KELVEDON AND TOLLESBURY LIGHT RAILWAY (For regulations for working see Appendix.)

Single line worked by train staff without tickets, and by only one engine in steam (or two or more engines coupled together).

Miles from Kelvedon M.	C.	DOWN WEEK DAYS.		1 Gds.	2 Mxd.	3 Pass.	4 Pass. WSO	5 Pass.	6
				a.m.	a.m.	p.m.	p.m.	p.m.	
—	—	Kelvedon ...... Ⓢ	dep.	6 40	9 41	12 25	1 48	5 40	—
—	33	Feering Halt	„	—	9 44	12 28	1 51	5 43	....
2	62	Heath Siding	„	7 10	—	—	—	—	—
2	69	Inworth	„	—	9 51	12 35	1 58	5 50	....
3	31	Tiptree	arr.	7 15	9 56	12 40	2 3	5 55	—
			dep.	7 30	10 1	12 41	2 4	5 56	....
3	72	Tudwick Rd. Siding	„	*	—	—	—		—
4	6	Tolleshunt Knights	„	—	10 4	12 44	2 7	5 59	....
5	48	Church Siding	„	*	—	—	—	—	—
6	45	Tolleshunt D'Arcy	arr.	7 45	10 12	12 50	2 13	6 5	....
			dep.	7 55	10 17	12 51	2 14	6 6	—
7	62	Old Hall Siding	„	*	....	....	....	....	....
8	35	Tollesbury ... Ⓢ	arr.	8 5	10 22	12 56	2 19	6 11	—

Passenger trains are worked on the "Conductor Guard" principle.

UP WEEK DAYS.		1 Pass.	2 Mxd.	3 Pass. WSO	4 Mxd	5 Mxd. SX	6 Mxd. SO	7
		a.m.	a.m.	p.m.	p.m.	p.m.	p.m.	
Tollesbury ... Ⓢ	dep.	8 32	10 40	1 1	3 15	6 30	6 42	....
Old Hall Siding	„	—	—	—	* *	—	—	—
Tolleshunt D'Arcy	arr.	8 38	10 46	1 7	3 21	6 36	6 48	....
	dep	8 40	10 48	1 8	3 30	6 43	6 55	—
Church Siding	„	....	....	....	* *	....	....	....
Tolleshunt Knights	„	8 46	10 54	1 14	3 36	6 49	7 1	—
Tudwick Rd. Siding	„	....	....	....	* *	....	....	....
Tiptree	arr.	8 51	10 59	1 19	3 46	6 54	7 6	—
	dep.	8 53	11 4	1 20	4 5	7 0	7 12	....
Inworth	„	8 56	11 7	1 23	4 8	7 3	7 15	—
Heath Siding	„	....	....	....	* *	....	....	....
Feering Halt	„	9 4	11 16	1 31	4 16	7 11	7 23	—
Kelvedon ...... Ⓢ	arr.	9 8	11 20	1 34	4 20	7 15	7 27	....

=4 To call at Old Hall, Church Sdg., Tudwick Rd., & Heath Siding, if reqd., to attach important traffic. Other traffic to be worked on 6.40 a.m. goods train ex Kelvedon.

=5 To convey traffic in fitted vehicles for 6.15 p.m. Goods ex Chelmsford.

The LNER Working Timetable, 1939.

KELVEDON AND TOLLESBURY LIGHT RAILWAY. (For regulations for working see Appendix.)

Single line worked by train staff without tickets, and by only one engine in steam (or two or more engines coupled together).

Miles from Kelvedon. M.	C.	DOWN WEEK DAYS.		1 Gds.	2	3 Mxd	4	5 Mxd	6	7	8	9 Pass	10	11	12
				a.m.		a.m.		p.m.				p.m.			
—	—	**Kelvedon** ...... Ⓢ	dep	6 40	....	9 25	....	12 29	....	....	....	5 54	....	....	....
—	50	Brooklands Siding...	„	6 55	—	—	—	—	—	—	—	—	—	—	—
2	62	Heath Siding	„	7 15	....	....	....	....	....	....	....	....	....	....	....
2	69	Inworth	„	—	—	9 35	—	12 39	—	—	—	6 4	—	—	—
3	31	Tiptree................	arr.	7 20	....	9 40	....	12 44	....	....	....	6 9	....	....	....
			dep.	7 30	—	9 45	—	12 49	—	—	—	6 10	—	—	—
3	72	Tudwick Rd. Siding	„	*	....	....	....	....	....	....	....	....	....	....	....
4	6	Tolleshunt Knights	„	—	—	9 48	—	12 52	—	—	—	6 13	—	—	—
5	48	Church Siding........	„	*	....	....	....	....	....	....	....	....	....	....	....
6	45	Tolleshunt D'Arcy	arr.	7 45	—	9 56	—	1 0	—	—	—	6 21	—	—	—
			dep.	7 55	....	10 1	....	1 5	....	....	....	6 22	....	....	....
7	62	Old Hall Siding	„	*	—	—	—	—	—	—	—	—	—	—	—
8	35	**Tollesbury** .. Ⓢ	arr.	8 5	....	10 6	....	1 10	....	....	....	6 27	....	....	....

Passenger trains are worked on the "Conductor Guard" principle.

UP WEEK DAYS.		1 Pass.	2	3 Mxd	4	5	6 Mxd	7	8 Mxd	9	10	11	12
		a.m.		a.m.			p.m.		p.m				
Tollesbury ... Ⓢ	dep.	8 24	....	10 36	....	....	3 15	....	6 42	....	....	....	....
Old Hall Siding	„	—	—	—	—	—	*	—	—	—	—	—	—
Tolleshunt D'Arcy	arr.	8 30	....	10 42	....	....	3 21	....	6 48	....	....	....	....
	dep.	8 32	—	10 44	—	—	3 30	—	6 55	—	—	—	—
Church Siding	„	....	....	....	....	....	*	....	....	....	....	....	....
Tolleshunt Knights	„	8 38	—	10 50	—	—	3 36	—	7 1	—	—	—	—
Tudwick Rd. Siding	„	....	....	....	....	....	*	....	....	....	....	....	....
Tiptree................	arr.	8 43	—	10 55	—	—	3 46	—	7 6	—	—	—	—
	dep.	8 45	....	11 0	....	....	4 5	....	7 12	....	....	....	....
Inworth	„	8 48	—	11 3	—	—	4 8	—	7 15	—	—	—	—
Heath Siding	„	....	....	....	....	....	*	....	....	....	....	....	....
Brooklands Siding...	„	—	—	—	—	—	*	—	—	—	—	—	—
Kelvedon ...... Ⓢ	arr.	9 0	....	11 16	....	....	4 20	....	7 27	....	....	....	....

=1 & 8. Horse and carriage traffic will be conveyed from Tollesbury only by these trains.
=6 To call at Old Hall, Church Sgs., Tudwick Rd., Heath and Brooklands Sgs., if required, to attach important traffic. Other traffic to be worked on 6.40 a.m. goods ex Kelvedon.

The LNER Working Timetable, 1928.

KELVEDON AND TOLLESBURY LIGHT RAILWAY

(NO SUNDAY SERVICE)

(For regulations for working, see Appendix)

Single line worked by train staff without tickets, and by only one engine in steam (or two or more engines coupled together).

These trains are worked on the "Conductor Guard" principle.

DOWN WEEKDAYS

Miles from Kelvedon	No.	1	2	3	4
	Class		K	B	B
	Description			Mxd.	Mxd.
M. C.			am	am	PM
— —	**Kelvedon** (S)		6 40	10 10	5 45
33	Feering Halt		..	10 13	5 48
2 62	*Heath Siding*		7 10	..	..
2 69	Inworth		..	10 20	5 55
3 31	Tiptree		7 15	10 25	6 0
— —	Tiptree		7 30	10 29	6 4
3 72	*Tudwick Road Siding*		*	..	..
4 6	Tolleshunt Knights		..	10 33	6 8
5 48	*Church Siding*		*	..	..
6 45	Tolleshunt D'Arcy		7 45	10 41	6 16
— —	Tolleshunt D'Arcy		7 55	10 45	6 20
7 62	*Old Hall Siding*		*	..	..
8 35	**Tollesbury** (S)		8 5	10 50	6 25

UP WEEKDAYS

Miles from Tollesbury	No.	5	6	7	8
	Class	B		B	B
	Description	Mxd.		Mxd.	Mxd
M. C.		am		PM	PM
— —	**Tollesbury** (S)	8 30	..	12 50	6 37
— 53	*Old Hall Siding*	..	..	*	..
1 70	Tolleshunt D'Arcy	8 36	..	12 56	6 43
— —	Tolleshunt D'Arcy	8 38	..	1 5	6 50
2 67	*Church Siding*	..	..	*	..
4 29	Tolleshunt Knights	8 44	..	1 11	6 56
4 43	*Tudwick Road Siding*	..	..	*	..
5 4	Tiptree	8 49	..	1 21	7 1
— —	Tiptree	8 54	..	1 35	7 7
5 46	Inworth	8 57	..	1 38	7 10
5 53	*Heath Siding*	..	..	*	..
8 2	Feering Halt	9 5	..	1 46	7 18
8 35	**Kelvedon** (S)	9 9	..	1 50	7 22

2 ECS for 8.30 a.m. Up runs attached.

The final passenger service from British Railways (Eastern Region) Working Timetable, 1950.

The 1935 working timetable gave paths for two passenger, one mixed and one goods train in the 'down' direction, and one passenger and three mixed on the 'up' road. The 'down' goods timing remained at 6.40a.m. ex-Kelvedon calling at Tudwick Road, Church and Old Hall sidings, if required, with mandatory stops at all other yards. Two additional passenger trains ran on Wednesdays and Saturdays only, departing from Kelvedon at 1.48p.m. and 8.31p.m., although the latter ran on Saturdays only from 15th June 1936. In the 'up' direction the 3.15p.m. mixed train, as well as shunting the larger sidings, also called at Old Hall, Church, Tudwick Road, and Heath sidings, if required, to attach important traffic. An additional passenger train ran on Wednesdays and Saturdays only, departing from Tollesbury at 1.02p.m., whilst the return working of the 8.31p.m. (WSO) 'down' (SO after 15th June 1936) ran as e.c.s. and departed from Tollesbury at 9.17p.m., calling at all stations to enable the guard to extinguish the oil lamps.

By 1939 the working timetable showed two passenger, one mixed and one goods train in the 'down' direction, with an additional passenger train running on Wednesdays and Saturdays only. In the 'up' direction the service provided was one passenger and three mixed trains, with an additional passenger train on Wednesdays and Saturdays. The 'down' goods continued to depart from Kelvedon at 6.40 a.m., calling at Tudwick Road, Church and Old Hall sidings, as required, whilst the 9.41a.m. ex-Kelvedon train ran as mixed, the Wednesdays and Saturdays only passenger train departing from the junction at 1.48p.m. In the 'up' direction the WSO return working departed from Tollesbury at 1.01p.m. whilst the 3.15p.m. mixed train called at Old Hall, Church, Tudwick Road and Heath sidings, if required, to pick up important traffic, all other stops being mandatory. The 6.30p.m. (SX) mixed ex-Tollesbury working was permitted to convey goods traffic in fitted wagons, to connect with the 6.15p.m. ex-Chelmsford goods service, whilst the SO working departed from Tollesbury at 6.42p.m.

Class J67/1 No. 68616 approaches Kelvedon with the 12.50p.m. Tollesbury to Kelvedon mixed train, on 29th July 1950. The main Liverpool Street to Norwich main line ran parallel to the light railway, for a short distance, along the embankment on the left. Behind the signal post the branch can be seen curving towards Feering.
LCGB/Ken Nunn Collection

Class J69/1 0-6-0T No. 68578 waits to depart from Tollesbury with a two coach train, formed of ex-Stoke Ferry vehicles Nos. E62262 and E62261. The former vehicle had the smaller guard's look-out and was originally a composite vehicle, but was rebuilt to a brake third prior to transfer to the Tollesbury Light Railway in 1931.
Photomatic

Soon after the outbreak of World War II the services were reduced to two passenger and one goods train in the 'down' direction, and two passenger and one mixed on the 'up' road. The 'down' goods departed from Kelvedon at 6.40a.m. while passenger trains followed at 10.10a.m. and 5.43p.m., being allowed forty minutes for the journey to Tollesbury. On the 'up' road, trains departed from Tollesbury at 9a.m., 12.50p.m. mixed and 6.35p.m. Subject to slight adjustments in timing, the same service pattern sufficed throughout the years of hostility until 1945.

The LNER passenger timetable for 1946 showed only two passenger services in the 'down' direction, these departing from Kelvedon at 10.15a.m. and 5.48p.m., with a timing of forty minutes for the 8½ mile journey. In the 'up' direction, trains departed from Tollesbury at 8.30a.m., 12.40 p.m. (SX), 12.50p.m. (SO) and 6.37p.m., with timings varying from 39 minutes to 1 hour. The one goods train of the day continued to depart from Kelvedon in the early morning, this conveying the coaching stock for the first 'up' working.

The working timetable for June 1950 and, in fact, the last to exhibit passenger services, was a poor shadow of former times. In the 'down' direction two mixed and one freight service, running under Class K code, were balanced by three mixed trains in the 'up' direction. The goods train, as throughout the history of the line, was the first departure from Kelvedon at 6.40a.m., making mandatory calls at Heath Siding, Tiptree and Tolleshunt D'Arcy before arriving at Tollesbury at 8.05a.m. This train also conveyed the coaching stock for the first 'up' working, the 8.30a.m. ex-Tollesbury service, and called at Tudwick Road, Church and Old Hall sidings, if required. In the 'up' direction, the afternoon mixed train, the 12.50p.m. ex-Tollesbury working, called at these intermediate sidings, if required, to clear any traffic.

After the withdrawal of the passenger service, a weekdays only freight service continued to serve all sidings until the line south of Tudwick Road to Tollesbury was closed to all traffic on 29th October 1951. The 1952 working timetable showed the 'down' Class K goods working departing

85

KELVEDON AND TOLLESBURY LIGHT RAILWAY.

(NO SUNDAY SERVICE)

(For regulations for working see Appendix.)

Single line worked by train staff without tickets, and by only one engine in steam (or two or more engines coupled together).

These trains are worked on the "Conductor Guard" principle.

Miles from Kelvedon. M. C.	DOWN WEEK DAYS.		1 Gds. and Cars. a.m.	2 Mxd a.m.	3 Mxd p.m.
	Kelvedon .... Ⓢ	dep.	6 40	10 15	5 48
— 33	Feering Halt	,,	—	10 18	5 51
2 62	Heath Siding	,,	7 10	.....	.....
2 69	Inworth	,,	—	10 25	5 58
3 31	Tiptree	arr.	7 15	10 30	6 3
		dep.	7 30	10 34	6 7
3 72	Tudwick Rd. Siding	,,	*	.....	.....
4 6	Tolleshunt Knights	,,	—	10 38	6 11
5 48	Church Siding	,,	*	.....	.....
6 45	Tolleshunt D'Arcy	arr.	7 45	10 46	6 19
		dep.	7 55	10 50	6 23
7 62	Old Hall Siding	,,	*	—	—
8 35	Tollesbury .... Ⓢ	arr.	8 5	10 55	6 28

Miles from Tollesbury M. C.	UP WEEK DAYS.		1 Mxd a.m.	2 Mxd p.m.	3 Mxd p.m.
— —	Tollesbury .... Ⓢ	dep.	8 30	12 45	6 37
53	Old Hall Siding	,,	—	*	—
1 70	Tolleshunt D'Arcy	arr.	8 36	12 51	6 43
		dep.	8 38	1 0	6 50
2 67	Church Siding	,,	.....	*	.....
4 29	Tolleshunt Knights	,,	8 44	1 6	6 56
4 43	Tudwick Rd. Siding	,,	.....	*	.....
5 4	Tiptree	arr.	8 49	1 16	7 1
		dep.	8 54	1 30	7 7
5 46	Inworth	,,	8 57	1 33	7 10
5 53	Heath Siding	,,	.....	*	.....
8 2	Feering Halt	,,	9 5	1 41	7 18
8 35	Kelvedon .... Ⓢ	arr.	9 9	1 45	7 22

The LNER Passenger Working Timetable, 1945.

KELVEDON AND TOLLESBURY LIGHT RAILWAY

WEEKDAYS

Single line worked by train staff without tickets, and by only one engine in steam (or two or more engines coupled together). (For regulations for working see "Appendix.")

Miles from Kelvedon M. C.			1 Gds. a.m.	2	3
— —	Kelvedon .... Ⓢ	dep.	6 40	.....	.....
2 62	Heath Siding	,,	7 10	—	—
3 31	Tiptree	arr.	7 15	.....	.....
		dep.	7 30	—	—
3 72	Tudwick Rd. Siding	,,	*	.....	.....
5 48	Church Siding	,,	*	—	—
6 45	Tolleshunt D'Arcy	arr.	7 45	.....	.....
		dep.	7 55	—	—
7 62	Old Hall Siding	,,	*	.....	.....
8 35	Tollesbury .... Ⓢ	arr.	8 5	—	—

1 To work cars from Kelvedon for 8.30 a.m. mixed train Tollesbury to Kelvedon.

The LNER Freight Working Timetable, 1944.

Table 16 KELVEDON and TOLLESBURY (Light Railway)—(One class only)

Miles	Week Days only	a.m		p.m			
—	Kelvedon .... dep	1010	..	5 48	..	..	..
½	Feering Halt	1013	..	5 51	..	..	..
2¾	Inworth	1020	..	5 58	..	..	..
3½	Tiptree	1029	..	6 7	..	..	..
4	Tolleshunt Knights	1033	..	6 11	..	..	..
6½	Tolleshunt D'Arcy..	1045	..	6 23	..	..	..
8½	Tollesbury ..... arr	1050	..	6 28	..	..	..

Miles	Week Days only	a.m		p.m		p.m
—	Tollesbury ..... dep	8 30	..	1250	..	6 37
2	Tolleshunt D'Arcy..	8 38	..	1 5	..	6 50
4¼	Tolleshunt Knights..	8 44	..	1 11	..	6 56
5	Tiptree	8 54	..	1 35	..	7 7
5¾	Inworth	8 57	..	1 38	..	7 10
8	Feering Halt	9 5	..	1 46	..	7 18
8½	Kelvedon ...... arr	9 9	..	1 50	..	7 22

E Except Saturdays
S Saturdays only

Tickets (single only) and Local Tickets are issued on the train

The LNER Passenger Timetable, October 1947.

from Kelvedon at 12 noon (SO) and 3.20p.m. (SX), arriving at Tiptree twenty minutes later. Heath Siding and Tudwick Road Siding were served only if required. The 'up' train departed from Tiptree at 1.15p.m. (SO) and 5p.m. (SX), arriving at Kelvedon fifteen minutes later, as no call was made at Heath Siding.

In the final years of freight working, the diesel shunting locomotive, after travelling light from Witham at 1.10 p.m., shunted Kelvedon Yard until 3.30p.m. when it departed with the branch goods train for Tiptree and Tudwick Road. The return journey departed at 4.35p.m., with twenty minutes permitted for the run to Kelvedon, allowing time for shunting at Heath Siding. During summer months the train departed from Kelvedon 'up' Yard at the earlier time of 1.35p.m., returning from Tiptree at 2.50p.m. In the last few months there was often insufficient traffic to justify running the goods train, and the trip working was frequently cancelled.

Fares

Only third class single fares were offered on the Tollesbury Light Railway, with the Conductor Guard issuing tickets on the train. No fares were bookable at Kelvedon (High Level) Station. The fare structure offered by the GER, when the line opened to traffic on 1st October 1904, was as follows:

Class R24 0-6-0T No. 391 descends the 1 in 50 'down' Inworth Bank, with the 11.16a.m. Tollesbury to Kelvedon train; on 31st May 1910. No. 391 is running with front coupling rods removed, making it a 2-4-0T locomotive. The train is formed of a four wheel two compartment brake third and four wheel five compartment third, originally built between 1877 and 1882 and converted for use on the light railway in 1904. It was then that the compartment partitions were removed and a central gangway with end doors was provided, to enable the guard to collect fares.

LCGB/Ken Nunn Collection

Kelvedon to		*Tiptree to*		*Tolleshunt D'Arcy to*	
Tiptree	4d	Tolleshunt D'Arcy	3d	Tollesbury	2d
Tolleshunt D'Arcy	7d	Tollesbury	5d		
Tollesbury	9d				

After the opening of Inworth on 1st May 1905, Tolleshunt Knights on 12th December 1910 and Tollesbury Pier on 15th May 1907, the revised fare structure was as follows:

Kelvedon to		*Inworth to*		*Tiptree to*	
Inworth	3d	Tiptree	1d	Tolleshunt Knights	1d
Tiptree	4d	Tolleshunt Knights	2d	Tolleshunt D'Arcy	3d
Tolleshunt Knights	5d	Tolleshunt D'Arcy	4d	Tollesbury	5d
Tolleshunt D'Arcy	7d	Tollesbury	6d	Tollesbury Pier	7d
Tollesbury	9d	Tollesbury Pier	8d		
Tollesbury Pier	11d				
Tolleshunt Knights to		*Tolleshunt D'Arcy to*		*Tollesbury to*	
Tolleshunt D'Arcy	2d	Tollesbury	2d	Tollesbury Pier	2d
Tollesbury	4d	Tollesbury Pier	4d		
Tollesbury Pier	6d				

After the opening of Tollesbury Pier, in an endeavour to generate holiday traffic and develop the area as a sailing resort, the GER issued through weekend tourist tickets between Liverpool Street and Tollesbury Pier stations. Available on Friday or Saturday to the following Tuesday, the fares were first class (third class on the light railway) 12s 0d, third class 5s 6d.

The fare structure on the light railway at the time of closure continued to offer third class single fares, although monthly return tickets were also available:

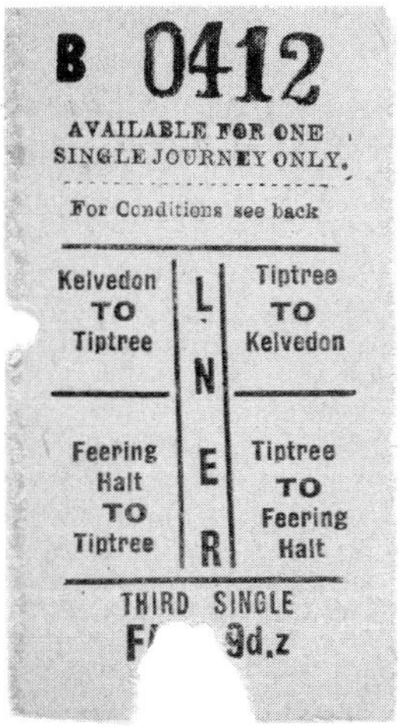

Kelvedon to		*Feering Halt to*		*Inworth to*	
Feering Halt	3d	Inworth	6d	Tiptree	3d
Inworth	6d	Tiptree	9d	Tolleshunt Knights	5d
Tiptree	9d	Tolleshunt Knights	10½d	Tolleshunt D'Arcy	1/-d
Tolleshunt Knights	10½d	Tolleshunt D'Arcy	1/6d	Tollesbury	1/5d
Tolleshunt D'Arcy	1/6d	Tollesbury	1/11d		
Tollesbury	1/11d				
Tiptree to		*Tolleshunt Knights to*		*Tolleshunt D'Arcy to*	
Tolleshunt Knights	3d	Tolleshunt D'Arcy	6d	Tollesbury	5d
Tolleshunt D'Arcy	9d	Tollesbury	11d		
Tollesbury	1/2d				

Sample monthly returns were Kelvedon or Feering Halt to Inworth — 10½d.

Tickets were of the bell punch type, roughly printed on white paper and bearing the legend GER, LNER or British Railways, and were similar to bus tickets, while monthly returns were green in colour. The guard cancelled tickets on issue with the orthodox bell punch.

So few were passengers in later years, that the guard came round the train asking people for the ticket they required. He then returned to the brake and cancelled the tickets, before returning along the train to collect the fares. The antics of the guard clambering across the drop plate between coaches, whilst the train pitched and swayed along the light railway, was always a source of amusement to passengers.

South of Station Road level crossing at Tollesbury, was the run-round loop, situated on the 'up' side of the main single line. Here locomotives ran round and re-formed their trains before making the return trip to Kelvedon. Here, Class J67/1 No. 68616 prepares to set off with her train on the main single line, over the level crossing and into Tollesbury Station.

The 12.50p.m. mixed train from Tollesbury approaches the branch 'up' home signal, at Kelvedon, on 28th August 1950, hauled by Class J67/1 0-6-0T No. 68616. The only passenger accommodation on the train is provided by ex-Stoke Ferry brake third No. 62261.
LCGB/Ken Nunn Collection

Freight Traffic

Before the advent of the railway, local carriers conveyed goods to and from neighbouring towns and markets. From Tiptree, Bennett served Colchester on Tuesdays and Saturdays and Maldon on Thursdays, whilst Runnicles journeyed to Colchester on Wednesdays and Saturdays. Bacon conveyed goods from Tiptree to Kelvedon, Tolleshunt D'Arcy and Tollesbury on Mondays and Fridays, while from Tollesbury, Collins served Colchester and Maldon on Tuesdays, Thursdays and Saturdays, with George Anthony serving Colchester only on Mondays, Wednesdays and Fridays. The same carriers also called at Tolleshunt D'Arcy en route to Colchester and Maldon. Anthony did not, however, provide a service from Tolleshunt D'Arcy to Colchester on Mondays.

The Tollesbury line was conceived and built essentially to provide an effective outlet for growers, and the growth of the initial freight traffic handled soon confirmed to the GER and the Treasury, that the construction of the line was, indeed, an asset to the district. Barley, wheat, hay, straw, vegetables, fruit, hops, malt, paper, coal and coke traffic was quickly transferred from the slow ponderous carriers' carts to rail, although some small traffic for local journeys was still conveyed by carriers' waggons.

To encourage local landowners and growers to dispatch and receive traffic by rail, a number of sidings was provided on the branch in addition to the sidings at Tiptree, Tolleshunt D'Arcy and Tollesbury stations. The sidings at Heath (2 miles and 62 chains from Kelvedon), Tudwick Road (3 miles and 72 chains from Kelvedon), Church (5 miles and 48 chains from Kelvedon) and Old Hall (7 miles and 62 chains from Kelvedon) were designated for public use, but Brooklands Siding (50 chains from Kelvedon) near Feering, although initially designated public, was a private siding used by W. Blyth & Sons and W. D. Deal. It ran across a field to terminate in Threshfords Farm, although it was closed in the 1930s and subsequently lifted.

Of the more specific items, fruit traffic loaded at various sidings, and export of jam from Britannia Fruit Farms factory, owned by Mr. Wilkin, of Tiptree, provided considerable traffic for the branch. Established in 1885, the Tiptree factory was producing 450 tons of jam per annum by 1907 and over the years this increased considerably, much of it being dispatched by rail and often requiring a daily supply of seven or eight covered vans in season. Wilkin's company also imported a considerable tonnage of stable manure by rail in the early years of the branch, and this was offloaded not only at Tiptree but at other intermediate sidings for distribution to the fruit fields and orchards. Other landowners in the area, especially those served by Brooklands Siding, followed the trend and supplies of manure from London became a regular feature on the branch freight trains, until the traffic ceased soon after World War I.

Notable freight traffic carried by the branch train in the first decade were oysters and fish, and on one day it is reported that over 110,000 oysters were dispatched from Tollesbury. Oysters were also loaded with other fish traffic for a short while at Old Hall Siding, when boats brought their catch up Old Hall Creek for rapid dispatch to the London markets. Shrimps and sprats were included in the consignments of the latter, caught between November and March, in the Blackwater and Colne estuaries.

The railway company attempted to encourage and increase dairy farming in the area with milk being regularly dispatched from Tollesbury and Tiptree, conveyed to the dairies at Colchester in the familiar seventeen gallon churns. Two loads were dispatched during the summer months by the early morning and late afternoon trains, but during the winter months only one collection was made, this being by the early morning service. This area of Essex was not noted for dairy farming, and the relatively small amounts of traffic conveyed by the branch train was quickly lost to road transport by the early 1930s.

Livestock was also handled in small quantities, and horse traffic was regularly conveyed in wagons or horse-boxes attached to the specific mixed or passenger trains noted in the working timetable, but even then, only between Kelvedon and Tollesbury or return. Horse traffic declined, by the early 1930s, with the advent of the road motor/horse-boxes but cattle wagons were a common feature on the line, until the outbreak of World War II, for the conveyance of livestock to Colchester market on Saturdays, and Chelmsford market on Fridays. After the war very little cattle traffic was handled.

Coal traffic was offloaded at Tiptree, Tolleshunt D'Arcy and Tollesbury on a regular basis and, to a fluctuating degree, at some of the intermediate sidings. Most arrived in privately-owned wagons routed from the Midlands and Yorkshire coalfields via Stanground Sidings, Peterborough, or Whitemoor and Temple Mills, with empties being returned via the same route. Local merchants included Moys, Frosts and Garwoods.

Malt traffic was taken to the brewery at Tiptree and, from the late 1920s, quantities of sugar beet were loaded at the various sidings on the light railway during the period October to January, and forwarded to the British Sugar Corporation factories at Felstead, Ipswich or Bury St. Edmunds. Conveyance of this crop continued on a declining scale, until the branch was closed to freight.

The use of a tow rope was authorised at all stations to enable the locomotive to shunt vehicles in the adjacent siding and, when not in use, was carried in the Tollesbury branch goods brake van. All goods accounts work for the branch was handled at Kelvedon, where the goods office was enlarged when improvements were made to the main line station.

During World War I the branch train conveyed several hundreds of soldiers to the shores of the Blackwater for military training and manoeuvres, with equipment and stores being carried by additional freight trains to Tollesbury. In World War II the overgrown Tollesbury Pier extension was taken over by the War Department and became of strategic importance, as defences were established to nullify any possible enemy landing. Munitions and some personnel were conveyed to Tollesbury to man and supply the shore batteries and, in addition, at various times during hostilities, armoured WD locomotives were worked across the branch and operated on the Tollesbury Pier extension, with anti-aircraft guns mounted on flat wagons as a defence line against Luftwaffe air attacks or coastal landings.

The rapid decline of freight traffic on the railway, after World War II, saw much of the remaining goods traffic transfer to road haulage as the end of petrol rationing brought more lorries on to the road. Very often, the goods train ran with few wagons whilst the mixed trains ran with only coaching stock, with coal traffic and the ever-important fruit and jam traffic from Tiptree being the only regular consignments. Soon after the withdrawal of the passenger services from the line, British Railways announced the closure of the line to all traffic beyond Tudwick Road Siding, and freight facilities were subsequently withdrawn from Church Siding, Tolleshunt D'Arcy, Old Hall Siding and Tollesbury on and from 29th October 1951.

The remaining section of the line, from Tudwick Road to the junction, remained open for a further eleven years, mainly for the conveyance of coal and coke traffic to Tiptree, for the fuel merchants of Frosts and Garwoods who distributed fuel throughout the area. Outgoing commodities included spasmodic vegetable traffic, usually peas and potatoes for Spitalfields, and sugar beet as well as jam traffic from Wilkin's factory. Initially, the coal traffic conveyed totalled 2,000 tons per annum, whilst jam exports totalled some 600 tons. Road traffic with door-to-door service, however, gradually attracted traffic from the line and, as maintenance deteriorated, the truncated section of the branch became more of a liability until the GE Line Management at Liverpool Street announced, in the spring of 1962, their intention to withdraw the freight service and close the branch completely. Alternative facilities were offered initially at Kelvedon and then Witham, and freight facilities were subsequently withdrawn from Heath Siding, Tiptree and Tudwick Road Siding, on and from 1st October 1962.

The following facilities were available for goods and livestock traffic at the branch stations:

Kelvedon (High Level)	Fixed crane 1½ ton capacity
	20 ton capacity wagon weighbridge
	Weighing machine 1 ton 2 cwt.
	Goods shed with capacity for storage of 100 quarters of grain
	Water supply for cattle
	Loading gauge
Tiptree	Weighing machine 10 cwt.
	Loading gauge
Tolleshunt D'Arcy	Weighing machine 10 cwt.
	Loading gauge
Tollesbury	Loading dock
	Weighing machine 1 ton
	Loading gauge

Sidings were equipped with a loading gauge, and all the above stations (but not sidings) also had lock-up premises for small parcels. In GER days, the latest time for receipt of animals or goods for forwarding the same day was as follows:

	Saturdays excepted	*Saturdays only*
Kelvedon	4.30p.m. to London, 5p.m. to other stations	12.30p.m.
Brooklands Siding	3.30p.m. all stations	12.30p.m.
Heath Siding	3.15p.m. all stations	12.30p.m.
Tiptree	4.30p.m. to London, 5p.m. to other stations	12.30p.m.
Tudwick Road Siding	3p.m. all stations	12.30p.m.
Church Siding	3p.m. all stations	12.30p.m.
Tolleshunt D'Arcy	4.30p.m. to London, 5p.m. to other stations	12.30p.m.
Old Hall Siding	3p.m. all stations	12.30p.m.
Tollesbury	4.30p.m. to London, 5p.m. to other stations	12.30p.m.

The loads of freight authorised to be hauled by locomotives between Kelvedon and Tollesbury, in GER days, was as follows:

Class of locomotive	*Minerals 'down' and 'up'*	*Goods 'down' and 'up'*	*Empties 'down' and 'up'*
C	12 wagons	17 wagons	24 wagons

On mixed trains, one passenger vehicle was considered equal to one loaded truck of goods. The following locomotives regularly allocated to the branch were classified as under:

GER Class	*LNER*	*Classified*
Y14	J15	C
R24	J67/1	C
C72	J68	C
R24R	J69/1	C
S56	J69/1	C

Under the LNER, the freight train loads on the Tollesbury branch were not permitted to exceed 24 wagons in length, with individual loadings as under:

	Minerals	*Goods*	*Empties*
Class 1 engine	12	13	24
Class 2 engine	13	19	24
Class 3 engine	14	21	24
Class 4 engine	16	24	24
Class 5 engine	18	24	24
Class 6 engine	20	24	24

A Class 3 goods engine was a J15.

Traffic Staff

Motive power and Civil Engineering staff are covered in their respective sections, but a brief mention must be made of traffic staff.

When the light railway opened to traffic, the responsibility for administration and operation of the line came under the control of the Kelvedon stationmaster C. E. Jarvis, who was stationmaster at that time. He received a higher grading for his additional responsibilities. Jarvis was soon promoted elsewhere and his place was taken by Mr Johnson who, in turn, relinquished his responsibility for the Tollesbury branch on promotion to the post of stationmaster at Manningtree, in January 1914. The resultant vacancy was taken by Stationmaster Jordan, who was transferred from Haughley to Kelvedon.

On the branch proper, staffing was kept to a bare minimum, with a total of seven wages grade personnel. At Kelvedon a porter/shunter was initially allocated to full time duties at the low level station, being relieved in the event of sickness or absence by a member of the main line station staff. Tiptree boasted a staff of two; a porter in charge, later designated leading porter, and a porter/shunter. At Tolleshunt D'Arcy a porter/shunter was appointed, whilst Tollesbury boasted a porter in charge. The branch staff was complemented by two conductor guards, who issued tickets on the trains and lit and extinguished the oil lamps at unstaffed stations or halts, in addition to their normal duties. Staff on the light railway were a close-knit community and when Porter/Shunter H. Dodd of Kelvedon (Low Level) was married, in March 1914, his companions presented him and his wife with a dinner service.

Soon after the Grouping, the LNER sought to cut the cost of staffing the line, and reduced the establishment by withdrawing the posts of porter/shunter at Kelvedon (Low Level), Tiptree and Tolleshunt D'Arcy, leaving only leading porters at Tiptree and Tollesbury. Duties at Kelvedon (Low Level) were incorporated into the duties of leading porters on the main line station.

At the time of closure to passenger traffic, the following staff were employed on the line; Leading Porter Ted Pearse, who had been at Tiptree since 1936 and had previously served fifteen years in the Carriage & Wagon Department, Porter William Papworth at Kelvedon (Low Level), whilst at Tollesbury, Porter in charge Arthur Lawrence had been only the second man in that post, succeeding J. Gallant on his retirement who was appointed porter in charge at Tollesbury when the line opened in 1904. The two conductor guards on the final establishment were Bill Manning, who joined the GER in 1916 and worked for nine years in the Carriage & Wagon Department (no relation to Driver Manning), and M. Petchey who worked the last train.

All the staff on the branch were keen railwaymen and gave of their best, but most took an interest in their local trade union and belonged to the Colchester branch of the National Union of Railwaymen.

GER Class R24 0-6-0T No. 391 stands outside the diminutive Kelvedon Shed, on 31st March 1910. The jib water crane (foreground) was fed from a water tank located behind the shed. In the background is the covered walkway connecting the high level main line station with the low level station.
LCGB/Ken Nunn Collection

Class J67/1 No. 68616, at the head of a mixed train at Kelvedon (Low Level), on 19th September 1950. The passenger vehicles are bogie tram No. E60461, brake third No. E62262 and brake third No. E62261, followed by two vans, an open wagon, the LNER four wheel full brake and, bringing up the rear, the branch goods brake van. No. 68616 has, by this time, received the BR lion and wheel emblem on the side tanks.
Ian L. Wright

Class J67/1 0-6-0T No. 68616 stands at Kelvedon (Low Level) Station with the 12.50p.m. Tollesbury to Kelvedon train, formed of an ex-Stoke Ferry brake third, a Wisbech & Upwell bogie tram, a four wheel Gresley parcels van and the branch goods brake, on 29th July 1950.
LCGB/Ken Nunn Collection

Chapter Six

Locomotives and Rolling Stock

The light construction of the Tollesbury branch, with its relatively steep gradients, numerous curves and 14 ton maximum axle loading, restricted the choice of locomotives available to work the services. This restriction posed no problems for the GER and, from the day of the official opening until closure, the services were worked by diminutive tank locomotives supplemented by lighter tender engines.

The LNER route availability permitted the following locomotives to work across the light railway between Kelvedon and Tollesbury; Class J15 tender engines for working ballast and breakdown trains at reduced speed and Class J65, J67 and J70 tank engines. Later, for route availability, the branch was unclassified (RA-), permitting only the following classes on the line; Class J15 (working ballast and breakdown trains at reduced speed) and Classes J65, J67/1 and J70. British Railways continued to show the route as unclassified with diesel locomotive Classes DY1, 2, 5 and 11 and steam locomotive Class J15. In practice, however, and in complete contravention of instructions, restricted locomotives of Classes J68 (GER C72 class) and J69 (GER R24R class) with axle loading of 15tons 2cwt., often worked the services.

Scott &Middleton,the contractor, initially used a Manning Wardle 0-6-0 saddle tank in the final stages of construction. For the opening of the line to passenger traffic, however, the GER allocated one of the Class K9 0-4-2Ts, No. 25, to Kelvedon Shed. Designed by William Adams, the class, totalling ten locomotives, was built in 1877/8 with No. 25 being constructed at Stratford Works in June 1877, at a cost of £1,795. She was re-boilered in October 1894 at a cost of £840 and, at the same time, received a backplate to the open cab, and coal rails on the bunker to increase coal carrying capacity. This diminutive tank was one of the last of the class to remain in service but, after working on the light railway with little relief for six months or so, she was transferred early in 1905 to the Norwich District where she spent the rest of her days as yard pilot at Thorpe, before withdrawal later in the year.

From the spring of 1905, the GER allocated members of the sturdy Class R24 0-6-0 tank locomotives, with an axle loading within the stipulated limit, to the branch and the 'Buck Jumpers' as they were nicknamed from thereon, handled most of the traffic. Originally designed by James Holden, and built at Stratford Works between 1890 and 1904, the locomotives were fitted with Westinghouse brakes for passenger work and gained fame on the 'Jazz' suburban services from Liverpool Street to Enfield Town and Chingford. Most depots throughout East Anglia had this class in its allocation, and it was from Colchester Motive Power Depot that the Tollesbury branch locomotive was supplied. Many of the locomotives were rebuilt with new boilers, with a working pressure of 180p.s.i. instead of 160p.s.i., and wider side tanks for increased water capacity, and because of this were known as the Class R24 (rebuilt). In 1904 twenty more 0-6-0Ts were introduced for passenger work, these Class S56 locomotives having higher boiler pressure and larger tanks when built.

Class J69/1 No. 68578 hauled the last passenger train along the branch on 5th May 1951 and, by coincidence, sister locomotive No. 68579 (ex-GER No. 271) hauled the last passenger service on the other GER Essex light railway, from Elsenham to Thaxted, on 13th September 1952. Two of the class wandered further afield after service on the light railway, No. 68560 being allocated to Boston (40F) whilst No. 68567 spent its final years at Parkhead Shed (65C), in the Scottish Region. The most noted of all was No. 68619, which finished its days as East Side pilot at Liverpool Street, where she was maintained in spotless LNER apple green livery, and later BR lined black and finally GER blue livery.

The following locomotives were regularly used on the Kelvedon to Tollesbury Light Railway services and when not so, they performed shunting or station pilot duties at Colchester, Witham, Maldon and Braintree.

GER Class	*Rebuilt to Class*	*LNER Class*	*GER No.*	*LNER No.*	*LNER 1946 No.*	*BR No.*	*Withdrawn from Service*
S56	-	J69/1	53	7053	8619	68619	October 1961
S56	-	J69/1	89	7089	8635	68635	September 1962
S56	-	J69/1	90	7090	8636	68636	January 1959
R24	R24R	J69/1	160	7160	8607	68607	May 1958
R24	-	J67/1	161	7161	8608	68608	October 1958
R24	R24R	J69/1	165	7165	8612	68612	June 1961
R24	-	J67/1	169	7169	8616	68616	November 1958
R24	R24R	J69/1	267	7267	8575	68575	October 1960
R24	R24R	J69/1	270	7270	8578	68578	January 1961
R24	R24R	J69/1	364	7364	-	-	January 1931
R24	R24R	J69/1	384	7384	8560	68560	January 1961
R24	R24R	J69/1	391	7391	8567	68567	August 1957

Evidently little notice was taken of the route availability limitations by the Colchester running foreman, as the majority of locomotives were, in fact, the restricted Class R24R or S56 0-6-0Ts.

Although officially restricted from working over the light railway, another class associated with the 'Crab and Winkle', especially in later years, was the GER Class C72 (LNER Class J68) 0-6-0Ts, introduced by A. J. Hill and built at Stratford between 1912 and 1914. These locomotives, distinguishable from the Class R24s by their cab with high-pitched roof, side windows and large square front and rear cab spectacles instead of round, represented the final stage of the development of the original Holden 0-6-0 tank locomotives dating from 1886. The following were regularly sub-shedded at Kelvedon for use on the branch services:

GER Class	*LNER Class*	*GER No.*	*LNER No.*	*LNER 1946 No.*	*BR No.*	*Withdrawn from Service*
C72	J68	42	7042	8638	68638	February 1959
C72	J68	45	7045	8641	68641	November 1959
C72	J68	48	7048	8644	68644	November 1960

In the early years, the 'Buck Jumpers' operating the Tollesbury services had the coupling rods removed from the leading pair of driving wheels to convert them to 2-4-0T. It was thought that this would allow greater movement of the leading pair of wheels on the sharp curves and undulating gradients of the branch, thus reducing the fixed wheelbase of the locomotive and thereby minimising flange and tyre wear and also excessive wear on the outer rails of the sharp curves. The inconvenience and additional time required to remove or replace the coupling rods every time a locomotive was changed over, soon made the practice unpopular with fitting staff at Colchester. It then became routine to send a 'Buck Jumper' to Kelvedon without this modification, and when it was found the removal of the coupling rods made hardly any difference to the wear on tyres, flanges or track, the practice ceased. It was also the concern of the Locomotive Department that engines so modified suffered additional wear on the boxes, and also had slight frame distortion.

For many years special freight and ballast trains were hauled by the GER Class Y14 (LNER Class J15) 0-6-0 tender locomotives, designed by T. W. Worsdell and introduced in 1883. The success of the class can be gauged by the fact that construction continued for thirty years until 1913. All except nineteen of the class of 272 locomotives were built at Stratford Works, the others being built by Sharp Stewart & Co. The ubiquitous class was occasionally sent to Kelvedon to deputise for the regular branch locomotive, provided they were fitted with Westinghouse brakes, but only as a last resort in the event of Colchester being unable to provide a 'Buck Jumper'. The Class J15 as well as working freight services were also used on enthusiasts' specials across the branch, and members of the class known to have worked on the branch after nationalisation include Nos. 65369, 65402, 65424, 65427, 65431, 65432, 65440, 65441, 65443, 65444, 65445, 65446, 65448, 65454, 65456, 65465, 65468, 65470, 65473 and 65476. No. 65443 hauled the Railway Enthusiasts' Club train of open wagons and brake van on the visit to the branch on 6th April 1957.

One of the most celebrated class of locomotives to visit the 'Crab and Winkle', albeit on a enthusiasts' special, was one of the GER Class T26 locomotives, nicknamed 'Intermediates'. A total of 100 was built to the design of J. Holden, between 1891 and 1902. Most were assigned for mixed traffic duties, long cross-country routes and slower traffic on the main line. The LNER classified them as E4, but in the 1920s and 1930s most were scrapped. By 1942 the class was reduced to a total of eighteen, most of them being allocated to the Cambridge and Norwich districts although

From the opening of the line in 1904, the GER allocated Adams Class K9 0-4-2T No. 25 to work the services. Built in 1877, at a cost of £1,795, she was re-boilered and modified in 1894 and subsequently worked the initial services over the Tollesbury Light Railway for about six months, before transfer to Norwich in 1905. No. 25 is shown here, at Norwich, just before withdrawal.
LCGB/Ken Nunn Collection

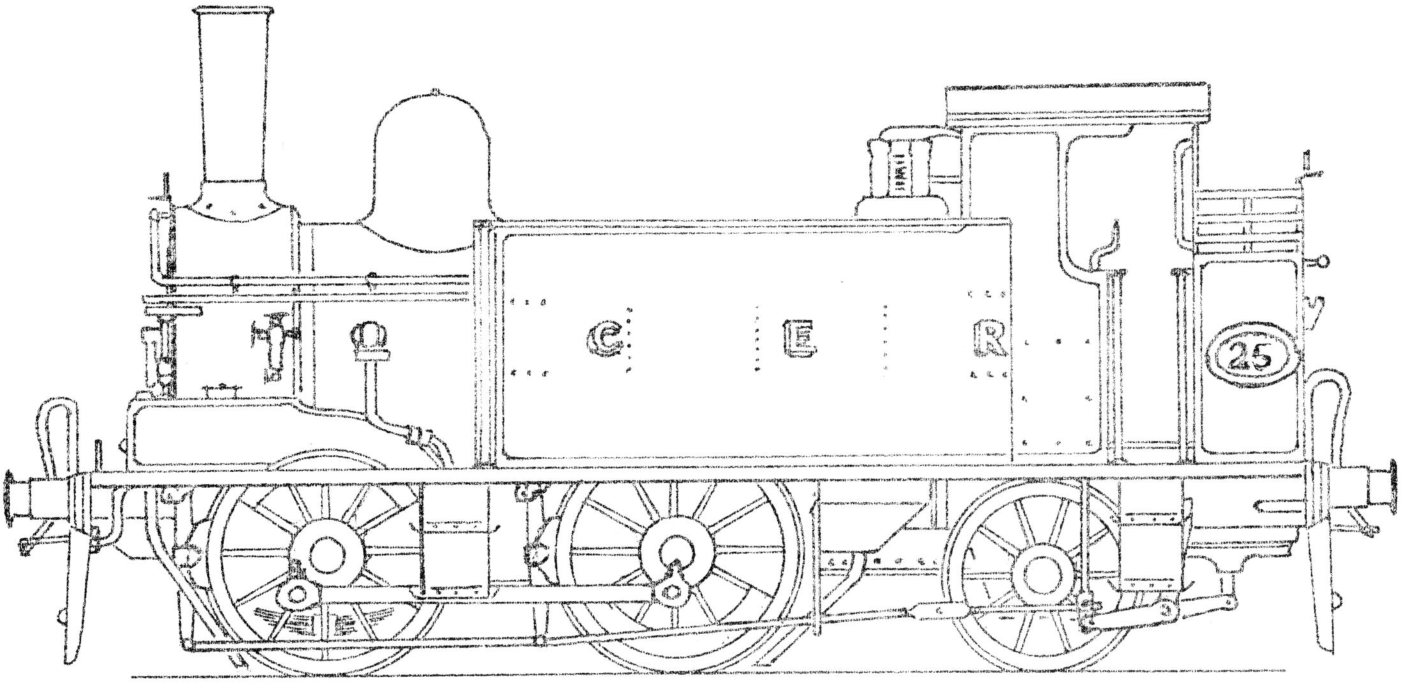

William Adams Class K9 0-4-2T No. 25, used on the initial Tollesbury Light Railway services.

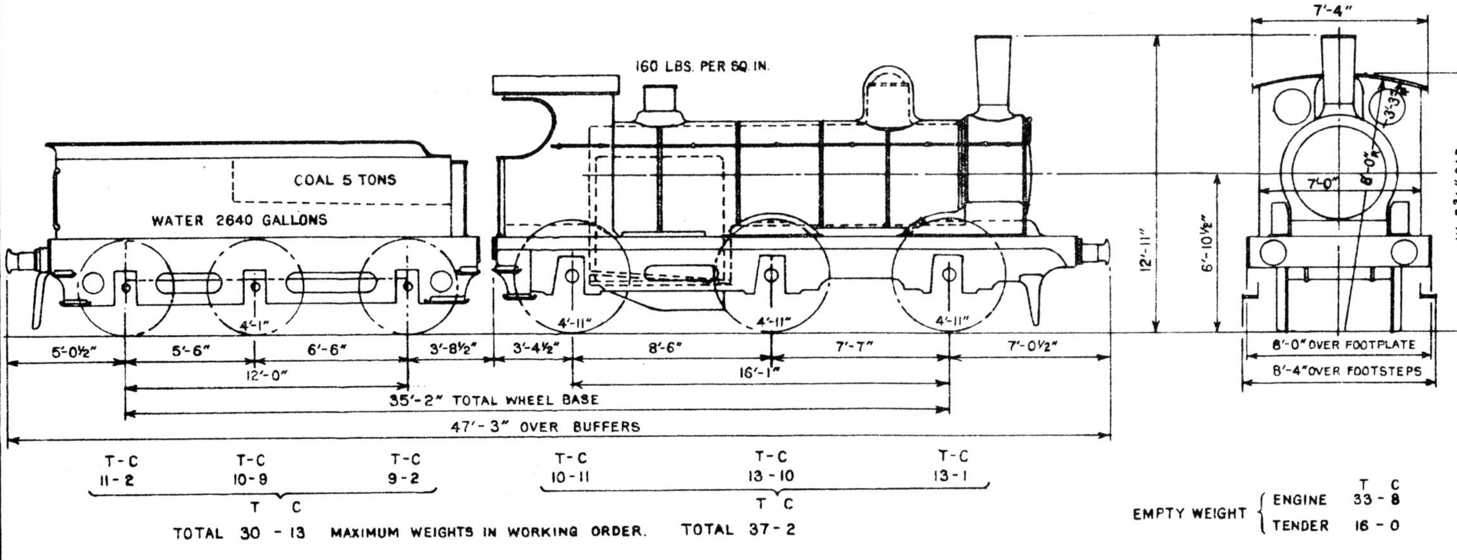

T. W. Worsdell's GER Class Y14 tender 0-6-0 (LNER Class J15) which occasionally worked the Tollesbury branch.

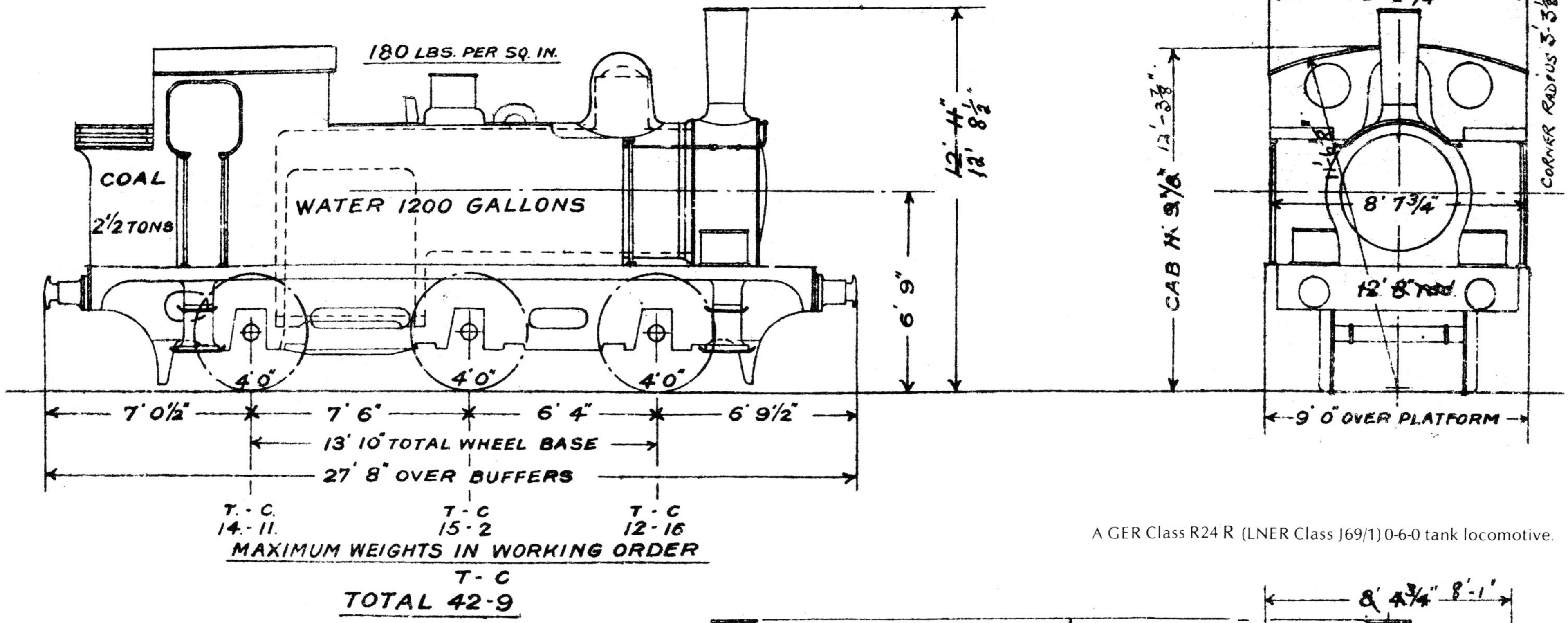

A GER Class R24 R (LNER Class J69/1) 0-6-0 tank locomotive.

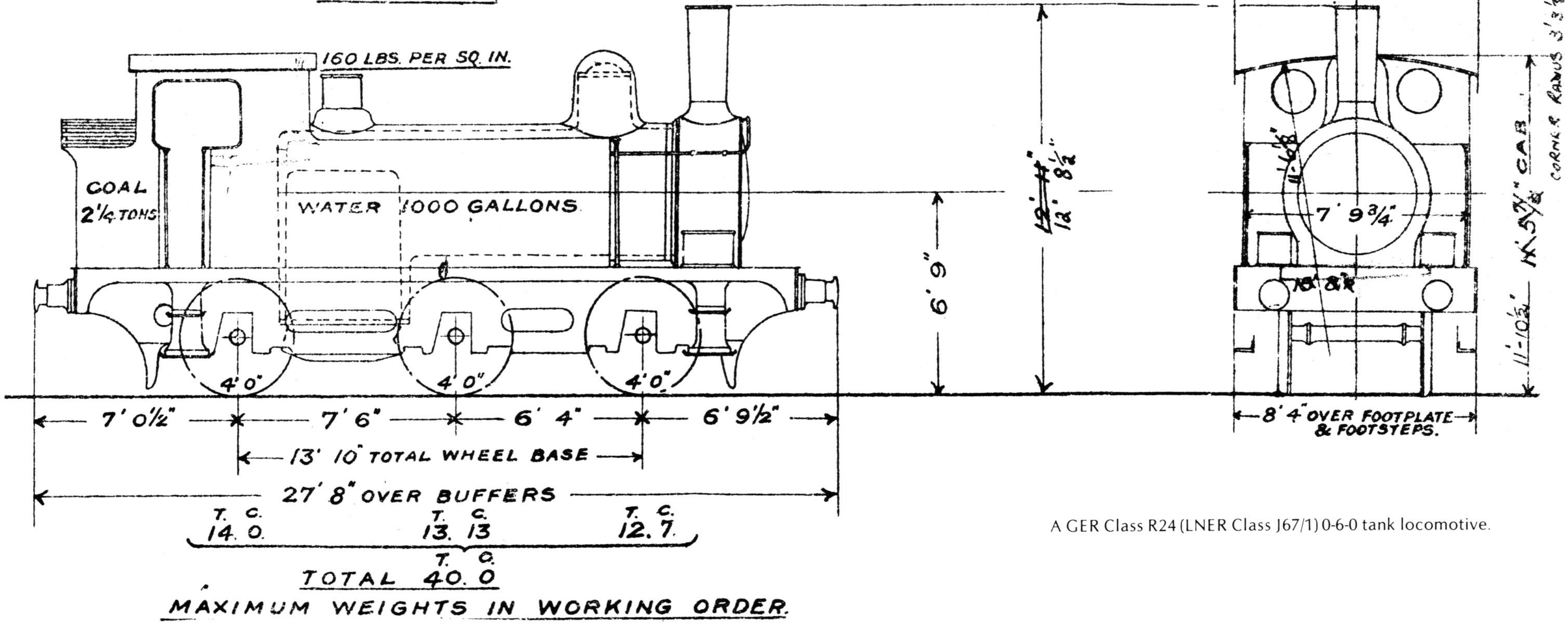

A GER Class R24 (LNER Class J67/1) 0-6-0 tank locomotive.

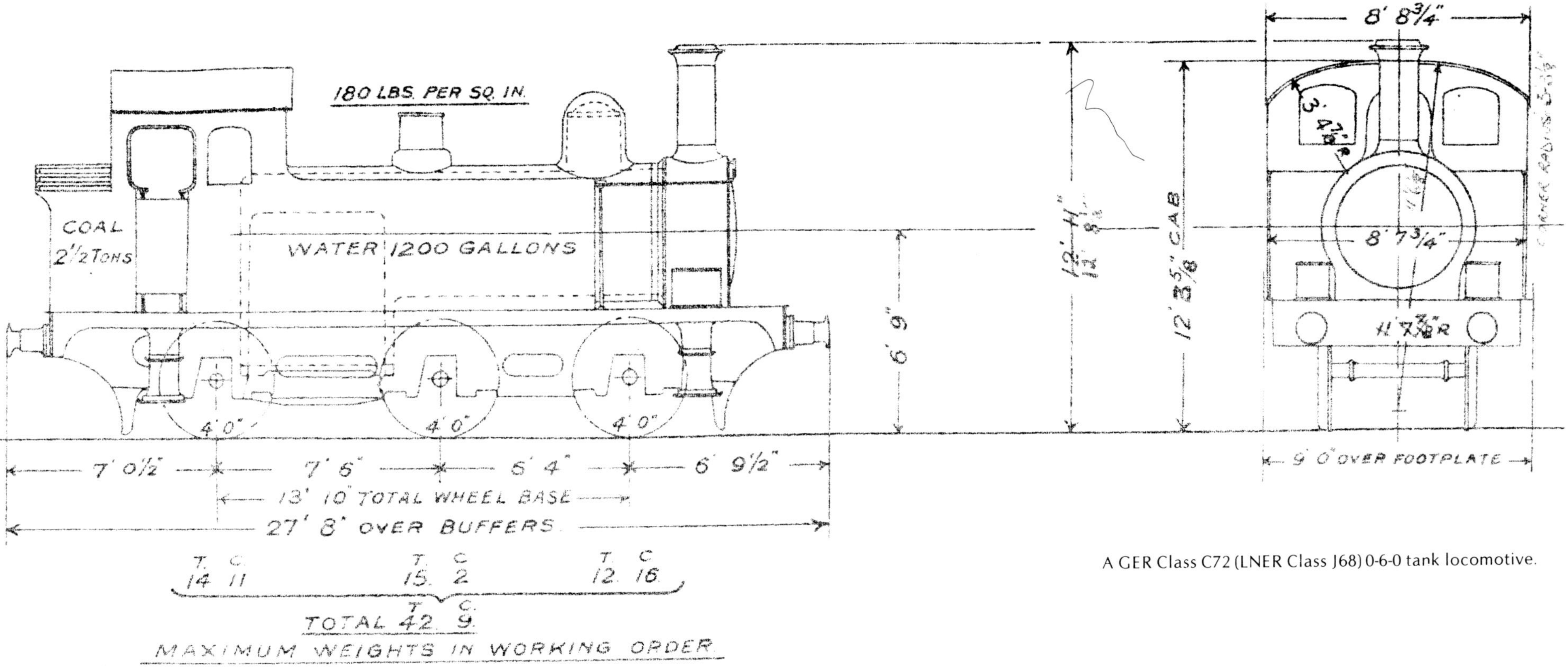

A GER Class C72 (LNER Class J68) 0-6-0 tank locomotive.

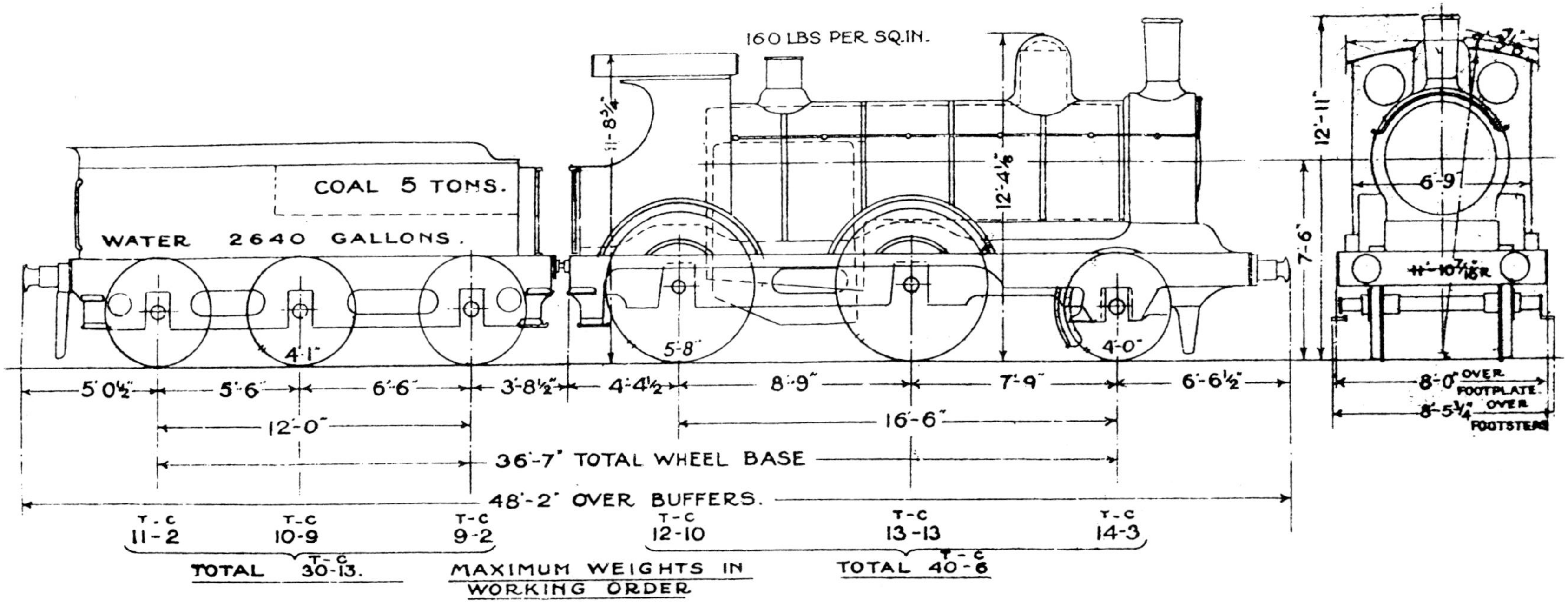

A GER Class T26 2-4-0 (LNER Class E4). This class of locomotive was used on an enthusiasts' special on the line in 1957.

GER Class R24 0-6-0T No. 267 pulls into Tiptree Station with the two coach 1.40p.m. Tollesbury to Kelvedon train, on 9th April 1910. No. 267 has the front pair of coupling rods removed, and is running as a 2-4-0T. This practice persisted during GER days, when it was thought that it would save flange and tyre wear on the coupled wheels. The practice was later abandoned.

LCGB/Ken Nunn Collection

Class R24 0-6-0T No. 391, running as a 2-4-0T with its front coupling rods removed, eases the two coach 12.30p.m. Kelvedon to Tollesbury train over Feering Crossing while the guard waits to close the gates across the railway, on 31st March 1910. The head-code disc, red with a white outer ring, is positioned on the incorrect lamp bracket and should be up by the chimney. No. 391, in its later life as No. 68567, spent its final years at Parkhead Shed (65C) in Scotland.

LCGB/Ken Nunn Collection

No. 8636 stands by the run-round loop at Tollesbury in 1948. The train is waiting to run forward over the level crossing into Tollesbury Station.

Dr I. C. Allen

Class J69/1 0-6-0T No. 8636 prepares to leave Tollesbury with a mixed train on 19th September 1950. After the late 1920s the practice of removing the front coupling rods to make the locomotives into 2-4-0Ts was abandoned, after it was found the flanges and rails suffered equal wear whatever the wheel arrangement.

H. G. Lawlor

LNER Class J68 No. 7045 stands at Tollesbury with a two coach train, formed of an ex-Stoke Ferry six wheel brake third and an ex-Wisbech & Upwell bogie tram, in the mid-1930s. Note the headcode disc of purple with white outer ring, which superseded the GER code of red with white outer ring. The LNER soon altered the disc and light to the standard white disc or light for stopping passenger trains. No. 7045 was GER Class C72 No. 45, and later became BR No. 68641.

LNER Class J68 0-6-0T No. 7048 stands at Tollesbury, prior to shunting the freight section of its mixed train in the mid-1930s. The Class J68s were officially banned from the light railway because of an axle loading above the required limit but, in fact, were often utilised by Colchester Motive Power Depot and allocated to Kelvedon Shed in the event of a shortage of Class J67 'Buck Jumpers'.

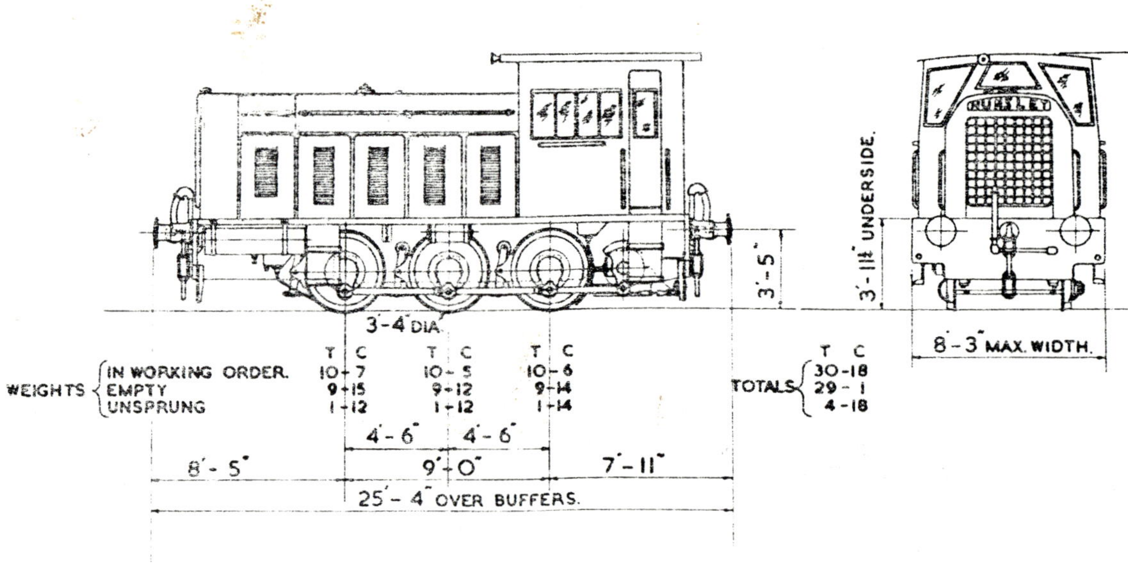

A 204hp Hunslet 0-6-0 diesel-mechanical Class 05 shunter. The type was used on freight services to Tiptree after the withdrawal of steam on the Light Railway.

during 1950/1 No. 62791 was allocated to Colchester Shed for a short period. As the class succumbed to the cutter's torch the survivors were in demand for use on special trains and, on 27th September 1958, No. 62785 hauled the Railway Enthusiasts' Club brake van special across the branch. This locomotive was condemned in December 1959 and restored to its former GER livery as No. 490, and is now in the National Railway Museum collection at York.

In 1958 the 'Buck Jumper' or J15 diagrammed for pilot duties at Witham, which included in its working the Tiptree freight train, was replaced by a diesel-mechanical 0-6-0 shunting locomotive. From then onwards, the weekdays only goods working on the branch was hauled by 204hp diesels. The Hunslet 204hp locomotives, initially introduced in 1955 and allocated to Parkeston Depot for maintenance and repairs, were classified by the Eastern Region of British Railways as D2/8. Weighing 30 tons, the locomotives were powered by Gardner 8L3 engines, giving a rating of 204hp at 1,200 r.p.m., whilst the transmission was Hunslet patent friction clutch and Hunslet four speed gearbox, incorporating reverse and final drive gears. The driving wheels were 3ft. 4in. in diameter, and maximum tractive effort was 14,500lb. Initially, the diesel proved unpopular but its 'all-enclosed' warm cab soon changed the attitude of locomotivemen, especially in winter months. Their use on the branch coincided with deteriorating permanent way and on more than one occasion, a Class J15 0-6-0 or sister diesel locomotive was sent with tool vans, from Colchester, to assist in re-railing. On one occasion, in 1960, a Hunslet shunter succeeded in colliding with a car on the open crossing near Tiptree Station. Initially numbered in a series commencing 11136, under the standard BR renumbering procedure, the class received the numbers D2550 onwards. Regular visitors to the branch included Nos. D2550 (11136), D2551 (11137), D2552 (11138), D2553 (11139), D2554 (11140), D2555 (11141), D2564 (11167) and D2571 (11171), the latter hauling the last freight on the branch on 28th September 1962. Only one of the class survived to become BR Class 05 when No. D2554 was exiled, for use on ballast and engineering trains, on the electrified section of the Isle of Wight line between Ryde (Pier Head) and Shanklin. The locomotive allocated to Ryde (RY on the BR coding) initially carried the number D2554 but was then renumbered 05001, and was then transferred to Departmental Stock as No. 97803. Seldom used, it often spent considerable time in the 'up' back platform siding at Sandown before being withdrawn. It has now been purchased by the Isle of Wight Steam Railway and is based at Haven Street.

Occasionally, in the event of the non-availability of a Hunslet shunter for the Tiptree working, a Drewry 0-6-0 diesel-mechanical locomotive was substituted. Introduced in 1952, and classified D2/3 by the Eastern Region, these locomotives also had Gardner 8L3 engines giving an output of 204hp at 1,200r.p.m. Transmission was a Vulcan-Sinclair type 23 fluid coupling, with Wilson-Drewry CA5 type five speed epicyclic gearbox and type RF11 spiral bevel reverse and final drive unit. Weighing 29 tons 15cwt., and with 3ft. 3in. driving wheels, maximum tractive effort of these engines was 16,850lb. Only two of the class are known to have been used on the Tiptree goods service, Nos. 11100 and 11110, which were later renumbered D2200 and D2209. The class was designated 04 by British Railways.

Kelvedon Shed was a sub-shed of Colchester Motive Power Depot, which always supplied locomotives to the light railway. In BR days the code '30E' was given to Colchester Shed, which was part of the Stratford district, and most branch locomotive carried the 30E shed plate on the smokebox door.

When the line was opened to traffic, two sets of footplate staff were based at Kelvedon, supplement by a cleaner and, later, a coalman who was usually booked on at night to coal and water the locomotive for the following day's duties. The early turn set of footplatemen signed on at 3.45a.m. to prepare the locomotive and work the early morning goods

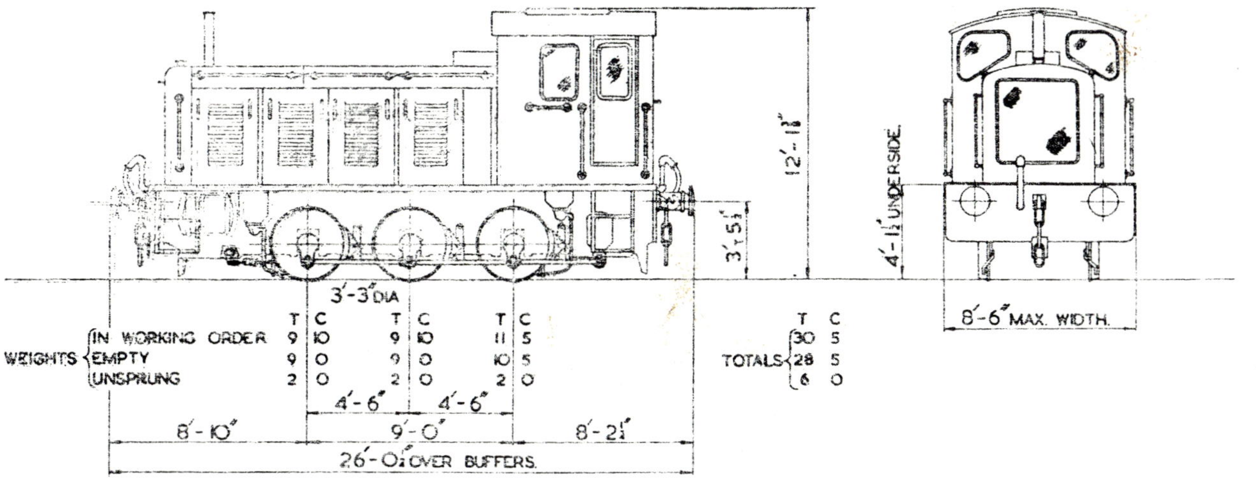

A Drewry 204hp diesel-mechanical Class 04 shunter.

Class J67/1 0-6-0T No. 68608 approaches Tollesbury with a train from Kelvedon in 1950.

Dr I. C. Allen

Class J67/1 0-6-0T No. 68616 stands at Tollesbury, with the 12.50p.m. mixed train to Kelvedon, on 11th July 1950.

P. N. Williams

and passenger/mixed trips, being relieved by the back shift men who signed on at 12 noon to work the remainder of the service, before disposing of the locomotive and signing off at 8.15p.m. In addition to his normal footplate duties, the fireman was responsible for opening all gated level crossings on the branch, a task during an eight hour shift that included the opening of sixteen gates. If working light engine, he also closed the gates across the line as well.

The locomotive foreman (or driver in charge as he was later called) at Kelvedon received a half day's extra pay per week for administrative duties, which included the submission of drivers' tickets and coal and oil returns to the locomotive shedmaster at Colchester, who ultimately passed much of the information on to the District Motive Power Office at Ipswich and later Stratford. The majority of drivers at Kelvedon only signed route knowledge sheets for the branch and the main line between Kelvedon and Colchester, although some also signed to Witham and between Colchester and St. Botolphs. Some Colchester footplatemen signed 'the road' between Kelvedon and Tollesbury, as they were responsible for working special freight workings and engineering and ballast trains. At one time, at least two Stratford crews also signed for the branch for the same reason.

Affairs of the heart, and the love of a pint and a game of darts at a local hostelry, combined to bring about some typical branch line malpractice among footplate staff. A certain fireman based at Kelvedon was so captivated by a young lady who lived in Tiptree that the late turn was almost unbearable to work, and after one or two attempts to transfer to the permanent early turn were scotched by his opposite number, the affair appeared to be heading for an early end. Fortunately, however, his driver at that time was a member of the darts team at a local pub, and required at least two early finishes for practices and matches. One large obstruction to both men was the fact that the branch

Principal Dimensions of Locomotives

GER class	K9	R24	S56 R24R	C72	Y14	T26
LNER class	-	J67/1	J69/1	J68	J15	E4
Wheel arrangement	0-4-2T	0-6-0T	0-6-0T	0-6-0T	0-6-0	2-4-0
Cylinders	15" x 22"	16½" x 22"	16½" x 22"	16½" x 22"	17½" x 24"	17½" x 24"
Motion	Stephenson with Slide Valves					
Boiler max. diameter	4' 2"	4' 2"	4' 2"	4' 2"	4' 4"	4' 4"
Boiler barrel length	9' 1"	9' 1"	9' 1"	9' 1"	10' 0"	10' 0"
Firebox	4' 5⅜" 3' 11"	4' 6"	5' 2 1/16"	5' 2 1/16"	6' 0"	6' 0"
Heating tubes	203 x 1¾"	227 x 1⅝"	227 x 1⅝"	227 x 1⅝"	242 x 1⅝"	242 x 1⅝"
Surface (sq. ft.)	874.87	909.40	909.40	909.40	1,063.8	1,063.8
Firebox (sq. ft.)	75.43	78.0	86.77	86.77	105.5	100.9
Total (sq. ft.)	950.03	987.40	996.17	996.17	1,169.3	1,164.7
Grate Area (sq. ft.)	12.3	12.4	14.5	14.5	17.9	18.0
Boiler pressure (lbs)	140p.s.i.	160p.s.i.	180p.s.i.	180p.s.i.	160p.s.i.	160p.s.i.
Leading wheels	-	-	-	-	-	4' 0"
Coupled wheels	4' 10"	4' 0"	4' 0"	4' 0"	4' 11"	5' 8"
Trailing wheels	3' 8"	-	-	-	-	-
Tractive effort		16,970lb.	19,091lb.	19,091lb.	16,942lb.	14,700lb.
Length over buffers		27' 8"	27' 8"	27' 8"	35' 2"	48' 2"
Wheelbase	14' 0"	13' 10"	13' 10"	13' 10"	16' 1"	16' 6"
Weight in working order	38t. 11cwt.	40t.	42t. 9cwt. 42t. 3cwt. 42t. 7cwt.	42t. 9cwt.	37t. 2cwt.	40t. 6cwt.
Max. axle load	13t. 5cwt.	14t.	15t. 2cwt. 14t. 19cwt. 15t. 1cwt.	15t. 2cwt.	13t. 10cwt.	14t. 3cwt.
Tender wheelbase					12' 0"	12' 0"
Wheel diameter					4' 1"	4' 1"
Weight in working order					30t. 13cwt.	30t. 13cwt.
Water capacity	850 gall.	1,000 gall.	1,200 gall. 1,140 gall. 1,180 gall.	1,200 gall.	2,640 gall.	2,640 gall.
Coal capacity	15cwt.	2t. 5cwt.	2t. 10cwt. 2t. 5cwt.	2t. 10cwt.	5t.	5t.

Class R24 0-6-0T No. 391, running with front coupling rods removed as a 2-4-0T, pulls into Kelvedon (Low Level) with the 8.07a.m. service from Tollesbury, on 31st March 1910.

LCGB/Ken Nunn Collection

locomotive required disposal after the last 'up' working but the two, with some aiding and abetting from the coalman at Kelvedon Shed, came to a satisfactory compromise, and on darts practise and match nights the driver, immediately on arrival at Kelvedon (Low Level), departed for his 'local' leaving the lovelorn fireman to dispose of the 0-6-0T with the help of the coalman. In return, on three nights of the week, the fireman hopped off the locomotive at Tiptree, on the last 'up' working, leaving the train to be worked forward by driver and guard only to Kelvedon where the driver, again with the help of the coalman, disposed of the locomotive.

These 'arrangements' went on undetected for some months, with the aid of some free beer or cigarettes for the coalman and guards until one evening, unannounced and with complete surprise, the Colchester shedmaster paid a visit to Kelvedon Shed, just as the one-man operated 'Buck jumper' pulled into Kelvedon (Low Level) Station. Various excuses that the fireman had been left to shut the gates at Feering, and would walk along the line to the station were met with suspicion. After an hour and a half the locomotive had been disposed of for the night by the shedmaster, driver and coalman, and halfhearted attempts to persuade authority that the fireman was 'still walking' failed to convince, and the game, in all but detail, was well and truly up. For the next month or so a motive power inspector was sent to Kelvedon at frequent intervals, especially when the intrepid pair were on late turn, necessitating alternative arrangements to be made for girlfriend and darts.

The two sets of men based at Kelvedon at the time of closure were Driver Jim Gardner (24 years at the shed), Driver George Manning, Fireman Norman Woriker and a vacancy which was filled daily by a relief fireman from Colchester.

The drivers in GER days were strict with firemen and cleaners, especially if the branch engine was not spotlessly clean. A common test was to wipe a clean rag along the footplate, or on the inside of wheels and frame, to make sure that the cleaning had been carried out correctly and thoroughly. In the 1920s, during the coal shortage, the cleaner was delegated to make briquettes from coal and cement, to supplement the meagre coal supplies, and to cut up old sleepers for firelighters to light up the fire in the firebox. The cleaner/coalman also offloaded coal from wagons on to the coaling stage at Kelvedon Shed although, in the latter years, coal was frequently transferred direct from wagon into the locomotive bunker; a practice frowned upon by authority if traffic wagons were used instead of locomotive coal wagons.

Boiler washing was never carried out at Kelvedon Shed but, in GER days, tube cleaning was occasionally performed by footplate staff at this rural depot when the branch locomotive remained here over the weekend. The senior fireman was paid four hours Sunday rate for the work, and the task was usually carried out using home-made or purloined tools. The branch locomotive normally returned light engine to Colchester on Saturday evenings after the last train and its relief ran light from Colchester Shed on Monday mornings, when all maintenance and repairs, including tube cleaning, was performed at the parent depot.

Motive power facilities at Kelvedon included a timber-framed concrete and corrugated iron-built single road engine shed, just large enough to accommodate a 'Buck Jumper' 0-6-0T, with a tank house and an enginemens' mess-room. On the north side of the building outside the shed was the water tank, mounted on cast-iron columns on the 'up' side, and a timber coaling stage on the 'down' side of the locomotive shed road. The timber stage deteriorated in later years, and was eventually replaced by a brick structure.

The Tollesbury branch engine rarely travelled beyond the branch limits, unless returning to Colchester for change-over. It was also used for trip working, between Kelvedon main line goods yard and the low level station, when transferring loaded and empty wagons to and from the branch. Unlike many branches, there appears to have been no particular preference with regard to the working of the locomotive 'engine first' to Kelvedon and 'bunker first' to Tollesbury. If snow threatened, the engine was kept in steam and ran light up and down the branch throughout the night in an endeavour to keep the line clear, although this practise ceased in the 1930s.

The headcode carried by branch trains, when the line first opened, was one red light at the top of the smokebox. Later, during daylight hours, a red circular disc with white outer rim was displayed on the same lamp bracket. After the Grouping, the LNER phased out the red light and disc as a possible source of a danger, and replaced them with purple discs with white outer rim or a purple light. By 1936, however, the standard stopping passenger train code, of a white light or white disc under the chimney, was used on the Tollesbury branch services, and remained in use until the closure of the line. Freight trains on the branch carried the appropriate class headcode. In accordance with good branch line malpractice, very often no headcode was carried at all, whilst at other times, if a lamp or disc was displayed, the wrong headcode was exhibited.

The whistle code for engines requiring to run to or from the main line from the branch at Kelvedon was 3 short 1 long, whilst 1 long whistle had to be given approaching each level crossing on the branch.

Coaching Stock

For the new light railway, the GER provided 6 four wheel five compartment thirds and 2 four wheel two compartment brake thirds as coaching stock. Built between 1877 and 1882, they were converted at Stratford Works in 1904 when the compartment partitions were removed and a central gangway was provided, leading to a door at each end of the open coaches opening out on to a drop plate, to enable the guard to walk through the train to issue tickets. On the brake thirds, the central gangway was provided with a door to the guard's compartment, and at the opposite end, a door gave access to the drop plate. During conversion the 3ft. 6½in. Mansell wooden-centred wheels were replaced by those of 2ft. 9in. diameter, to provide a lower floor level as compensation for the low station platforms. At the same time the headstock was modified to maintain the drawbar and buffers at the same level as standard coaching vehicles. On third class vehicles, three of the five doors on each side were blanked off, whilst in the brake third two doors on each side were blanked off, leaving only the end doors available for passenger use. To help passengers alight and step down on to the platforms, exterior steps were provided under each opening door. These coaches remained in use until 1928, when replacement stock was transferred from the Wisbech & Upwell Tramway. Six of the original coaches were withdrawn by the LNER between 6th May 1928 and March 1929, four without being renumbered.

Diagram	*GER No.*	*LNER No.*	*Built*	*Transferred to Kelvedon-Tollesbury Line*	*Withdrawn*
605	212	-	July 1878	14th May 1904	6th May 1928
605	716	-	March 1879	14th May 1904	6th May 1928
605	728	60463	March 1879	2nd April 1904	2nd March 1929
606	775	60465	November 1882	2nd April 1904	2nd March 1929
606	777	-	November 1882	1904	30th September 1928
606	810	-	April 1883	1904	2nd March 1929
607	337	62261	April 1877	1904	24th October 1931
608	356	62262	May 1877	1904	20th October 1931

With the closure of the Wisbech & Upwell Tramway, on 2nd January 1928, the nine tram coaches used on that line became surplus to requirements. Their suitability as replacements for use on the Tollesbury Light Railway soon became apparent and, between September 1928 and January 1929, six vehicles were transferred from Cambridgeshire to Essex for further use. Two types of coach were offered: LNER Nos. 60463-6 were four wheel 23ft. 7in. long saloons whilst Nos. 60461 and 60462 were 33ft. 10½ in. long saloon bogie vehicles, all constructed in 1884 and 1890.

Originally Nos. 60461-4 were composite vehicles, but were down-rated to thirds on transfer to the Kelvedon & Tollesbury line. As with the original stock, the newcomers had 2ft. 9in. wooden-centred wheels, but were distinguishable by having balconies at each end with wrought-iron railings, and gates and steps for passenger use. The drop plate was also provided, to enable the guard to walk between vehicles, whilst seating was arranged along each side of the vehicle facing towards the central gangway.

Three of the four wheel tramcars saw little service between Kelvedon and Tollesbury, as Nos. 60463, 60464 and 60466 were withdrawn on 16th May 1936. The fourth, No. 60465, completed almost twenty years on the line before being withdrawn on 20th March 1948, although it left Kelvedon for the last time on 7th January 1948. The two bogie coaches remained in use on the branch until the withdrawal of passenger services, and even then they were not removed from capital stock until 1st October 1951. No. 60461 was used in the Ealing Studios film 'The Titfield Thunderbolt' in 1952 and was then sold on 24th January 1953 but has since been saved for preservation by the Rutland Railway Museum, Cottesmore. No. 60462 was restored to GER livery as No. 8 for preservation, the main attraction being the end balconies with wrought-iron railings. It was stored at Bounds Green Carriage Depot but, unfortunately, through lack of storage space and later misunderstanding, the vehicle was scrapped on 9th March 1957 and the body was burned.

On 22nd September 1930, the passenger service between Downham and Stoke Ferry (Norfolk) was withdrawn. Because of the sparse area served; from 1896 the line had been operated with two tramcar vehicles, a composite and brake third. The vehicles were initially put into store pending a decision as to their future but, early in 1931, the authorities thought they could find use for them on the Tollesbury services as replacements for the original brake vehicles, Nos. 62261 and 62262, then being 54 years old. The pair were subsequently taken into Stratford Works, where composite GER tram No. 10 (LNER No. 63255) was converted into a brake third, similar in style to sister vehicle GER No. 11. Each vehicle then seated 24 passengers, and was fitted with steps and end doors for passenger use. The centre gangway door to end plate, for use by the guard, was retained. With their 3ft. diameter wheels and 30ft. long body, the pair were ideal for the Tollesbury line, and were transferred to Kelvedon in September 1931. Upon their arrival, the old original brake third trams were withdrawn.

Together with the ex-Wisbech & Upwell bogie vehicles, the ex-Stoke Ferry coaches worked out their life on the line. No. 63255 was renumbered 62262 by the LNER, taking the number of the former vehicle. Both were officially withdrawn from service on 1st October 1951, spending the period between the closure of the line to passenger traffic and their dispatch to Stratford, adjacent to Kelvedon Shed.

Diagram	*GER No.*	*LNER No.*	*Built*	*Transferred to Kelvedon-Tollesbury Line*	*Withdrawn*
601	2	60464	June 1890	12th January 1929	16th May 1936
601	3	60465	June 1890	9th December 1928	20th March 1948
601	4	60466	June 1890	9th December 1928	16th May 1936
601	6	60463	July 1884	9th December 1928	16th May 1936
603	7	60461	September 1884	30th September 1928	1st October 1951
603	8	60462	September 1884	30th September 1928	1st October 1951
609	10	63255 (later 62262)	December 1896	September 1931	1st October 1951
610	11	62261	December 1896	September 1931	1st October 1951

The branch coaching stock received heavy repairs at Stratford Works, and minor repairs and maintenance at Colchester. When travelling on the main line, the side steps of the vehicles were removed to enable them to run within loading gauge limits. All coaches on the branch were replenished with gas for lighting at Kelvedon.

Non-passenger carrying stock used on the branch, ranged from fitted vans for perishable produce, fruit and fish, cattle wagons for the conveyance of livestock to neighbouring markets, horse-boxes, carriage wagons and milk vans. The great majority of wagons consisted of GER five plank or high-sided opens for general merchandise and manure, and covered vans for grain, fruit and flowers. Coal traffic was handled in local merchants' wagons or privately-owned colliery wagons. Repairs to private wagons were effected by Wagon Repairs Ltd. and Lincoln Wagon Repairs Ltd., whilst the GER/LNER dealt with repairs to their railway-owned wagons, minor repairs being effected at Kelvedon and heavier repairs at Colchester. A goods brake van was also allocated to the branch for use on mixed or freight trains. When not in use it was based at Kelvedon.

The run-round loop and low level junction at Kelvedon, photographed on the last day of passenger working, 5th May 1951. Nos. E62262, E60462 and E62261 wait at the platform to form the last 'down' train to Tollesbury.

J. Watling Collection

Contrary to regulations, passengers on the last train, on 5th May 1951, were permitted to remain in the coaches when the locomotive ran beyond Tollesbury Terminus to the run-round loop. Here No. 68578 makes her way back round her train, watched and photographed by railway enthusiasts and local people.

Former Wisbech & Upwell bogie tram, No. 60461, is pictured standing with the two ex-Stoke Ferry vehicles. This photograph shows a close up of the balcony end with wrought ironwork and gates, and the steps for passengers' use. Because 2ft. 9in. diameter wooden centre wheels were provided on the Wisbech & Upwell vehicles to provide a low floor level as compensation for the low station platforms, it was also necessary to provide a modified headstock, to maintain the drawbar and buffers at the same level as standard coaching vehicles.

Ian L. Wright

Coaching Stock : Principle Dimensions

GER Diagram No.	601	603	605	606	607	608	609	610
	Third class 4 wheel tram	*Bogie third tramcar*	*Four wheel third*	*Four wheel third*	*Four wheel brake/third*	*Four wheel brake/third*	*Six wheel brake/third*	*Six wheel brake/third*
Length over buffers	27′ 1″	37′ 4½″	30′ 6¾″	30′ 6¾″	30′ 6¾″	30′ 6″	33′ 6″	33′ 6″
Length over body	23′ 7″	33′ 10½″	27′ 0¾″	27′ 0¾″	27′ 0¾″	27′ 0″	30′ 0″	30′ 0″
Height overall	10′ 2½″	10′ 2½″	10′ 5¼″	10′ 6¾″	10′ 4¾″	10′ 4¾″	10′ 6⅝″	10″ 6⅝″
Body height	7′ 0½″	7′ 0½″	6′ 8″	6′ 9¾″	6′ 8″	6′ 8″	7′ 0½″	7′ 0½″
Width over guard's look-out	-	-	-	-	9′ 0″	9′ 0″	-	9′ 0″
Width over body	8′ 0″	8′ 0″	8′ 0″	8′ 0″	8′ 0″	8′ 0″	8′ 0″	8′ 0″
Wheel dia.	2′ 9″	2′ 9″	2′ 9″	2′ 9″	2′ 9″	2′ 9″	3′ 0″	3′ 0″
Wheelbase	11′ 0″	4′ 6″ *	15′ 3″	15′ 3″	15′ 3″	15′ 3″	20′ 0″	20′ 0″
Seating	22	34	40	40	16	16	24	24
Luggage	-	-	-	-	10cwt.	10cwt.	10cwt.	10cwt.
Weight empty	7t. 14cwt.	12t. 5cwt.	8t. 17cwt.	8t. 17cwt.	9t. 2cwt.	9t. 2cwt.	9t. 19cwt.	11t. 6cwt.

* Indicates bogie wheelbase

The interior of an ex-Wisbech & Upwell bogie tramcar, showing the seating along the sides of the vehicle. Note the roof straps, and the drop side windows with leather straps.

John H. Meredith

Above: Ex-Stoke Ferry branch brake third, No. E62261, at Tiptree in July 1950, showing the end door used by the guard to walk between vehicles. Note the side steps, used by passengers to board and alight from vehicles at the low platform.

P. N. Williams

Top left: This ornate end balcony and side steps were for use by passengers at low platform stations on the Tollesbury Light Railway. Illustrated is ex-Wisbech & Upwell bogie tram (LNER No. 60461), ex-GER No. 7. Also of note are the buffer heights, to enable the coaches to work with normal railway rolling stock.

Left: Bogie tramcar No. E60461, pictured after the addition of the 'E' prefix by BR and the obliteration of the legend LNER on the panel side.

J. H. Aston/G. Pember

Former Wisbech & Upwell bogie third tramcar (GER No. 8, LNER No. 60462) was transferred upon closure of the Cambridgeshire Tramway for further use on the Tollesbury line, arriving at Kelvedon on 30th September 1928. This vehicle was used right up to the day of closure for passenger services and was finally withdrawn on 1st September 1951, being later restored to GER livery.

J. H. Aston/R. C. Riley

Former Stoke Ferry branch brake third No. 62261 with prefix E added by BR, and the LNER legend obliterated from the panel sides. After closure of the Stoke Ferry branch in September 1930 this vehicle, together with composite 63255, later 62262, was placed in store pending a decision as to its future. With the poor condition of the original K&TLR stock, it was decided to ressurect the pair for further service and after modifications, they were transferred to the Tollesbury line in September 1931. Note only one door is available for passenger access.

Lens of Sutton

A Wisbech & Upwell bogie tramcar (GER No. 8), as restored for preservation, seen at Stratford. As LNER No. 60462, this vehicle was tranferred to the Kelvedon to Tollesbury line in 1928, and was finally withdrawn on 1st September1951. Unfortunately,through lack of storage space and, later, misunderstandings, the vehicle was scrapped and the body burned.

J. Watling Collection

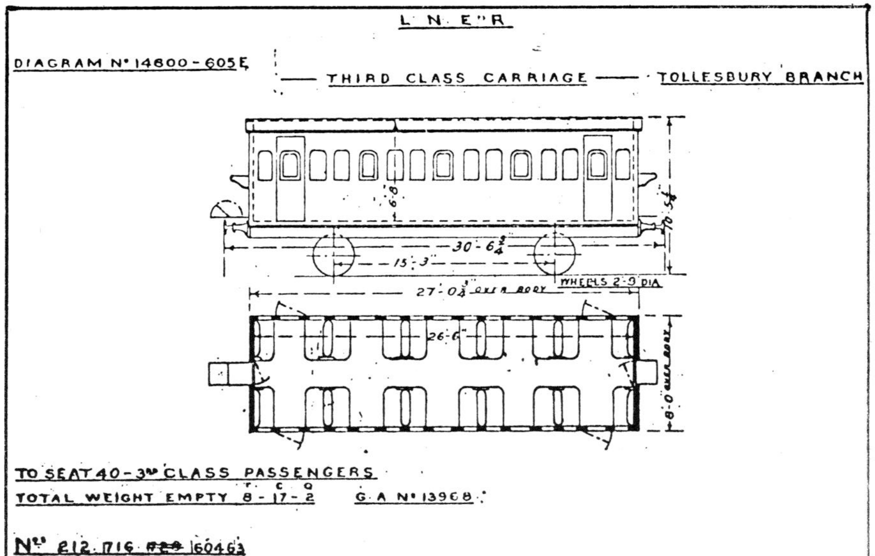

LNER diagram 605 for a four wheel third carriage built between 1878 and 1879. It was converted in 1904 for use on the Kelvedon to Tollesbury Light Railway. Of the GER vehicles numbered 212, 716 and 728, only 728 was renumbered by the LNER to 60463.

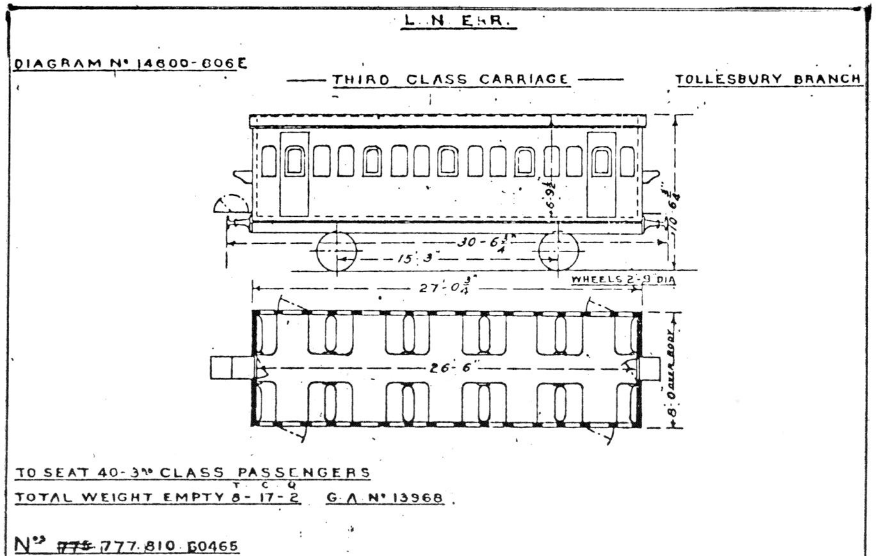

LNER diagram 606 for a four wheel third carriage built in 1882/3. It was converted in 1904 for use on the Tollesbury Light Railway. GER numbers were 775, 777 and 810, but only No. 775 survived to be renumbered by the LNER to 60465.

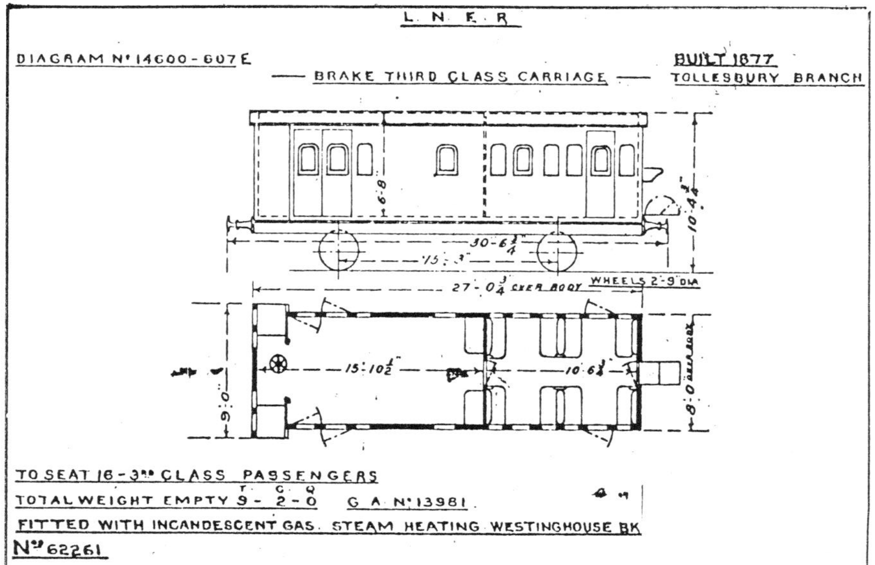

LNER diagram 607 for a four wheel brake third carriage built in April 1877. GER No. 337 was converted in 1904 for use on the Tollesbury Light Railway and renumbered by the LNER to 62261.

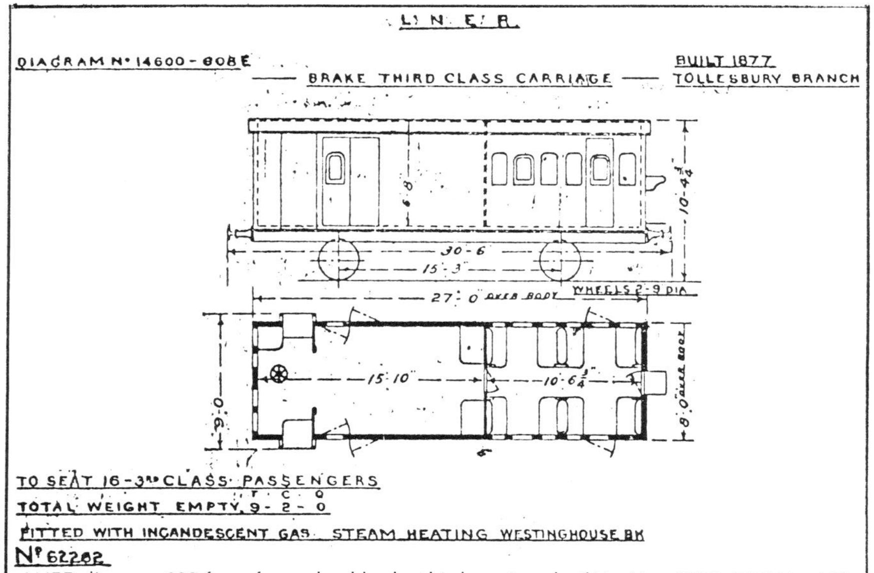

LNER diagram 608 for a four wheel brake third carriage built in May 1877. GER No. 356 was converted in 1904 for use on the Tollesbury branch and renumbered by the LNER to 62262.

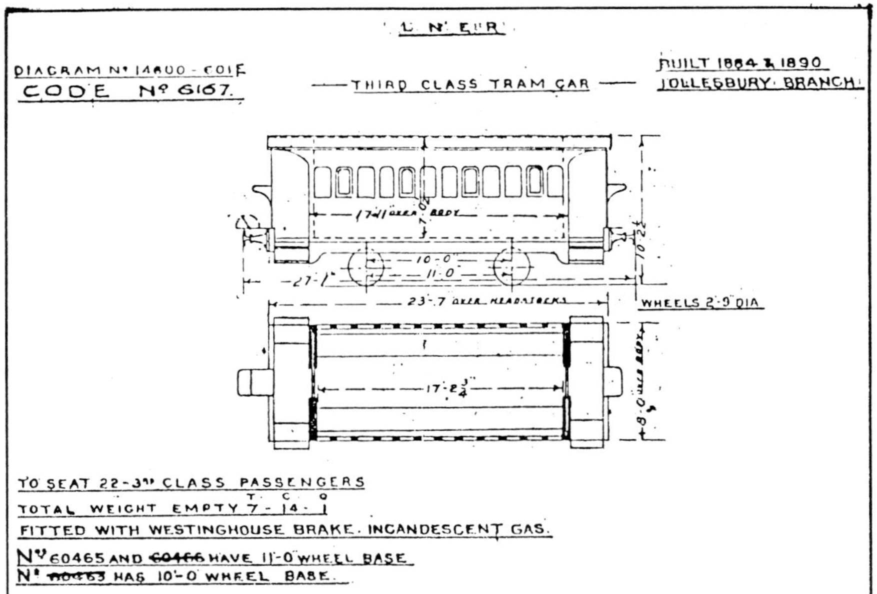

LNER diagram 601 for a third class four wheel tramcar (ex-Wisbech & Upwell Tramway). Vehicles Nos. 60463/4/5/6.

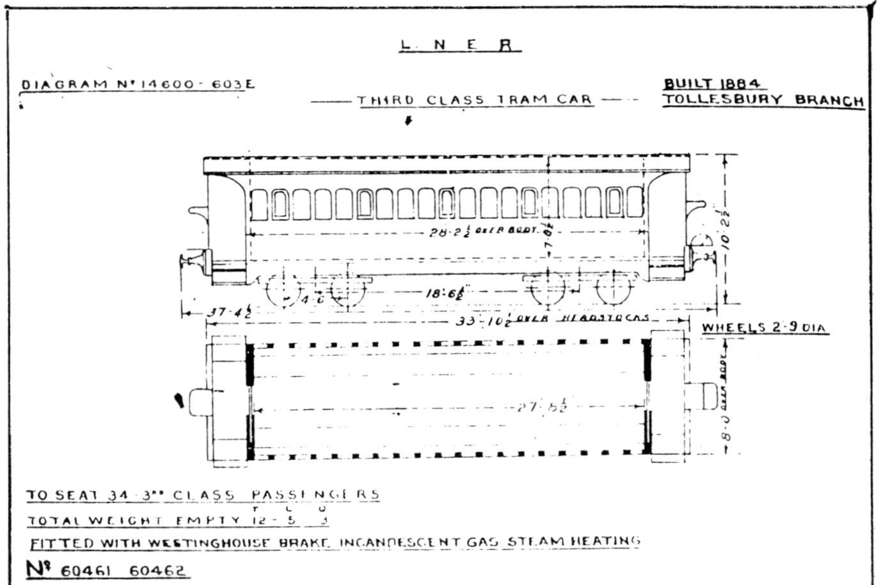

LNER diagram 603 for bogie third tramcar No. 60461/2, transferred from Wisbech & Upwell Tramway.

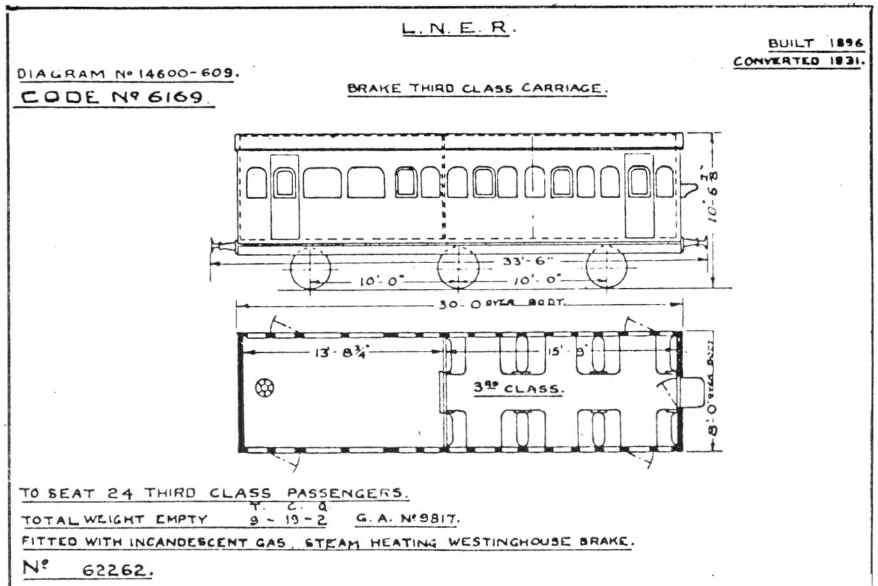

LNER diagram 609 for a six wheel brake third carriage. No. 62262 was converted from a composite tramcar, GER No. 10, in 1931 (ex-Stoke Ferry branch).

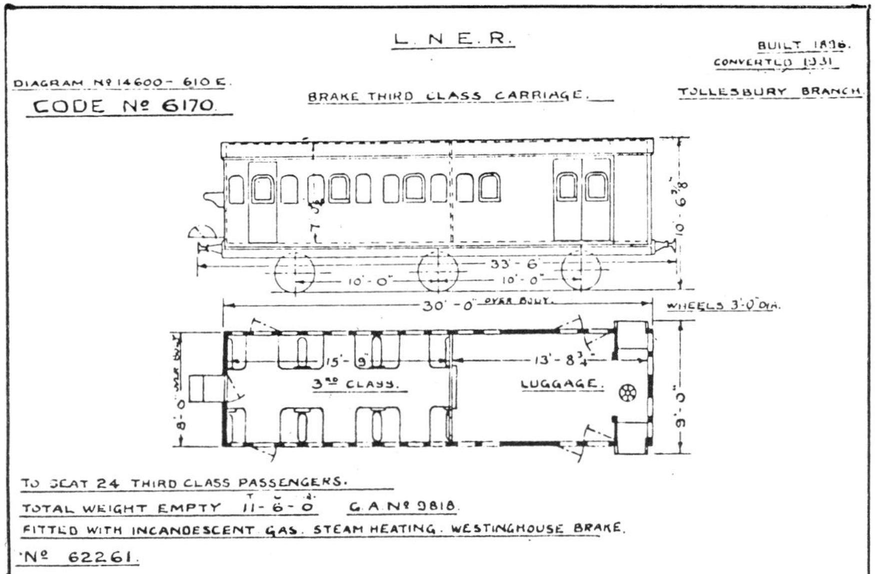

LNER diagram 610 for a six wheel brake third carriage No. 62261 (ex-Stoke Ferry branch).

Ex-Wisbech & Upwell bogie tramcar (GER No. 8, LNER No. 60462) was transferred to the Kelvedon to Tollesbury line in September 1928, and is seen at Tollesbury in January 1949.

John H. Meredith

Ex-Wisbech & Upwell bogie tram (GER diagram No. 603, GER No. 7 and LNER No. 60461) was transferred to the Tollesbury Light Railway in September 1928, and is seen on a branch train in July 1950. Note the end balconies, the drop plate and also the difference in height between No. E60461 and the adjoining ex-Stoke Ferry vehicle.

P. N. Williams

The end balcony, with ornate ironwork and side steps, on ex-Wisbech & Upwell bogie tramcar No. 60461.

Ian L. Wright

An April 1951 view between ex-Stoke Ferry branch coaches on the Kelvedon & Tollesbury Light Railway, showing the central gangway and drop plate used by the guard when walking between vehicles.

G. R. Mortimer

The two ex-Stoke Ferry Vehicles, and former Wisbech & Upwell tram No. 60462, form a passenger train for Tollesbury, at Kelvedon (Low Level) Station, in September 1939. The side steps on the light railway vehicles can be seen to advantage, as can the raised drop plate, positioned by the wrought ironwork of the end balcony on No. 60462. Whilst the train was in motion no passengers were permitted to ride on the balconies of the two Wisbech & Upwell tramcars.

Ex-Wisbech & Upwell bogie tramcar No. E60461 at Kelvedon on 29th July 1950. This vehicle, in 1952, was used in the film 'The Titfield Thunderbolt', located on the former GWR Camerton branch. It is now preserved at the Rutland Railway Museum, Cottesmore.

LCGB/Ken Nunn Collection

Ex-Stoke Ferry branch six wheel composite tram, converted to a brake third in 1931 for use on the Tollesbury service. Originally GER No. 10, it became LNER No. 63255 (later being renumbered 62262) and was withdrawn on 1st October 1951.

J. H. Ashton

Bogie tramcar no. E60462, as repainted brown and relettered by British Railways, pictured on the light railway on 19th September 1950.

Ian L. Wright

Former Stoke Ferry branch brake third (GER No. 11) was later renumbered by the LNER as 62261 and is seen at Tollesbury on 26th June 1948, while still in LNER teak livery. This vehicle, built to GER diagram No. 610 in 1896, weighed 11tons 6cwt., had seating for 24 third class passengers and accommodation for 10cwt. of luggage. It was transferred to the Tollesbury Light Railway in 1931.

H. C. Casserley

Appendix One

Kelvedon to Tollesbury Pier: Bridges & Culverts

No.	M. Ch.	Between	Local Name	Under/or Over	Status	No. of Spans	Square Span/ Between Abutments or Supports ft. in.	Skew Span/ Between Abutments or Supports ft. in.	Construction
	0 16	Kelvedon & Feering		Under			1 0	dia.	GER pipe skew under line
873	0 67	Feering & Inworth	Stream	Under		2	6 0 6 0	6 2 6 2	Brick abutments and piers segmental arches and concrete Two spans L R
	1 21	Feering & Inworth		Under			1 0	dia.	GER pipe
	1 32	Feering & Inworth		Under	'Up' side of line		1 0	dia.	GER pipe under approach road to level crossing No. 5
	2 14	Feering & Inworth		Under			1 0	dia.	GER pipe skew under line
	2 59½	Feering & Inworth		Under	'Up' side of line		1 0	dia.	GER pipe under footpath approach to public level crossing No. 14
	2 60	Feering & Inworth		Under	'Up' side of line		1 0	dia.	GER pipe under approach road to public level cross-ing No. 14
	2 71	Inworth Station		Under			1 0	dia.	GER pipe skew under line
	2 71	Inworth Station		Under	'Up' side of line		1 0	dia.	GER pipe under approach road to level crossing No. 15
	3 70	Tiptree & Tolleshunt Knights		Under	'Down' side of line		1 0	dia.	GER pipe under approach to level crossing No. 24
	3 70	Tiptree & Tolleshunt Knights		Under	'Up' side of line		1 0	dia.	2 GER pipes under approach road to public level cross-ing No. 24
	3 70½	Tiptree & Tolleshunt Knights		Under	'Down' side of line		1 0	dia.	GER pipe under approach road to traders' siding
874	3 74	Tiptree & Tolleshunt Knights	Stream	Under		1	6 0	7 0	Brick abutments segmental arch and concrete, faced with blue brindled bricks LR
	4 29	Tolleshunt Knights & Tolleshunt D'Arcy		Under			3 0	dia.	Brick barrel skew under line
875	4 71	Tolleshunt Knights & Tolleshunt D'Arcy	Blind Lane	Over	Public	2	25 4 16 0	25.8 16 2	Brick abutments piers and parapets. Width between parapets 5ft. Two spans over running line, RS joists and brick jack arches

						of cutting. Brick segmental arches. All brickwork blue brindled bricks
5 26	Tolleshunt Knights & Tolleshunt D'Arcy		Under	1 0	dia.	GER pipe
6 05	Tolleshunt Knights & Tolleshunt D'Arcy		Under	1 0	dia.	GER pipe
6 54	Tolleshunt D'Arcy Tollesbury		Under	1 0	dia.	GER pipe under running line
6 72	Tolleshunt D'Arcy & Tollesbury		Under	1 0	dia.	GER pipe
7 26	Tolleshunt D'Arcy & Tollesbury		Under	1 0	dia.	GER pipe under running line and approach to field gate on 'down' side of line at public level crossing No. 30
7 70	Tolleshunt D'Arcy & Tollesbury		Under	1 6	dia.	GER pipe
8 23	Tolleshunt D'Arcy & Tollesbury		Under	1 6	dia.	GER pipe
8 77	Tollesbury & Tollesbury Pier		Under	1 0	dia.	GER pipe
9 58	Tollesbury & Tolllesbury Pier	Stream	Under	5.0	dia.	Timber cells on earth bank, supported by sleeper sheeting. Timber longitudinals carrying track on cross sleepers

Class R24 0-6-0T No. 267 bursts from under Blind Lane Overbridge with the 11.16a.m. Tollesbury to Kelvedon train, on 9th April 1910. No. 267 is running as a 2-4-0T, with its front coupling rods removed. Blind Lane Overbridge No. 875 (4 miles and 71 chains from Kelvedon) was the only overbridge on the branch and had two skew spans of 25ft. 4in. over the running line and 16ft. 0in. over the embankment.

LCGB/Ken Nunn Collection

Looking towards Kelvedon, through the cutting near Blind Lane Overbridge (No. 875), with the 5 mile post on the 'down' side of the line in the foreground. The branch is laid on a mixture of ashes and clinker.

D. Trevor Rowe

Class J15 0-6-0 No. 65470 waits with the branch freight at Kelvedon branch 'up' home signal, in August 1958, for BR Class 7MT 4-6-2 No. 70037 *Hereward the Wake* to pass on the 'up' main line with a Clacton to Liverpool Street express. Note the altered layout of Kelvedon (Low Level) Station with only the single branch line remaining.

Dr I. C. Allen

Class J15 No. 65443 stands in Kelvedon 'up' Yard, with a brake van and open wagons, and forms the Railway Enthusiasts' Club special to Tiptree on 6th April 1957. The participants on the tour had arrived in the Gresley and GER bogie coaches, stabled alongside the special.

R. C. Riley